PRAISE FOR *Leslie Mackie's Macrina Bakery & Cafe Cookbook*

"From the day it opened, Leslie Mackie's Macrina Bakery & Cafe has bee[n] great food in Seattle. Now, with this treasure of a book, anyone not lucky arily good breads and homey cakes, her can't-get-enough-of-them tarts a[nd] can savor her specialties at home. All our favorites are here in recipes th[at] easy to follow. What a treat."

    —DORIE GREENSPAN, author of *Paris Sweets: Great Recipes fro[m...]*

"Leslie Mackie's sparkle, raw energy, talent, humor, and integrity combine to not only produce one of America's greatest bakers and pastry cooks, but someone who cooks as well as any chef today. When I picked up *Leslie Mackie's Macrina Bakery & Cafe Cookbook*, there was that same sparkle, energy, and inspiration! It is *wonderful*. I did peek to make sure the steamed chocolate pudding cake was there . . . It WAS!"

    —LYDIA SHIRE, chef and co-owner, Locke-Ober restaurant in Boston

"Leslie Mackie has long been one of the professional bakers I most admire in the whole country. Everything she prepares is imbued with honesty, freshness, flavor, and love, and I can't resist stopping by Macrina Bakery & Cafe every time I am in Seattle. Now we're lucky enough to have her inspired recipes to use at home, and everyone's home baking skills will rise—just like Leslie's wonderful doughs!"

    —NICK MALGIERI, author of *Perfect Cakes and Chocolate*

"I have known Leslie Mackie for over twenty-five years, and after reading her book, I can say it embraces what she does so well with passion, simplicity, and excellence. She is a true master, and this book represents years of work that can now be brought into any aspiring baker's home or professional kitchen."

    —CORY SCHREIBER, author of *Wildwood: Cooking from the Source in the Pacific Northwest*

"Leslie Mackie has all the ingredients of a baker's baker: a natural understanding of the crafts of bread baking, pastry making, and cooking; a thoughtful and curious mind; and a big heart. I know this is a lot to read into a loaf of bread or a tart or a crostoni, but it's all there. And in these recipes Leslie's spirit shines through. You want to eat what she makes. You want to make what she makes. And with this book you can—and you should."

    —NOEL COMESS, owner of Tom Cat Bakery in New York City

Leslie Mackie's

MACRINA
BAKERY & CAFE
COOKBOOK

Leslie Mackie's

MACRINA BAKERY & CAFE COOKBOOK

Favorite Breads, Pastries, Sweets & Savories

Leslie Mackie with *Andrew Cleary*
Foreword by *Carol Field*

SASQUATCH BOOKS
SEATTLE

To Saint Macrina the Younger

Text copyright ©2003 by Leslie Mackie
"Most-Requested Recipes" copyright ©2006 by Leslie Mackie
All rights reserved. No portion of this book may be reproduced or
utilized in any form, or by any electronic, mechanical, or other means, without
the prior written permission of the publisher.

Printed in Canada
Published by Sasquatch Books
Distributed by Publishers Group West
14 13 12 11 10 09 08 07 06   9 8 7 6 5 4 3 2 1

Book design: Kate Basart/Union Pageworks
Cover photograph: John Granen
Interior photographs: Dennis Wise
Interior illustrations: Leslie Mackie

Library of Congress Cataloging-in-Publication Data
Mackie, Leslie.
Macrina Bakery and Cafe cookbook / by Leslie Mackie.
p. cm.
ISBN 1-57061-372-9 (hardcover) / 1-57061-504-7 (paperback)
1. Baking. 2. Macrina Bakery and Cafe. I. Macrina Bakery and Cafe. II. Title.

TX765.M315 2003
641.8'15—dc21

2003045663

SASQUATCH BOOKS
119 South Main Street, Suite 400 • Seattle, Washington 98104 • 206/467-4300
www.sasquatchbooks.com • custserv@sasquatchbooks.com

CONTENTS

PREFACE TO THE NEW EDITION

The release of the first edition of this book, in the fall of 2003, coincided with Macrina's tenth anniversary, and I was thrilled with the response it received. Our loyal customers carried the book into their homes and started baking. Many came into the cafes grinning from ear to ear, eager to share their tales of success or to ask for advice. It was a pleasure to hear their stories and to know that the recipes were finding new life.

In producing this second edition, I am very happy to be able to add a chapter containing new recipes our customers have been asking for. I've also provided recipes for our updated, trans fat–free pie dough and a gluten-free bread that we've developed. The beautiful new cover features one of our most-requested recipes—the elegant Macrina's Tuxedo Cake. I hope what you find inside this book brings many hours of happiness to your kitchen and your table. Enjoy.

FOREWORD

Whenever I come home from a trip to Seattle, I am likely to dream that a branch of Leslie Mackie's Macrina Bakery & Cafe has opened in my neighborhood. I wake up ready to leap out of bed and walk around the corner. I think of the loaves of raisin bread and ciabatta that are waiting, the house bread I want to tuck under my arm and take home. At some point, of course, reality reasserts itself, and I am inevitably crestfallen when the moment of truth arrives. It is hard to accept that I have to do without the bread puddings, fougasse, and ginger pear upside-down cakes that line the shelves and counters of Cafe Macrina, and it doesn't really seem fair that those delicious tastes are only available in my memory. Yes, that moment of realization has always been a blow, but I am happy to say that consolation has now arrived in the form of Leslie's new book, which makes it possible to re-create Macrina Bakery & Cafe specialties and bring their sparkling tastes and flavors into my life.

I can't overstate my enthusiasm for *Leslie Mackie's Macrina Bakery & Cafe Cookbook*. Leslie's passion for bread and her commitment to preparing soul-satisfying food shines out from every page. When I first met her, Leslie was preparing for her bread pilgrimage to Italy, and I was immediately impressed by her knowledge, her passion, and her desire to learn everything she could from masters of bread baking. Her approach to finding the local and regional specialties all over the country paralleled my own a few years before, and I was thrilled to think that she was planning to open a bakery devoted to recipes learned from those inspired artisans. Leslie's adventurous spirit carried her all over the peninsula. She absorbed more than the formulas and techniques she saw and brought home with her not only memories of exceptional tastes but a commitment to reproducing them with fresh, organic, local, and seasonal ingredients.

Little did she know when she enlisted friends, local artisans, and artists to help build her neighborhood bakery that she would soon expand from being a bakery with breads, three kinds of tarts, two kinds of cookies, and a single biscotto to baking multiples of all those and then to becoming a community restaurant offering delicious dishes that are meant to be eaten with the breads that are still at the heart of her vision.

Leslie's passion translates directly into her easy-to-follow recipes. They are straightforward and clear, so full of encouragement and good-natured observations that she moves us easily through the baking process. We know what the dough should look and feel like, and we are reassured at every step. As I read my way through the book, I found it almost impossible not to reach for flour, sugar, and eggs, not to pull down bowls and measuring spoons and cups and get to work. My copy bristles with stick-it notes marking the numerous alluring possibilities that I want to bake and taste for myself. I can almost see the bubbling starters, smell the sweet breads, feel the heat and steam in the air as breads, summer berry muffins, and coffee cakes come out of the ovens. Macrina Bakery & Cafe has made a place for itself in Seattle's heart. Leslie's gifts to her neighborhood and the larger community are well known. She extends the idea of family by embracing the whole neighborhood and city itself in the warm home-like ambiance she has created. No one who has ever been there will be surprised that Leslie thinks of the bakers as family or that she has persuaded her own mother to come into Macrina's kitchen, roll up her sleeves, and show the staff how to make the American classic sweets that Leslie grew up eating. In preserving the recipes of her own childhood and other bakers' traditions, in making and preserving the breads of Italian bakers and the classic tastes of American desserts, Leslie has given us all a special gift. With this book she is preserving important traditions and encouraging the next generations to participate in the magic of baking. When she went to her three-year-old daughter's preschool, I could feel the excitement of the children plunging into the bread-making process, "their little fists pounding the dough . . . like a drum roll," and then heard that drum roll grow louder and louder in appreciation of Leslie's dedication and talents. Brava Leslie, brava again and again.

CAROL FIELD
Author of *The Italian Baker* and *In Nonna's Kitchen*

ACKNOWLEDGMENTS

The writing of this book was quite an undertaking, requiring the hands and eyes of many people. It is with great appreciation that I first thank Andrew Cleary, my collaborator and General Manager of Macrina. He took my handwritten recipes and stories and converted them into the pages that fill this book. Andrew's attention to detail, as well as his talent for prose, made this book possible. Our editor, Suzanne DeGalan, was invaluable and served as our coach. Her expertise and vision, along with her enthusiasm and love for Macrina, led us through one deadline after another. We were also fortunate to work with several great photographers. Dennis Wise's pictures truly capture the feeling of Macrina Bakery & Cafe, conveying what words couldn't. I'm equally pleased with John Rizzo's beautiful work for the cover of the first edition, and John Granen's on the paperback. It's a great honor to have such a beautifully written foreword by Carol Field. A fellow baker, Carol has been an inspiration to all of us involved in baking artisan breads. This project finally gave me the opportunity to work with my longtime friend Kate Basart, a designer of beautiful books for Sasquatch. She was able to capture the feel of our cafes in the overall design of this book. Many thanks to the managers at Macrina: Kimberly Johnson, Rebecca Mason, Karra Wise, Kim Abrams Marshall, Clark Griffin, Phuong Hoang Bui, and Jessica Fields. Thank you for all the extra work in Andrew's and my absence. Thank you to you all.

I would also like to thank a few important people who have greatly influenced my career. A special thank you to Lydia Shire, whom I worked with for many impressionable years. She shared her gift of wonderful cooking and flavor building, and stressed the importance of travel and authenticity in recipes. I would also like to thank Gwen Bassetti and Alan Black, co-owners of Grand Central Bakery, for the opportunity to work with them. Artisan bread was just arriving in Seattle when I started working at Grand Central back in 1989. It was there that I worked with Tomas Solis, who had been hired as a consultant to get the bakery started. Tomas shared his vast knowledge with me, and introduced me to the amazing range of "browns" on the crust of each loaf of bread. I'm also deeply thankful for my friend Susan Regis (chef extraordinaire). Her presence in my life has added a second pair of eyes, making my world twice its size.

Finally, I would like to express my gratitude to my mother and father. My mother used to take my sister and me to San Francisco for spring breaks. We would have breakfast, lunch, and dinner in different restaurants every day. I would beg her to take a break and skip a meal. "And miss going to Tadich Grill for sand dabs?" Thanks to my mother, good food has always been a part of my life. The existence of Macrina Bakery & Cafe would not have been possible without my father. After many years of convincing, he took a chance and invested in his daughter's dream. He set up my accounting books and met equipment deliveries while the bakery was being built. After the opening he was the extra set of hands and advice that I couldn't afford to hire. Many thanks for your loving support and encouragement.

That said, I hope you all enjoy this book!

LESLIE MACKIE

A heartfelt thank you to Leslie for the opportunity to work on this project with you. It has been a year I'll never forget. We've been working together for a decade now, and during this time I've enjoyed a work life that most people only dream of. Thank you for your patience and encouragement, and thank you for your friendship.

Thank you to Suzanne DeGalan for your guidance and support, and for your sense of humor.

Thank you to Kimberly Johnson and all of my coworkers at Macrina. Without your help this book would never have been possible. I'm glad I get to see your faces every day.

Special thanks to Douglas Orsini and all of my friends and family.

ANDREW CLEARY

INTRODUCTION

". . . to me being a baker is just about the most important, most honest profession there is in the world . . . along with teaching and farming . . ."

ALICE WATERS

The idea for Macrina Bakery & Cafe existed long before we actually opened our doors. The seed was planted in my brain many years earlier. I had kept a journal all through cooking school, throughout my early restaurant career, and during my travels, filling a stack of notebooks with ideas for what I hoped would someday be my own business. The books chronicled my early culinary days and included notes on everything from memorable meals to favorite lighting fixtures and retail counters. Not wanting to forget a thing, I lined the pages with sketches of the beautiful pastries and loaves of bread that I saw along the way. I was absorbing as much information as I could, and the concept of Macrina was starting to take shape.

I finally opened Macrina Bakery & Cafe in the summer of 1993. I had relocated to Seattle several years earlier, the city had become my home, and it was time to bring my dream to life. Being the conservative Scottish girl that I am (a conservative girl with grand ideas!), I leased a small space in Belltown, a neighborhood that was then considered "transitional." It seemed like the perfect location for what I wanted to create—not just a bread bakery but a place where the community could gather all day long. I planned to incorporate all of my passions. Bread would be the focus, of course, but we would also serve classic European pastries and good coffee, and our cafe would offer simple, savory lunches. This is a combination that you don't often find under one roof, and it's part of what makes Macrina unique.

As soon as people realize that my name isn't Leslie Macrina they want to know how I chose the name for the bakery. For me, the process of baking bread is inherently spiritual, so it seemed only natural to name my bakery after a Saint. Saint Macrina the Younger lived in Greece during the fourth century, working to improve the quality of life for the people of her community. She schooled her brothers, Saints Basil and Gregory, and then sent them out to educate others about the injustices of their day. This was exactly the kind of gal I wanted on my side. And frankly, I needed someone to be accountable to during the process of starting and operating my own business!

We opened with six employees, a French Bongard oven as our centerpiece, a stack of convection ovens, one mixer, an espresso machine, an antique display case, and a lot of ambition. Right off the bat we offered a full line of artisan breads, ranging from full-flavored, naturally leavened sourdoughs to American favorites like our Rustic Potato Loaf. The pastry selection was limited to a few muffins, coffee cakes, and tarts. The neighborhood responded favorably, and we were fortunate to get some great reviews in the local press. The following January *Sunset Magazine* featured Macrina in an article about sourdough breads. This coverage put us on the map. Business increased immediately, enabling us to hire more employees and introduce more products. My father moved to Seattle from Portland, Oregon, to help me with the bookkeeping end of the business, and I put all of my energy into baking.

Our cozy bakery was soon bursting at the seams. We definitely needed more space. In July 1994 I took over an adjoining retail space and started construction on what would become our cafe. (This expanded our breathing room from 847 square feet to a luxurious 1,755!) I brought the neighborhood into the project, hiring local artists to produce our tabletops, chairs, light fixtures, cabinetry, and welded signs. My friend Susan Hamilton and I stained the floor and did the painting. When the work was finished, I had finally achieved my goal. Macrina Bakery & Cafe was complete. Eight years later we put all that we had learned to use opening our second bakery and cafe in Seattle's Queen Anne neighborhood.

This book came together just in time for the bakery's tenth anniversary. Inside these pages you'll find recipes representing a sampling of everything Macrina Bakery & Cafe produces. All the favorites are here, from Buttermilk Biscuits, Rocket Muffins, and Morning Rolls, to Apple Cinnamon Monkey Bread, Mom's Chocolate Cake, and our popular Lemon Chess Tart. There's also a large section entitled Macrina Cafe Favorites, filled with recipes for simple, satisfying lunches and brunches.

The first section of the book is dedicated to bread baking—my passion—and I've included recipes for our signature loaves. There are step-by-step instructions for preparing loaves such as Ciabatta, the classic Italian "slipper" bread. You'll also learn how to make your own Biga and Natural Sour Starter, the key ingredients in rustic European breads.

This book is about the magic I experience at the bakery every day. It's about being part of an exciting workplace, a thriving neighborhood, and a baking tradition. Our devoted customers have become part of my extended family, and their contributions to Macrina are many. The book is also an opportunity to share my favorite memories and to celebrate the talented employees who have persevered through a series of awkward growth spurts to make Macrina the unique and special place that it is. I'm grateful for the opportunity to share our story.

KITCHEN MUST-HAVES

There are a few pieces of equipment I think are essential to successful baking—as well as cooking in general. Simply put, the right tools make every job easier. Each of the items on this list is affordable and readily available at kitchen supply stores such as Sur la Table and Williams-Sonoma.

- **Baking Stone.** A good baking stone is one of the keys to successful bread baking. When it is preheated in your oven, a ceramic or cement-composite baking stone provides an ideal surface for baking rustic breads and pizzas. Almost all of the bread recipes in this book call for the use of a baking stone. Buy the best one you can find,

  but make sure you know your oven's dimensions before you go shopping—it's disappointing to bring home a new baking stone and discover it does not fit in the oven.

- **Bamboo Skewers.** For testing the centers of muffins and cakes for doneness.

- **Cake and Tart Pans**. I bake most of my cakes in 9-inch springform pans, and I always prepare tarts in pans with removable bottoms. In both cases it's nice to have the easy-to-remove sides. If you are going to buy only one tart pan, I would recommend a 10-inch pan, but it's nice to have a variety ranging from 8- to 12-inch sizes. Buy the highest-quality pans you can afford.

- **Cooling Racks or Wire Racks**. These are important for quick and even cooling of breads and pastries. Buy a sturdy one. An unused oven rack will do nicely in a pinch.

- **Cutting Boards**. I like to keep at least two cutting boards in my kitchen, one for sweet ingredients and one for savory.

- **Dishtowels and Canvas Proofing Rags**. I like to keep extra dishtowels in my kitchen for covering loaves of bread while they proof. Often a recipe will call for wrapping a loaf in a floured dishtowel, which helps the loaf maintain its shape and keeps a skin from forming on the surface of the dough. At the bakery we use strips of canvas, which can be purchased at most neighborhood fabric stores, to wrap baguettes and bâtards (oval-shaped loaves). When not in use, the canvas needs to be scraped free of excess flour, then hung out to dry before being stored.

- **Knives**. At the very least, I like to have a good chef's knife, a bread knife, and a paring knife. Keep them sharp.

- **Measuring Cups and Measuring Spoons**. I like the stainless steel variety.

- **Microplane**. Perfect for zesting citrus fruits and grating ginger.

- **Mixing Bowls**. I prefer the stainless steel variety. They're lightweight, easy to clean, and even easier to store. It's good to have a couple of each size on hand.

- **Offset Spatula**. Perfect for frosting cakes and smoothing fillings into tart shells.

- **Parchment Paper**. Parchment paper is available in rolls or sheets and is a must-have item for bakers. I line cake pans with parchment paper to prevent sticking and always bake cookies on parchment paper–lined baking sheets. Placing a piece of parchment paper under a juicy tart or quiche while it bakes makes cleanup a breeze.

- **Parchment Paper for Lining Cake Pans**. Lining cake pans with parchment paper is the best way I know to keep cakes from sticking to their pans. It takes a few minutes of extra preparation time, but the results are worth the effort. Start by brushing the bottom and sides of the pan with canola oil. Cut a circle of parchment paper 1 inch bigger than the bottom of the pan you are using. (For example, cut a 10-inch circle of paper to line a 9-inch cake pan.) Fit the circle into the bottom of the pan, smoothing out any air bubbles with your fingers and pressing the extra paper firmly against the sides of the pan. The paper should rise ½ inch up the sides of the pan. Cut a strip, or collar, of parchment paper big enough to line the sides of the pan. (A 9 × 3-inch springform pan would require a 29 × 3-inch collar.) It's okay to use two pieces of overlapping paper. Some recipes may call for the collar to extend above the rim of the pan. If so, simply make the strip wider. Before lining the sides of the pan, brush a little more canola oil where the bottom round of paper rises up the sides. This will help the collar and bottom pieces to stick together. Press the paper collar against the sides of the pan, making sure that the paper fits snug against the bottom of the pan. In addition to keeping cakes from sticking, this method of lining the pan with overlapping pieces of paper helps keep cake batter from leaking out of the bottom of a springform pan.

- **Pastry Bags and Tips.** I recommend plastic-coated pastry bags, which are easy to clean and don't leak. It's worth buying a good set of tips in various sizes.

- **Pastry Brushes.** Buy the kind with natural bristles, in a variety of sizes.

- **Rimmed Baking Sheets**. Also referred to as jelly-roll pans or half-sheet pans, these are truly a kitchen essential. They're perfect for toasting nuts and seeds, and the raised sides prevent wet ingredients from spilling and making a mess of the oven. I recommend having at least two.

- **Rolling Pin**. A good one is essential. I recommend the heavy, wooden ball-bearing variety, at least 15 inches long. This size is big enough for just about any project. Make sure the handles are sturdy and comfortable.

- **Rubber Spatulas**. You can't have too many. I recommend buying the heat-safe kind in a variety of sizes.

- **Scale**. It's a good idea to have a basic pounds-and-ounces scale in your kitchen. One that converts to grams is even better. Some ingredients, such as Natural Sour Starter for example, are best measured by weight. Giving a cup or tablespoon measurement of these ingredients often isn't accurate enough. The scale doesn't have to be fancy, but I do recommend getting one with a digital screen.

- **Slotted Spoons**. Necessary for removing items such as poached pears from a pan of hot liquid.

- **Spray Bottle.** This is one of the key tools for baking bread at home. I use a simple plastic spray bottle, filled with fresh filtered water. Misting the inside of your oven keeps the surface of the loaf moist during the all-important first 15 minutes of baking. This prevents the loaf from splitting open and aids in the development of a perfect crust.

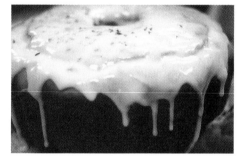

- **Stand Mixer.** My kitchen wouldn't be complete without a stand mixer. It's the most expensive piece of equipment on this list, but worth every penny. Buy the best one you can afford (I've always liked KitchenAid) and consider purchasing a professional-strength model if you plan on mixing a lot of bread dough. Make sure your mixer includes all of the basic attachments, including a whisk, paddle, and dough hook.

- **Wooden Spoons**. For mixing dough and endless other uses.

KITCHEN NICE-TO-HAVES

- **Baker's Peel.** If you're going to do a lot of bread baking, it's worth buying a peel. These thin wooden paddles make sliding bread and pizza into the oven easier and faster.

- **Bench Scrapers.** Also known as bench knives or dough scrapers, these are a miraculous baking tool and as essential as whisks and bowls. A square piece of metal, usually fitted with a plastic or wooden handle, a bench scraper is helpful in lifting and dividing sticky bread doughs. I also use it for dividing scones and biscuits and for cleaning cutting boards and canvas proofing rags.

- **Blowtorch.** Pick one up at a kitchen supply store or neighborhood hardware store. A small blowtorch is great for browning the surface of tarts and crème brûlée.

- **Cake Stand.** This isn't an essential kitchen item, but it does make cake frosting easier and more fun. Treat yourself.

- **Food Processor.** Food processors are ideal for puréeing soups, sauces, and spreads, and they provide a quick and easy alternative to chopping nuts and seeds by hand. Some people like to make pastry doughs in their food processor, but I don't recommend it. The blades spin too quickly and tend to overwork the dough.

- **Proofing Baskets.** Used for proofing pre-formed loaves, these baskets help loaves maintain their shape. There are all kinds of proofing baskets, or *bannetons*, available at specialty stores these days. They come in a wide range of shapes and sizes and are even available lined with linen. I like to use woven plastic or wicker baskets, which are affordable and easy to clean. Simply dust the inside of a basket with flour, insert the pre-formed loaf, and cover the basket with a dishtowel.

INGREDIENTS

- **Butter.** All of the butter in these recipes is unsalted. Salted butter should not be substituted.

- **Canola Oil.** I use canola oil for brushing cake and tart pans, muffin tins, and other baking pans. It has a neutral flavor and can reach high temperatures without burning.

- **Chocolate.** We use different chocolates in our recipes, including bittersweet and unsweetened, all of which are available in most supermarkets. I recommend Guittard and Callebaut brands.

- **Cocoa Powder.** I recommend Dutch-process (or alkalized) cocoa powder, which is nice and dark and has a rich flavor that's perfect for baking.

- **Dried Fruit**. I like to use unsulfured dried fruits whenever possible. The color of the fruit is not as brilliant as fruits that have been chemically treated, but the taste is better and you don't have to worry about any health risks.

- **Eggs**. All of the recipes in this book call for large eggs. Support your local farmers whenever possible and buy the freshest eggs available.

- **Extracts**. Use only pure vanilla and almond extracts.

- **Flour**. Flour is the most frequently used ingredient in baking, and it is important to use the highest quality available. The recipes in this book call for several flours, from unbleached all-purpose to coarse rye to semolina. Most of these are now available in supermarkets, and those that are not can usually be found in gourmet stores and natural food stores. Whenever possible, I recommend supporting your local mills—we use Washington's Fairhaven Mill—when buying your flour. More widely distributed brands that I like include King Arthur and Bob's Red Mill brands, both of which offer a full line of flours. Experiment and find your own favorites.

- **Milk and Cream**. I always cook with fresh whole milk and heavy cream, and I prefer to use organic brands when they are available.

- **Nuts**. I recommend buying whole raw nuts, then toasting and chopping them as needed. (While cooking times vary, I usually toast nuts in a preheated 350°F oven for about 10 minutes.) Pre-packaged chopped nuts aren't likely to be fresh, and you'll taste the difference in your baked goods.

- **Salt**. I'm a big fan of kosher salt, which has a lighter flavor than iodized table salt. You will see it used in all of our bread recipes, as well as in the lunch and brunch items. A lot of the pastry recipes simply call for salt, by which I mean table salt.

- **Spices**. Use fresh spices and store them in airtight containers. Whole seeds are best toasted and freshly ground, either by hand or in a coffee or spice grinder.

- **Sugar**. The recipes in this book always specify which kind of sugar to use. We use granulated sugar, light brown sugar, powdered sugar, and coarse raw sugar.

- **Yeast**. When a recipe in this book calls for dried yeast, it is referring to active dry yeast, which is available in all supermarkets.

- **Zest**. Always use fresh citrus zest, taking care to use only the outermost skin of the fruit. (The white pith just below the surface can be quite bitter.) I recommend using a Microplane zester.

A FEW IMPORTANT TERMS

- **Crumb Coat**. The process of covering a cake with a thin layer of frosting, just enough to seal in the crumbs. A crumb coat is usually applied, then the cake is chilled, before the final layer of frosting is added.

- **Crust and Crumb**. When referring to a loaf of bread, the crust is the exterior and the crumb is the interior. The word crumb is also used to describe the texture of cakes.

- **Pre-Baking**. Also called blind baking, this is the process of lining a raw tart shell with parchment paper and baking weights and baking the shell before it is filled (see page 129).

- **Proofing**. The rising of a dough, whether in a bowl or once it has been shaped into a loaf.

- **Scoring**. The process of slashing the surface of a loaf, usually with ⅛- to ¼-inch-deep cuts, just before it goes into the oven. The slashes are decorative and also serve the purpose of letting gases escape from the dough as it bakes.

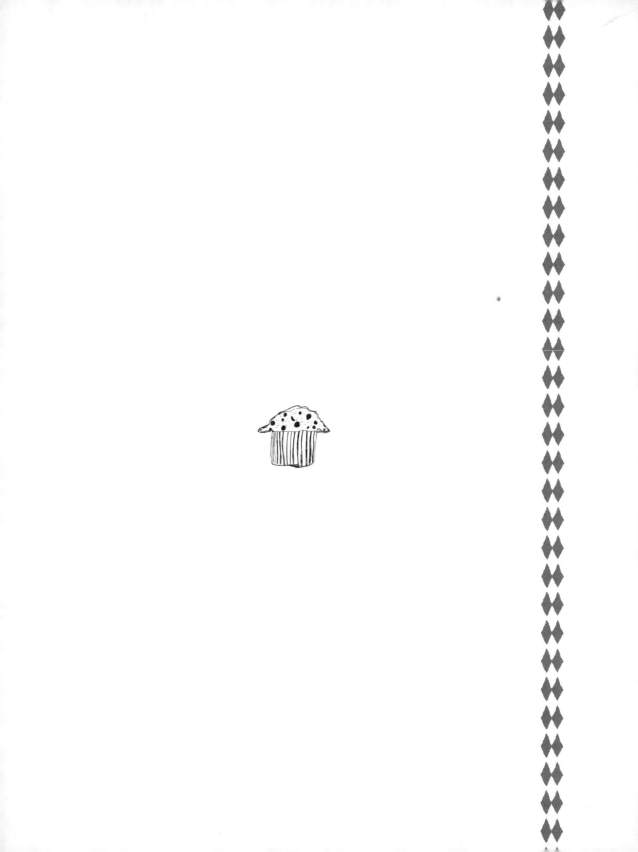

OUR DAILY BREAD

OUR DAILY BREAD

I have tasted loaves from some of the world's best bakeries and been inspired by bread baked in the simplest of home kitchens. I have baked in culinary school, in my home, and in restaurants and bakeries across America. One experience in particular helped shape my approach to bread baking; it was the catalyst for Macrina Bakery & Cafe. Before opening the bakery in 1993, I went on what I like to call a bread pilgrimage to Italy. Bread had become my passion, and I wanted to learn all I could. I consulted books, recent European travelers, and fellow chefs, all the while compiling my list of must-sees and must-tastes. Finally I set off in search of Italy's regional specialties and best breads.

In Milan I tasted a fantastic *ciambellone all' uva* at the bakery Gian Fornaio. The loaf was packed with plump muscat raisins, and I quickly devoured the entire thing. In Lucca I found an incredible focaccia. I watched the bakers cut the saltless dough into four-foot lengths and sprinkle them with coarse sea salt before loading them into the oven. The finished golden loaves were brushed with extra virgin olive oil as they were pulled from the oven and then sold by weight to eager customers, who simply held their hands apart to indicate what size pieces they wanted.

In Rome I discovered my all-time favorite bread. I was enjoying a simple dinner of wood-fired pizza when I noticed a gorgeous slice of bread on a nearby table. I asked the waiter for some and he proudly obliged. The crust's color ranged from caramel to almost black, the crumb had a beautifully irregular texture, and the flavor was much more developed than I had found in most Italian loaves. This was truly the best bread I had ever seen or tasted. After a few inquiries I was presented with a phone number and address of the source of this heavenly loaf: Panficio Arnesse Giuseppe.

The next morning my traveling companion, Susan Regis, and I made our way to this bakery. We arrived to find Giuseppe relaxing after the morning bake. He was seated in front of his warm oven, coffee in hand, reading a newspaper. We talked for hours about the bread and about his wood-burning oven, which was fueled by hazelnut shells. I discovered that his doughs were made with very little equipment and stored without any refrigeration (too expensive). Starters were developed in his mixers and held there for the next day. I went on and on about his wonderful bread, but he insisted that it was "only bread." With that he tore open a loaf, plunged some into a bowl of olive oil, and presented it to me. It was so good I couldn't speak for half an hour after we left. I was so inspired and grateful for having met this amazing baker.

I visited many bakeries during my stay in Italy. I met with as many bakers as I could and tasted more than a hundred loaves. What most moved me was each baker's commitment to making the best loaf possible in the given circumstances. Whether limited by space, lack of refrigeration, or the availability of certain ingredients, these bakers make the most of what they have available. They strive for beautiful bread, and it was that spirit that I brought home with me. All of the breads at Macrina were inspired by traditional recipes and adapted to our bakery's environment. We're lucky, for example, to have lots of refrigeration for storing and fermenting our doughs, and modern technology allows us to easily adjust the bakery's temperature. And while we are always experimenting with ways to improve our baking, the basics never change. We still form every loaf by hand.

The recipes in this section are meant to inspire you to bake your own beautiful loaves. Use these formulas as a starting point and adapt them to your home environment, your oven, your schedule, and your personal preferences. Try not to get discouraged if your first loaf isn't picture perfect. Mine certainly wasn't. Practice your craft and learn to trust your intuition. Enjoy the mixing, the hands-on forming of the loaves, and the joy of sharing the results with family and friends. Baking bread is an amazingly satisfying process. I can't imagine my life without it, and I hope you bring it into yours.

Enjoy.

Chapter 1

BAKING WITH
NATURAL SOUR STARTERS

For me, sour starters define the art of bread baking. They provide the natural leavening that helps to create rustic European-style breads, and their organic acids act as a natural preservative, adding several days to a loaf's shelf life. Similar to a reduction added to a great sauce, a natural starter is also a concentrated flavor builder. Letting starter-based doughs sit for a long fermentation time allows them to develop a marvelous complexity of flavor that is not found in loaves baked with dried yeast.

Unfortunately, naturally leavened breads are often undervalued and little understood. A variety of sourdough loaves are readily available in most supermarkets, but these breads are rarely made from scratch. Instead, large mills create easily prepared mixes that contain dried yeast and dehydrated sour flavor.

While these commercial mixes make it easier to bake large quantities of bread in little time, the finished loaves don't compare to those of an artisan bakery or dedicated home bakers who carefully nurture and maintain their natural starter.

Starters put your skills and intuition to the test; in many ways they are like children. They need to be fed regularly, they get fussy when ignored, and they are best kept on a routine schedule. A starter's leavening power, as well as its flavor, is directly affected by its surroundings and the quality of care that it receives. To best anticipate a sour starter's needs, you have to establish a relationship with it and get to know its personal characteristics. But once you've done this the results can be spectacularly satisfying.

Heat is the catalyst for any starter's development, and starters are very sensitive to erratic changes in temperature. I witnessed this firsthand at one of my past baking jobs. We had just moved our bread production to a new, larger facility, where the ambient temperature was much warmer than our starter was used to. After one week the starter became intensely sour, and the finished loaves were rising to only half their normal size. The increased heat had accelerated the starter's fermentation. To fix the problem, we began keeping the starter at a cooler temperature, thus slowing down the fermentation process. In no time at all our loaves had regained a beautiful round shape and a balanced sour flavor.

The five breads in this chapter are fine examples of baking with natural sour starters. All of the starters used in these recipes are simple mixtures of flour, water, and the natural yeast found on the skin of organic grapes. As you'll see, bakers are able to achieve a variety of flavors by adding different flours and grains to their starters. Using a whole-wheat starter in the Macrina Casera Loaf gives it a mild sour taste that complements any dish. The starter's sour flavor also provides a perfect balance to the sweet dried apricots in the Apricot Pecan Loaf. These recipes take time to prepare, but with a little planning and dedication, I think you'll produce some of the best breads you've ever baked.

Natural Sour Starter

Don't be intimidated by the time involved in creating a natural sour starter.
It may be a two-week commitment at the beginning, but you will need to contribute only a
few minutes every day. Nature does most of the work, and the results are worth the wait. Once
you have a starter you are able to use, you can bake with it for years or even decades to come.
For an accurate measurement, it's best to weigh starters when using them in recipes.

Makes approximately 13 ounces of starter

FOR THE STARTER:
6 ounces organic grapes
1¼ cups unbleached all-purpose flour
1½ cups filtered water, at room temperature

FOR THE FEEDING FORMULA:
1 cup unbleached all-purpose flour
1 cup filtered water, at room temperature

CREATING THE STARTER:

- **Day One:** Place grapes in the center of a 10-inch square piece of cheesecloth. Gather up the sides of the cloth and tie with string, creating a sachet. Leave a tail of string at least 10 inches long. Whisk flour and water together in a medium bowl until all lumps are fully dissolved and the consistency is like pancake batter. Using your hands, crush the sachet of grapes and lower it into the starter. Tape end of string to outside of bowl so that it doesn't fall into the mixture. Set the bowl, uncovered, in a warm room, about 70°F, and let sit for 2 days.

- **Day Three:** Small bubbles will appear on the starter's surface. Remove and discard the sachet of grapes. Now the starter is ready for its first feeding.

FEEDING THE STARTER:

- *Note:* You will need to make a new batch of feeding formula every time you feed the starter. Combine flour and water (amounts listed above) in a medium bowl and whisk until flour is dissolved. Stir this initial batch of feeding formula into the starter and let sit in a warm room for 1 more day.

- **Day Four:** Stir the starter with a whisk and discard half of the mixture. Stir in a batch of feeding formula and let sit at room temperature for 2 hours. Then place the starter, uncovered, in the refrigerator for 1 day. (Starters need oxygen, which is why they are usually left uncovered.) Store the starter on one of the refrigerator's highest shelves to keep objects from falling into it. If you have a busy kitchen, cover the starter with plastic wrap to protect it, and cut a few slits in the plastic to let in air.

- **Day Five:** Remove the starter from the refrigerator, stir it with a whisk, and again discard half of the mixture. Stir in another batch of feeding formula, let the starter sit at room temperature for 2 hours, then return it to the refrigerator. Repeat this process for 10 more days, feeding the starter at about the same time each day. Be sure to let the starter sit out for 2 hours after each feeding before returning it to the refrigerator. After these 10 days the starter will be ready for baking and will require less attention.

Watching the Coupe du Monde

In February 1999, Andrew and I had the pleasure of attending the Coupe du Monde in Paris. We went as spectators to cheer on the U.S. team at this World Cup of baking, a prestigious international baking competition that's held every three years in the French capital. Teams are carefully selected from each country's top bakers, and training can last for more than a year. This was only the second time that a U.S. team had participated, and we were very excited about their chances. The competition was held over several days and tested a baker's skills in three categories: artistic design, viennoiserie (sweet and laminated doughs), and baguettes and specialty breads. We sat in bleachers and supported our team like a group of high school kids at a football game. It was a blast.

When the judging was over the American team had won! We were all very proud of the team and gathered in a Paris restaurant for a wonderful party in their honor. Bakers from across the United States were in attendance, all beaming with pride and sharing their opinions on why the team had performed so well. It appeared to me that the U.S. team, not bound strictly to any one tradition, had been able to absorb techniques and customs from the world's best baking. That is precisely what Macrina and other artisan bakeries across America have aimed for. We've used organizations like the Bread Bakers' Guild of America to share our techniques, favorite recipes, and daily discoveries, and we've raised the quality of American baking along the way. Whatever the secret of the team's success, we were thrilled by their performance.

Variations on
Natural Sour Starter

You can create your own variety of sour starters simply by using different flours in the recipe. Experiment on your own, and you'll find that your finished loaves take on a new range of flavors and textures. Below are two variations on the Natural Sour Starter recipe.

Mild Whole-Wheat Starter

Whole-wheat flour imparts an apple-like flavor to the starter and will give your loaves a mild sour taste.

Makes approximately 16 ounces of starter

FOR THE STARTER:
6 ounces organic grapes
1 cup unbleached all-purpose flour
⅓ cup coarse whole-wheat flour
1½ cups filtered water, at room temperature

FOR THE FEEDING FORMULA:
⅔ cup unbleached all-purpose flour
⅓ cup coarse whole-wheat flour
1 cup filtered water, at room temperature

• Follow the instructions for Natural Sour Starter (*page 7*).

Campagne Natural Starter

This is a great starter for using in country-style ryes and is typical of traditional, naturally leavened French breads. Loaves made with this starter will have a fuller, more sour taste than bread made with Natural Sour Starter.

Makes approximately 16 ounces of starter

FOR THE STARTER:
6 ounces organic grapes
½ cup unbleached all-purpose flour
⅓ cup fine rye flour
¼ cup coarse whole-wheat flour
1½ cups filtered water, at room temperature

Maintaining a Natural Sour Starter

The process of creating a starter requires daily work, but once it has a life of its own you can relax a little. At the bakery, we feed our starters every 24 hours. But if you are not baking bread every day, and most people aren't, it's best to switch from a daily feeding schedule to a weekly one. Choose a day that works best for you, and try to stick to the schedule.

Once a week, remove the starter from the refrigerator and stir it with a whisk. If a crust has formed on the starter, simply remove it with a spoon before whisking. Discard half of the starter, stir in a batch of feeding formula, and let the bowl sit at room temperature for 2 hours before returning it to the refrigerator. *Note: Never use up more than half of your starter.*

Fed weekly, the starter will remain flavorful but its leavening power will become dormant. Before you use the starter in recipes it will require a jump-start. Remove the starter from the refrigerator 24 hours before you plan on baking. Stir it with a whisk, discard half the volume, and add a batch of feeding formula. Keep the starter at room temperature and feed it again 12 hours later. Let the starter sit at room temperature for another 8 to 12 hours before baking with it. Measure off as much starter as your recipe calls for, then feed the remainder 1 more time. Let the starter sit at room temperature for 2 hours before returning to the refrigerator.

Starters that are fed daily do not need an extra feeding before being mixed into doughs.

It is always best to use starters 8 to 12 hours after their most recent feeding. They should be at room temperature when used.

Don't lose hope if you let more than 1 week go by without feeding the starter. You may still be able to revive it. Remove the starter from the refrigerator and pour off any dark liquid that may have formed on the surface. Taste the starter to make sure it hasn't spoiled. (Bad starter will have a sulfuric taste and should be discarded.) If it hasn't spoiled, let the starter sit at room temperature for 24 hours. Feed it twice, at 12-hour intervals, during that time period. Bubbles should appear on the surface. Taste the starter again to confirm that it hasn't gone bad, then return it to the refrigerator and continue feeding weekly.

FOR THE FEEDING FORMULA:
½ cup unbleached all-purpose flour
⅓ cup fine rye flour
¼ cup coarse whole-wheat flour
1 cup filtered water, at room temperature

- Follow the instructions for Natural Sour Starter (*page 7*).

MACRINA CASERA LOAF

The word casera *means of this house, which is how this bread got its name. Our house loaf, it was the first bread we baked at Macrina, and it's my personal favorite. With a mild sour flavor, the Casera Loaf is meant to be eaten with any meal. Try it for cinnamon toast.*

Makes 1 large, round loaf

6 ounces Mild Whole-Wheat Starter (*page 9*), at room temperature
1½ cups filtered water, at room temperature
3½ cups unbleached all-purpose flour
2 teaspoons kosher salt
Spray bottle of water

- Place starter and water in the bowl of your stand mixer. Using the paddle attachment, mix on low speed for about 2 minutes. (If mixing by hand, place starter and water in a medium bowl and break up starter with a whisk.) Add flour and salt and mix on low speed for 2 minutes more, or until ingredients are combined. Switch to the hook attachment and mix on medium speed for 12 to 14 minutes. Try to keep dough mass at the base of the hook, lowering the bowl if necessary. (If mixing by hand, add flour and salt and stir with a wooden spoon. Knead with your hands for 12 to 15 minutes.) Finished dough will have a smooth finish and elastic texture.

- Transfer dough to an oiled, medium bowl and cover with plastic wrap. Set the bowl in a warm room, 70 to 75°F, and let rise for 4 hours. Dough will almost double in size.

- Pull dough from the bowl onto a floured surface and punch it down with your hands. Form dough into a ball by pulling the edges up and towards the center of the mass. Repeat this motion until you have a tight ball, then let it rest, seam side down, for 2 minutes. Line a medium bowl with a floured dishtowel and place loaf, seam side up, in the center. Fold ends of the towel over top of loaf to prevent a skin from forming. Let sit at room temperature for 1 hour. Loaf will rise slightly.

- Transfer bowl to refrigerator for 6 to 10 hours. It's during this time that the loaf fully develops its flavor.

- Take bowl from refrigerator and let sit at room temperature for 1 to 1½ hours. Place baking stone on center rack of oven and preheat to 400°F. I usually put the bowl on top of my oven while it's preheating.

- The loaf is ready to bake when it has come to room temperature and has a Jell-O-like feel. Remove loaf from bowl and place on a counter or baker's peel, seam side down. Using a sharp blade, cut a shallow crosshatch design on the top of loaf. Transfer loaf to center of preheated baking stone and, moving quickly to keep heat in the oven, mist inside of oven with a spray bottle of water. Bake for 45 to 50 minutes, misting the oven twice more during the first 15 minutes of baking. The finished loaf should be golden brown and sound hollow when tapped on the bottom. Let cool on a wire rack for 30 minutes.

Creating the Macrina Starter

One of Macrina's starters has a lot of sentimental value for me. I created it from grapes harvested in my own backyard. It was the autumn of 1991 and I was preparing for my harvest party, an annual gathering in which I invite friends and family to bring foods they've grown in their own gardens. Someone might bring a basket of vine-ripened tomatoes; another might bring sweet corn on the cob. We've enjoyed beautiful raspberry tarts and steaming apple crisps, the fruit harvested at the peak of ripeness. Anything goes at these parties, and we never know what the menu will be. The only guarantee is that it will be fresh and flavorful.

That year I wanted to bake bread for my guests, so I started preparing a couple of weeks earlier. I picked plump red grapes from my vines and smashed them with my hands. I added the grapes to flour and water, and I had the beginnings of a natural starter. After several days of love and regular feedings, the starter was alive and kicking. I was ready to do some baking. The loaf that I made for that party ultimately became our house bread, Macrina Casera. More than a decade later we are still feeding that same starter every day, and I'm proud to see the loaf served in so many homes and restaurants. The spirit in which it was conceived lives on.

RUSTIC BAGUETTE

We had always baked a variety of baguettes at Macrina, including
an Italian panini loaf, a crusty sour white ficelle, and a soft baguette with fresh herbs.
Our customers loved all of these, but they frequently asked us for a classic French baguette.
On a trip to Paris my general manager, Andrew Cleary, and I finally found the inspiration
we needed. The bread was from La Flûte Gana, an artisan bakery run by two sisters from a
long-admired family of artisan bakers. The sisters are involved in every part of the operation,
and this attention to detail shows in their pastries, cookies, and breads. Andrew and I tasted
as many as we could; we particularly liked the fresh demi-flûtes. These mini baguettes had a
wonderfully nutty flavor, and we could taste the creaminess of the flour. I returned to Macrina
and set out with our lead baker, Mel Darbyshire, to create our own version of this classic.

Makes 4 demi-baguettes

5 ounces Natural Sour Starter *(page 7)*, at room temperature
1½ cups filtered water, at room temperature
1 teaspoon dried yeast
¼ cup medium whole-wheat flour
3 cups and 2 tablespoons unbleached all-purpose flour
2 teaspoons kosher salt
Spray bottle of water

- Combine starter, water, and yeast in the bowl of your stand mixer. Using the paddle attachment, mix for 1 minute on low speed. (If mixing by hand, place starter, water, and yeast in a medium bowl and whisk together to break up the starter.) Add the whole-wheat flour, all-purpose flour, and salt and mix 1 minute more, or until ingredients are combined. Switch to the hook attachment and mix on medium speed for 12 to 14 minutes. (If mixing by hand, add the flours and salt and stir with a wooden spoon. Knead with your hands for 14 to 16 minutes.) The finished dough will be sticky and slightly wet and will have a satiny appearance.

- Pull dough from the bowl onto a floured surface and form it into a ball. Place ball in an oiled, medium bowl and cover with plastic wrap. Let dough rise in a warm room, about 70°F, for 2 hours. Dough will almost double in size.

- Remove the plastic wrap from bowl and give dough what bakers call a *turn:* stretch each of the dough's 4 edges outward and then back onto the center (see photos, page 14). Turn the left and right sides first, followed by the top and bottom. Flip the entire ball over, placing it, seam side down, in the bowl, and cover again with plastic wrap. Turning the dough in this manner is a gentle continuation of the mixing process, and will make the finished dough easier to handle. Let dough rise at room temperature

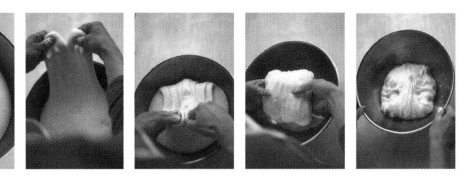

for 2 hours, then give it another turn. Re-cover the bowl with plastic wrap and let it rise at room temperature for 1 more hour. Dough will almost double in size. Place the covered bowl in the refrigerator for 1 hour. During this time the dough will develop more flavor.

- Remove bowl from the refrigerator and pull dough from bowl onto a floured surface. Using your hands, flatten the dough to release extra air. Shape into a rectangle and divide dough into 4 equal pieces with a knife. Loosely form each piece into a log, approximately 5 x 2 inches, and let rest for 10 minutes. One at a time, flatten the logs again and form into tighter baguettes: Use both hands and start in the center of the log. Using slight pressure, roll the dough back and forth, gently pulling to the right and left to lengthen the baguette. Repeat this motion until the baguette is approximately 12 inches long, adding small amounts of flour to the work surface as needed. Lift baguettes onto a floured dishtowel or canvas, leaving 3 to 4 inches between each loaf. Pull the gaps of cloth upwards so that each baguette is nestled snugly in the fabric. This will help to maintain the loaves' shape. Fold remaining fabric over top of baguettes, or cover with an additional piece of cloth. Let proof at room temperature for 1 to 1½ hours. Loaves will rise slightly.

- Place baking stone on center rack of oven and preheat to 425°F.

- Invert the baguettes onto a counter or baker's peel, and use a sharp blade to score one long line down the length of each baguette. Working quickly, transfer baguettes to the baking stone, taking care that the baguettes retain their shape. Mist inside of oven with a spray bottle of water. Bake for 30 to 35 minutes, misting oven twice more during the first 15 minutes. Finished baguettes will be medium brown and sound hollow when tapped on the bottom. Let cool on a wire rack for 30 minutes.

APRICOT PECAN LOAF

This recipe makes a rustic loaf similar to one we bake every weekend
at the bakery. It's packed with unsulfured apricots, which add a natural sweetness
and eliminate the need for added sugar. It's delicious with creamy cheeses such as
brie or ricotta. Customers rave that this is the perfect breakfast bread.

Makes 1 large, oval loaf

½ cup coarsely chopped pecans
4 ounces Mild Whole-Wheat Starter *(page 9),* at room temperature
1 cup filtered water, at room temperature
½ teaspoon dried yeast
¼ cup fine whole-wheat flour
2 tablespoons coarse rye flour
2 cups unbleached all-purpose flour
1½ teaspoons kosher salt
¾ cup unsulfured dried apricots, diced
Spray bottle of water

- Preheat oven to 350°F. Place pecans on a rimmed baking sheet and toast for 10 minutes. Let cool.

- Combine starter, water, and yeast in the bowl of your stand mixer. Mix with the paddle attachment for 1 to 2 minutes on low speed. (If mixing by hand, place starter and water in a medium bowl and whisk together to break up starter.) Add whole-wheat flour, rye flour, all-purpose flour, and salt and mix on low speed until ingredients are combined. Switch to the hook attachment and mix on medium speed for about 7 minutes. (If mixing by hand, add flours and salt and stir with a wooden spoon. Knead with your hands for 10 minutes.) Let dough rest in the bowl for 5 minutes, then add apricots and pecans and mix until evenly distributed.

- Transfer dough to an oiled, medium bowl and cover with plastic wrap. Let proof in a warm room, about 70°F, for 2 to 3 hours. Dough will increase 50 percent in size.

- Pull dough from the bowl onto a floured surface and form into a 5 x 8-inch rectangle. Position dough so that a short end is facing you. Starting with the closest end, roll dough away from you into a tight log. As you roll, apply extra pressure at the ends to taper them. The formed loaf should look similar to a small football. Wrap the loaf, seam side up, in a floured dishtowel or canvas to prevent a skin from forming on the loaf. (Wrapping the loaf also helps to maintain its shape.) Let proof at room temperature for 2 hours. Loaf will rise slightly.

- Place baking stone on center rack of oven and preheat to 400°F.

- Unwrap the loaf and set it, seam side down, on a counter or baker's peel. With a sharp blade, cut 7 diagonal lines across the top of the loaf. Place in center of baking stone and, moving quickly to keep heat inside oven, mist inside of oven with a spray bottle of water. Bake for 50 to 55 minutes, misting oven twice more during the first 15 minutes. The loaf's crust will be a deep, golden brown. Let cool on a wire rack for 30 minutes.

ONION RYE LOAF

*One of Macrina's former lead bakers, Evan Andres, accepted the
challenge of developing our version of this classic bread. He was obsessed
with ryes and created one of the best I've ever tasted.*

Makes 1 cylinder-shaped loaf

1 medium yellow onion, chopped into ½-inch pieces
2 tablespoons extra virgin olive oil
7 ounces Campagne Natural Starter *(page 9)*, at room temperature
1½ cups filtered water, at room temperature
1 teaspoon dried yeast
1 cup coarse rye flour
3 cups unbleached all-purpose flour
2 teaspoons kosher salt
1 tablespoon caraway seeds
Spray bottle of water

- Preheat oven to 400°F. Toss chopped onion with olive oil and spread evenly on a rimmed baking sheet. Roast for 25 to 30 minutes, or until edges of onion are golden brown. Let cool.

- Combine starter, water, and yeast in the bowl of your stand mixer. Mix with the paddle attachment for 2 minutes on low speed. (If mixing by hand, place starter, water, and yeast in a medium bowl and whisk together to break up the starter.) Add the rye flour, all-purpose flour, salt, caraway seeds, and cooled onions. Mix for 1 minute to combine, then change to the hook attachment and mix for 8 to 10 minutes on medium speed. (If mixing by hand, add flours, salt, caraway seeds, and onions and stir with a wooden spoon. Knead with your hands for 10 to 12 minutes.)

- Place dough in an oiled, medium bowl and cover with plastic wrap. Let proof in a warm room, about 70°F, for 1½ to 2 hours, or until dough has almost doubled in size.

- Pull dough from the bowl onto a floured work surface and flatten it with your hands, taking care to press out all the air. Form dough into a rectangle and position it so that a short end is facing you. Starting with the closest end, roll dough into a tight cylindrical loaf, tucking the ends underneath to give them a blunt finish. Wrap the loaf in a floured dishtowel or canvas, seam side up, and let proof at room temperature for 1 hour. Loaf will rise 50 percent.

- While the loaf is proofing, place baking stone on center rack of oven and preheat to 400°F.

- Unwrap loaf and set it, seam side down, on a counter or baker's peel. Using a sharp blade, score 4 lines across top of loaf. Moving quickly to keep heat in oven, lift loaf onto center of baking stone and mist inside of oven with a spray bottle of water. Mist oven 3 more times during the first 20 minutes of baking, which helps to keep the loaf moist and aids in the development of the crust. Bake for 50 to 60 minutes, or until bread has a deep brown color and sounds hollow when tapped on the bottom. Let cool on a wire rack for 30 minutes.

GREEK OLIVE LOAF

This bakery favorite was originally made only on weekends, but our customers insisted it be part of our daily bake. Our cafe chef likes to feature it as the base for an egg salad sandwich, topping it off with roasted tomatoes and a few anchovy fillets.

Makes 2 small, oval loaves

8 ounces Natural Sour Starter *(page 7)*, at room temperature
1½ cups filtered water, at room temperature
1 cup coarse rye flour
3¼ cups unbleached all-purpose flour
2 teaspoons kosher salt
2 teaspoons finely chopped fresh rosemary
1 cup pitted kalamata olives
Spray bottle of water

- Combine starter and water in the bowl of your stand mixer. Using the paddle attachment, mix for about 1 minute on low speed. (If mixing by hand, place starter and water in a medium bowl and whisk together to break up the starter.) Add the rye flour, all-purpose flour, salt, and rosemary and mix for another 2 minutes to combine. Switch to the hook attachment and mix on medium speed for 10 minutes. This dough is slightly wet, and it will take some time before developing into a ball. (If mixing by hand, add flours, salt, and rosemary and stir with a wooden spoon. Knead with your hands for 10 to 15 minutes.) Let dough rest in bowl for 5 minutes.

- Pull dough from the bowl onto a floured surface. Form into a rectangle about ½ inch thick and position dough so that a short end is facing you. Sprinkle olives over entire surface of dough. Starting with the closest end, roll dough away from you into a log. Let it rest, seam side down, for 1 to 2 minutes. Fold the 2 ends into the center and loosely form a ball. Place ball of dough in an oiled, medium bowl and cover with plastic wrap. Let proof in a warm room, about 70°F, for 4 hours. Dough will almost double in size.

- Pull dough from bowl onto a floured surface and punch it down with your hands to release air bubbles. Divide dough into 2 equal pieces and flatten one of the pieces into a rectangle. Starting with a short end, roll the dough away from you into a tight log. Taper the ends of the loaf to form a small football. Wrap the loaf, seam side up, in a floured cloth. Repeat this procedure with remaining piece of dough. Let proof at room temperature for 1½ hours. Loaves will rise slightly. Transfer wrapped loaves to the refrigerator for 6 to 10 hours.

- Remove loaves from refrigerator and let come to room temperature, about 1½ hours. While dough is coming to temperature, place baking stone on center rack of oven and preheat to 400°F.

- Unwrap loaves and set them, seam sides down, on a counter or baker's peel. Using a sharp blade, score a shallow line from end to end vertically on the surface of each loaf. Moving quickly to maintain oven temperature, lift loaves onto the preheated baking stone and mist oven with a spray bottle of water. Bake loaves for about 50 minutes, misting the oven twice more during the first 15 minutes of baking. Loaves are ready when they have a dark brown color and a firm crust. Let cool on a wire rack for 30 minutes.

Chapter 2

BIGA-STARTED BREADS

Traditional Biga Starter
Seed Dough
Classic Italian Loaf with Recipes for Focaccia and Pizzetta
Ciabatta Loaf
Semolina & Sesame Loaf
Olivetta Loaf

When I first started baking, I searched high and low for books that could answer my questions. It was difficult to find quality cookbooks that were dedicated to the art of bread baking, but I finally discovered Carol Field's *The Italian Baker*. I baked my way through the book, front to back, and it remains a favorite of mine to this day. The breads are wonderful, and I love the way Carol's joy and passion for baking comes through in her writing. It was Carol's book that first introduced me to biga-started breads.

A biga is a combination of flour, water, dried yeast, and a little time. While natural starters take two weeks to prepare and require weekly maintenance, a biga can be prepared in a matter of days, and leftovers are simply discarded. Much like natural sour starters, a biga provides leavening and a wonderful depth of flavor to rustic breads. Bigas also aid in the development of that beautiful, irregular texture that we find in classic Italian loaves. Results like these can't be achieved by simply dissolving dried yeast in water.

In a biga starter, yeast feeds on the wheat flour's natural sugars. This action results in the formation of carbon dioxide and alcohol, which give the starter a fuller, but not sour, flavor. The amount of yeast used in a biga is small, so allowing the biga to ferment for longer periods of time will allow more flavor to naturally develop.

The recipes in this chapter use two different biga starters, Traditional Biga Starter and Seed Dough. Seed Dough is essentially a firmer version of a biga starter, created by mixing in more flour. In my experience, firmer bigas give loaves more varied texture. The dried yeast in bigas is much stronger than the natural yeast found in sour starters, so loaves rise faster and are ready for baking quicker than those made with sour starters.

TRADITIONAL BIGA STARTER

Biga starters are a key ingredient in many rustic Italian loaves. They are easy to prepare and yield wonderful results. Using them in your baking will help you make breads that are filled with complexity of flavor and texture. I recommend preparing biga starter the day before baking. To assure an accurate measurement, it's best to weigh biga when using it in recipes.

Makes approximately 2½ pounds of biga starter

2 cups filtered water, at room temperature
1½ teaspoons dried yeast
2½ cups unbleached all-purpose flour

- Pour water into a medium bowl and sprinkle yeast on top. Mix with a whisk until all lumps are dissolved. Add flour and mix with whisk until smooth, about 3 minutes. Place uncovered bowl in a warm room, 70 to 75°F, and let sit for 2 to 3 hours. Bubbles will appear on the surface of the biga.

- Cover bowl with plastic wrap and transfer to refrigerator for at least 6 hours. It is during this time that the starter truly develops its flavor. Biga can be stored in the refrigerator for up to 4 days, but it will develop a more sour taste as fermentation continues. It will also lose some of its leavening power. Personally, I like to use starters within the first 2 days.

SEED DOUGH

Seed Dough is basically a biga starter with additional flour mixed in. Aging the dough for a day or more allows it to naturally develop a more complex flavor. Recipes that call for this firm version of a biga starter are best prepared in a stand mixer. To assure an accurate measurement, it's best to weigh Seed Dough when using it in recipes.

Makes approximately 2¼ pounds of seed dough

2 cups filtered water, at room temperature
2 teaspoons dried yeast
4½ cups unbleached all-purpose flour

- Place water in a medium bowl and sprinkle yeast on top. Mix with a whisk until yeast is completely dissolved. Add 2 cups of the flour and mix with a whisk until smooth, about 3 minutes. Let uncovered bowl rest at room temperature, about 70°F, for 2 hours.

- Transfer mixture to the bowl of your stand mixer. Add the remaining flour and mix with paddle attachment until fully incorporated, about 1 minute. Switch to the hook attachment and mix on medium speed for 7 minutes. Dough will remain quite wet and underdeveloped. It will lack elasticity and will break easily if stretched.

- Coat your hands with flour and transfer dough to an oiled, medium bowl and cover with plastic wrap. Set bowl in a warm room, 70 to 75°F, and let rise for 2 hours. Dough will double in size.

- Store covered bowl in the refrigerator for at least 12 hours or overnight. Seed Dough is best used when it is 1 day old, but it can be stored for up to 4 days in the refrigerator.

CLASSIC ITALIAN LOAF WITH RECIPES FOR FOCACCIA AND PIZZETTA

This bread is similar to the popular Giuseppe loaf we bake daily at Macrina.
Like the traditional Italian loaves that inspired it, this bread has a mild, full flavor
that is developed during a short but essential fermentation time. It boasts a hardy crust
and a medium-bodied interior texture that's accented by small, irregular holes.
This bread is truly a compliment to any meal. The dough can also be used
for making a variety of focaccia and pizzetta (recipes follow).

Makes 1 oval loaf

6 ounces Traditional Biga Starter *(page 21)*, 1 day old, at room temperature
½ teaspoon dried yeast
1½ cups filtered water, at room temperature
3½ cups unbleached all-purpose flour
2 teaspoons kosher salt
Spray bottle of water

- Place the starter, yeast, and filtered water in the bowl of your stand mixer. Using the paddle attachment, mix on low speed for 1 minute. (If you are mixing by hand, place starter, yeast, and water in a large bowl and mix with a whisk to break up starter and dissolve yeast). Switch to the hook attachment. Add flour and salt and mix on low speed until ingredients are combined, about 2 minutes. Increase speed to medium and mix for 12 to 14 minutes. (If mixing by hand, add flour and salt and stir with a wooden spoon. Knead with your hands for about 15 minutes). Finished dough will be slightly wet, but will pull away from sides of bowl and have an elastic texture.

- Transfer dough to a floured surface and form into a ball. You may need to lightly flour your hands to keep the dough from sticking. Place dough in an oiled, medium bowl and cover with plastic wrap. Let proof in a warm room, 70 to 75°F, for 2 hours. Dough will almost double in size.

- Pull dough from bowl onto a floured surface and flatten with your hands to release excess air. Form dough into a rectangle, then fold the short ends onto the top so they meet in the middle. Flatten dough again with your hands. Starting with the closest end, roll dough away from you into a tight log. As you roll, apply extra pressure at the ends to taper them. The final shape will resemble a football.

- Place loaf, seam side up, in the center of a floured dishtowel. Fold edges of towel so that sides of loaf are covered. If necessary, place extra towels around the loaf to make sure sides are well supported. The goal is to have the loaf rise, rather than spread, while it proofs. This can also be achieved by placing the loaf in an oblong basket that has been lined with a floured dishtowel.  Cover loaf with another towel to prevent a skin from forming on the surface. Let proof at room temperature for 1 hour, then transfer loaf to the refrigerator for 6 to 8 hours.

- Place baking stone on center rack of oven and preheat to 400°F.

- Remove loaf from refrigerator and unwrap. Place loaf, seam side down, on a counter or baker's peel. Using a sharp knife, score a shallow line from end to end vertically on the loaf's surface. Moving quickly, transfer loaf to center of baking stone and mist inside of oven with a spray bottle of water. Bake for 40 to 50 minutes, misting twice more during the first 15 minutes. The finished loaf will be medium brown and sound hollow when tapped on the bottom. Let cool on a wire rack for 30 minutes.

Macrina's Fancy Focaccia

Every day we offer our cafe's lunch customers savory focaccia.
It is sold whole or by the slice, and we rarely have leftovers. You can use as
many toppings as you like, but the idea is to keep it simple.

Makes 2 focaccias

1 recipe Classic Italian Loaf dough *(page 22)*
¼ cup cornmeal
⅓ cup extra virgin olive oil
5 Roma tomatoes, washed, cored, and cut lengthwise into ¼-inch slices
Kosher salt
Freshly ground black pepper
20 leaves fresh basil

- Prepare Classic Italian Loaf dough through the mixing process and let proof as instructed for 2 hours. Dough will almost double in size.

- Pull dough from bowl onto a floured surface and flatten with your hands. Form into a rectangle and, using a knife, divide dough into 2 equal pieces. Form each piece of dough into an oval by folding the corners onto the top.

- Dust a rimmed baking sheet with cornmeal. Transfer the loaves, seam sides down, onto the baking sheet. Cover with plastic wrap and let proof at room temperature for 1 hour. Loaves will rise slightly.

- While loaves are proofing, place baking stone on center rack of oven and preheat to 425°F.

- Remove plastic wrap and dimple the surface of each loaf with your fingers, leaving a 1-inch border around the edge of each loaf. Brush loaves with some of the olive oil and cover centers with a single layer of tomato slices. Season to taste with kosher salt and freshly ground black pepper. Moving quickly, transfer loaves to baking stone. Bake for 30 to 40 minutes, or until crusts are golden brown. Let cool on a wire rack for 10 minutes.

- Brush the edges of each focaccia with some more olive oil and garnish with fresh basil leaves.

MACRINA PIZZETTA

A daily favorite among customers and staff alike, these mini pizza shells are par-baked in advance, then we cover them with fresh toppings and bake each one to order. This is a great idea for kids' parties, where children can choose their toppings and devour their own creation.

Makes 8 pizzettas

1 recipe Classic Italian Loaf dough *(page 22)*
¼ cup cornmeal
½ cup extra virgin olive oil
2 cups Spicy Tomato Sauce *(page 181)*, or your favorite pizza sauce
3 cups grated fontina cheese
2 red bell peppers, washed, cored, and thinly sliced into rings
Kosher salt
Freshly ground black pepper
½ cup coarsely chopped fresh Italian parsley

● Prepare Classic Italian Loaf dough through the mixing process and let proof as instructed for 2 hours. Dough will almost double in size.

● Pull dough from bowl onto a floured surface and flatten with your hands into a rectangle. Divide dough into 8 equal pieces and form each piece into a ball.

● Dust a rimmed baking sheet with cornmeal. Place balls of dough, seam sides down, on top of the cornmeal. Brush tops with a little olive oil, then cover entire baking sheet with plastic wrap. Let proof in a warm room, 70 to 75°F, for 1 hour. Balls will double in size.

● Preheat oven to 425°F. Lightly oil 2 rimmed baking sheets.

● Once balls of dough have finished proofing, they can be formed into pizza crusts. I like to do this by hand rather than using a rolling pin. Place 1 ball of dough, cornmeal side down, on a floured surface and flatten center with your fingers. Pick up dough and, working your way out from the center, pinch and flatten dough, rotating as you go. Place crusts on a prepared baking sheet and repeat with remaining balls of dough. Four crusts should fit on 1 baking sheet.

● At this point the crusts can be covered with toppings and baked, but I prefer to pre-bake the shells before topping them. This gives the finished pizza a crispier crust. Place baking sheets in oven and bake for 7 to 10 minutes, or until shells are slightly golden. Be careful not to overcook the shells. Remove from oven and let cool. Depress any air bubbles with your fingers. Leave the oven on and place baking stone on center rack of oven.

- Brush cooled crusts with olive oil and cover with a little Spicy Tomato Sauce, fontina cheese, and red pepper rings. Drizzle a little more olive oil over the top and season to taste with kosher salt and freshly ground black pepper. Lift 4 pizzettas onto the baking stone and bake for 15 to 20 minutes, or until cheese is bubbling and crusts are golden brown. Let cool on a wire rack for 3 to 5 minutes, then sprinkle with chopped parsley. Repeat with remaining pizzettas.

An Impromptu Crostini & Crostoni Party

I feel that I share the same hectic lifestyle most people have these days. Sometimes it's hard to keep up with everything. One of my favorite ways to break up a fast-paced schedule is to throw an impromptu dinner gathering of friends. I've discovered I can keep a few ingredients in my freezer to help ease the pressure of last-minute menu planning. Of course, one of these essential items is bread.

I always start a party with a bread-based appetizer: My favorites are crostini and crostoni. The main difference between the two is the thickness of the slices, crostoni being thicker. Making either is a perfect way to use up day-old or frozen loaves.

Ciabatta is generally my bread of choice. I cut slices ranging from ¼ to ½ inches thick and sauté them in a skillet with olive oil. After I've browned both sides, I remove them from the pan and rub the slices with a raw clove of garlic. After that I top them with whatever cheeses, spreads, or seasonal vegetables I have available. One favorite is thinly sliced tomato, an anchovy fillet, a small wedge of avocado, and a drizzle of balsamic vinegar. Other slices might be topped with a leaf of fresh arugula and crumbled goat cheese. However they're topped, I always finish crostoni with a few drops of extra virgin olive oil, kosher salt, and a little freshly ground black pepper.

Enough slices with a variety of toppings can easily make a whole meal.

CIABATTA LOAF

*This classic Italian "slipper" bread is famous for its crisp, nutty-tasting crust
and the irregular texture of its interior. The use of milk, olive oil, and a long fermentation
time give ciabatta a special flavor all its own. It's perfect for sandwiches.
This is a wet dough and is best prepared in a stand mixer.*

Makes 2 rectangular loaves

½ teaspoon dried yeast
1½ cups warm filtered water
1 pound Seed Dough *(page 21)*, 1 day old, at room temperature
3 tablespoons extra virgin olive oil
3 tablespoons whole milk
3 cups unbleached all-purpose flour
2¼ teaspoons kosher salt
Spray bottle of water

- Place yeast and water in the bowl of your stand mixer and mix with a whisk until yeast is dissolved. Let sit for 2 minutes. Divide Seed Dough into 5 pieces and add to bowl. Attach bowl to stand mixer and add olive oil, milk, flour, and salt. Using the hook attachment, pulse mixture a few times to start bringing dough together. Switch to medium speed and mix for 10 to 12 minutes. Dough will form a ball around the hook and will remain wet and sticky.

- Transfer dough to an oiled, medium bowl and cover with plastic wrap. Place bowl in a warm room, 70 to 75°F, and let proof for 1½ hours. Dough will double in size.

- Uncover bowl and give dough what bakers call a *turn*: stretch each of the dough's 4 edges outward and then back onto the center (see photos, page 14). Turn the left and right sides first, followed by the top and bottom. Flip the entire ball over, placing it, seam side down, in the bowl and cover again with plastic wrap. Let proof in a warm room for another 1½ hours. Dough will double in size.

- Uncover bowl and give the dough one more turn, following the above instructions. Cover bowl and let proof for another 1½ hours. Next, place covered bowl in the refrigerator for 12 to 14 hours or overnight, to continue the fermentation process.

- Remove bowl from refrigerator and transfer dough to a floured surface, taking care not to fold dough. Using your fingertips, dimple the surface of the dough to release excess gases. Using a sharp knife, divide dough into 2 rectangular loaves. Place loaves on a heavily floured, rimmed baking sheet. It's a good idea to flour your fingers to avoid having them stick to the dough. Dust tops of loaves generously with flour and cover with a dishtowel. Let proof at room temperature for about 2 hours.

- While loaves are proofing, place baking stone on center rack of oven and preheat to 400°F.

- Loaves are ready to bake when they have come to room temperature and have increased 50 percent in size. Use both hands to slightly narrow loaves so that they regain their rectangular shape. (These loaves are meant to have an irregular shape, so don't worry about forming perfect rectangles.) Gently turn each loaf over and set back down on the baking sheet. Moving quickly to keep heat in the oven, transfer the loaves onto the baking stone, stretching loaves slightly, lengthwise, as you place them on the stone. Mist inside of oven with a spray bottle of water. Bake for about 40 minutes, misting twice more during the first 15 minutes. Finished loaves will have a deep brown crust and will sound hollow when tapped on the bottom. Let cool on a wire rack for 30 minutes.

SEMOLINA & SESAME LOAF

This golden bread is a spring tradition at the bakery. We bake it for three months every year to welcome the returning sun. Of course, here in Seattle, there's no guarantee that the sun will make an appearance. This dough is best prepared in a stand mixer.

Makes 1 round loaf

8 ounces Seed Dough *(page 21)*, 1 day old, at room temperature
1¼ cups filtered water, at room temperature
2½ cups semolina flour
2 teaspoons kosher salt
1 tablespoon raw sesame seeds
1 teaspoon coarse sea salt
Spray bottle of water

- Divide Seed Dough into 5 pieces and place in the bowl of your stand mixer. Add water, semolina flour, and kosher salt and mix with the paddle attachment for 1 to 2 minutes on low speed. Switch to the hook attachment and mix on medium speed for 8 to 10 minutes. Dough will form a ball at base of hook and sides of bowl will be clean.

- Place dough in an oiled, medium bowl and cover with plastic wrap. Set bowl in a warm room, 70 to 75°F, and let proof for 2 hours. Dough will almost double in size.

- Pull dough from bowl onto a floured surface and flatten it with your hands. Form dough into a ball by pulling the edges up and towards the center of the mass. Repeat this motion until you have a tight ball, then let it rest, seam side down, for 1 minute. Line a medium bowl with a floured dish towel and place loaf, seam side up, in the center. Fold ends of towel over top of loaf to prevent a skin from forming on the surface. Let proof at room temperature for 2 hours. Loaf will rise 50 percent in size.

- Transfer bowl to refrigerator and let sit for 3 hours. The fermentation process will continue during this time and the loaf will develop more flavor.

- Place baking stone on center rack of oven and preheat to 400°F.

- Remove bowl from refrigerator and place loaf, seam side down, on a counter or baker's peel. Using a sharp knife, score a shallow triangle across the top of the loaf (see photo, right). Mist top of loaf with a spray bottle of water and sprinkle with sesame seeds and sea salt. Moving quickly, place loaf in center of baking stone and mist inside of oven with water. Bake for 45 to 50 minutes, misting the oven twice more during the first 15 minutes. The finished loaf will be golden brown and sound hollow when tapped on the bottom. Let cool on a wire rack for 30 minutes.

OLIVETTA LOAF

This savory loaf is the perfect companion for soups and salads. Try serving it with a platter of roasted vegetables, cured meats, and your favorite cheeses. Delicious.

Makes 1 oval loaf

5 ounces Traditional Biga Starter *(page 21)*, 1 day old, at room temperature
1 cup filtered water, at room temperature
¼ teaspoon dried yeast
2¾ cups unbleached all-purpose flour
⅓ cup extra virgin olive oil
1 teaspoon finely chopped fresh rosemary
1 teaspoon finely chopped fresh oregano
2 teaspoons kosher salt
¾ cup pitted, halved green olives
Spray bottle of water

- Combine starter, water, and yeast in the bowl of your stand mixer. Using the paddle attachment, mix on low speed for 1 minute. (If you are mixing by hand, combine biga, water, and yeast in a medium bowl and mix with a whisk to break up starter and dissolve yeast.) Add all-purpose flour, ¼ cup of the olive oil, rosemary, oregano, and salt, and mix on low speed until ingredients are combined. Switch to the hook attachment and mix on medium speed for about 10 minutes. Dough will start forming a ball around the hook. (If mixing by hand, add flour, ¼ cup of the olive oil, herbs, and salt and stir with a wooden spoon. Knead with your hands for 10 to 15 minutes.) Let dough rest in bowl for 5 minutes.

- This dough is quite wet, so give your hands a generous dusting of flour before working with it. Pull dough from bowl onto a floured surface and form into a 6 x 10-inch rectangle, positioning dough so that a short end is facing you. Sprinkle olives over entire surface of dough. Starting with the closest end, roll dough away from you into a log. Make sure log is resting on its seam, then fold the ends underneath to form a loosely shaped ball. Place ball of dough in an oiled, medium bowl and cover with plastic wrap. Let proof in a warm room, 70 to 75°F, for 2 to 2½ hours. Dough will double in size.

- Pull dough from bowl onto a floured surface and gently flatten it with your hands to release excess air. Form flattened dough into an oval shape by folding the left and right sides onto the top. Place loaf, seam side up, on a floured rimmed baking sheet. Sprinkle top of loaf with flour and cover with a dishtowel to keep it from drying out. Let proof in a warm room for 1½ hours. Loaf will rise slightly and be soft to the touch.

- While loaf is proofing, place baking stone on center rack of oven and preheat to 385°F.

- Uncover loaf and dimple the surface with your fingertips. Turn loaf over and set it back on the baking sheet, dimpled side down. Moving quickly to keep heat in oven, transfer loaf to center of baking stone. Heavily mist inside of oven with a spray bottle of water. Bake for about 45 minutes, misting once more after the first 5 minutes. The finished loaf will have a reddish brown color and will sound hollow when tapped on the bottom. Let loaf cool on a wire rack for about 20 minutes, then brush top with more extra virgin olive oil.

Chapter 3

AMERICAN STANDARDS

Rustic Potato Loaf
Cracked Wheat Walnut Cider Loaf
Challah
Oatmeal Buttermilk Bread

The first time I ever baked bread was in Mrs. Johnson's first grade class. It was one of my favorite, and messiest, class projects. We dissolved packets of yeast in water and sugar, then mixed in flour and salt. With a lot of help from Mrs. Johnson, we kneaded the dough for what seemed like hours. Each student had a turn at forming dough into small balls, which we placed together into pie pans and baked in the cafeteria's oven. Soon the whole school was filled with the aroma of fresh baked bread. We devoured the bread while it was still warm, and I vividly remember the wonderful yeasty flavor.

Many Americans have similar baking memories that they hold dear. This style of baking is what we call the "direct method": dried yeast, and often a little sugar, are dissolved in warm water, the rest of the ingredients are added after about 5 minutes, and soon a loaf is ready for the oven. Since these loaves can be prepared relatively quickly, they are easy to fit into a hectic daily schedule. While "direct method" breads generally rely on yeast and sugar for their flavor, the addition of ingredients such as honey, potatoes, or oatmeal can yield delicious results.

The recipes in this chapter are great for busy families or anyone who wants to enjoy fresh bread without a lot of work. Bring back the memory of your first slice of warm, buttered bread and fill your home with its unforgettable aroma. The Rustic Potato Loaf is a perfect dinner companion, and the Oatmeal Buttermilk Bread is just right for your favorite sandwiches. Because these loaves don't contain the organic acids found in breads with a longer proofing time, they don't have as long a shelf life. They're best consumed within two days of baking, which simply encourages us to bake more frequently.

RUSTIC POTATO LOAF

Enjoyed by customers of all ages, this is Macrina's most sought-after loaf.
Some bakeries prefer to make potato bread with dried potato flakes, but this dough
is made with mashed whole potatoes. I also like to leave the potato peels on,
giving the bread a fuller flavor and more interesting texture.

Makes 1 large loaf

1¼ pounds russet potatoes
1 tablespoon kosher salt
1½ teaspoons dried yeast
2 tablespoons extra virgin olive oil
3 cups unbleached all-purpose flour
Spray bottle of water

- Scrub potatoes thoroughly and cut into 1-inch chunks. Place potatoes and 1 teaspoon of the kosher salt in a medium saucepan and cover with water. Bring to a boil, then reduce heat and simmer for about 15 minutes, or until potatoes are tender when poked with a knife. Measure out ½ cup of potato water and set aside. Drain potatoes in a colander and leave them to cool and dry for 20 minutes.

- Pour the ½ cup of lukewarm potato water into a small bowl and sprinkle yeast over the top. Mix with a whisk until yeast is dissolved. Let stand for 5 minutes.

- Place drained and cooled potatoes in the bowl of your stand mixer. Using the paddle attachment, mix on low speed for 1 minute to mash potatoes. Add olive oil and mix for another minute. Add potato water and yeast mixture and continue mixing until combined, 1 to 2 minutes. (If mixing by hand, place potatoes and olive oil in a medium bowl and smash with a potato masher. Add potato water and yeast mixture and mix with a wooden spoon until ingredients are combined.) Switch to the hook attachment and add flour and remaining 2 teaspoons of salt. Mix briefly on low speed to start bringing ingredients together, then increase speed to medium and mix for approximately 11 minutes. (If mixing by hand, add

flour and remaining salt and mix with a wooden spoon. Knead with your hands for 10 to 15 minutes.) Dough will appear firm at first, but will become wetter as mixing

Baking with Olivia's Class

When my three-year-old daughter's preschool decided to have a career day, her teacher asked if I would consider baking bread with the children. It sounded like fun. I arrived at the school dressed in my standard baking outfit, lugging in my KitchenAid mixer, all of my ingredients, and a display of wheat. The kids were so excited they could hardly sit still.

I started to explain how bread was made and where ingredients such as wheat come from, but the children wouldn't have it. They were more interested in the mixer and how it worked, and most of all they wanted to use their hands. Luckily I had thought to bring some potato dough from the bakery, so the kids didn't have to wait while I mixed a batch.

The teachers and I sprinkled flour on one of their play tables and gave each student a piece of dough. "It's like Play-Doh!" one of the kids squealed. They all agreed, repeating the phrase one after the other as they began flattening the dough. The sound of their little fists fiercely pounding the dough was like a drum roll. Shaping the dough into logs required concentration and patience, as it kept sticking to their hands, but the kids seemed determined to overcome their frustration.

One by one the children formed dough into their personal versions of a loaf. We watched the loaves rise and then baked them in the school's oven. The kids were beaming with pride as the room filled with that splendid aroma. It was a great group project, and the kids were able to share their loaves at that night's dinner tables. Olivia enjoyed hers, as usual, with a generous piece of butter.

continues. Check for elasticity by flouring your fingers and stretching some of the dough. Finished dough should stretch about 2 inches without breaking.

- Pull dough from bowl onto a floured surface and form into a ball. Place ball in an oiled, medium bowl and cover with plastic wrap. Let dough proof in a warm room, 70°F, for about 45 minutes. Dough will almost double in size.

- Place dough on a floured surface and flatten it with your hands. Form dough into a rectangle and, starting with a short end, roll dough away from you into a tight log. Stop rolling just before the log is sealed, then flatten the remaining inch of dough with your fingers and dust it with flour. This will prevent the loaf from fully sealing and will cause the seam to open slightly while baking. Wrap loaf, seam side down, in a floured dishtowel and let proof at room temperature for 45 minutes. Dough will rise slightly and feel spongy to the touch.

- Place baking stone on center rack of oven and preheat to 400°F.

- Carefully unwrap loaf and set it, seam side up, on a counter or baker's peel. Moving quickly, transfer loaf to center of baking stone and heavily mist inside of oven with a spray bottle of water. Bake for 45 minutes, misting oven once more after the first 5 minutes. Finished loaf will be golden brown and sound hollow when tapped on the bottom. Let cool on a wire rack for 30 minutes.

CRACKED WHEAT WALNUT CIDER LOAF

This hearty and flavorful loaf is perfect for your favorite sandwiches.
Try filling slices with roasted chicken, or reinvent the classic grilled cheese
by adding heirloom tomatoes and smoky bacon.

Makes 1 (9 x 5-inch) loaf

¾ cup cracked wheat*
1 cup boiling filtered water
1½ cups walnut halves
1¼ cups apple cider
1½ teaspoons dried yeast
2 tablespoons honey
1 cup and 1 tablespoon coarse whole-wheat flour
2¼ cups unbleached all-purpose flour
2 teaspoons kosher salt
½ cup canola oil
*available in specialty shops and some supermarkets

- Place cracked wheat in a small bowl and cover with boiling water. Stir with a spoon to make sure all wheat is moistened. Let sit, uncovered, for 10 minutes while liquid is being absorbed.

- Preheat oven to 350°F. Spread walnuts on a rimmed baking sheet and toast for 20 minutes. Let cool. Chop coarsely and set aside.

- Place apple cider in a medium saucepan and warm over low heat, just until it's warm to the touch. Pour warm cider into the bowl of a stand mixer. Add yeast and honey and mix with a whisk until yeast is dissolved. (If mixing by hand, place warm cider, yeast, and honey in a medium bowl and mix with a whisk.) Let mixture sit for 5 minutes. Add plumped cracked wheat, 1 cup whole-wheat flour, all-purpose flour, salt, and canola oil. Using the hook attachment, mix on low speed for 1 minute to combine ingredients. Switch to medium speed and mix for 10 minutes. Dough will form a loose ball at base of hook. Add walnuts and mix for 2 minutes. (If mixing by hand, add plumped cracked wheat, 1 cup whole-wheat flour, all-purpose flour, salt, and canola oil and mix with a wooden spoon until dough comes together. Knead with your hands for about 10 minutes, then add walnuts and continue kneading until nuts are evenly distributed.)

- Transfer dough to an oiled, medium bowl and cover with plastic wrap. Let proof in a warm room, 70 to 75°F, for 2 hours. Dough will almost double in size.

- Pull dough from the bowl onto a floured surface and punch it down with your hands to release air bubbles. Form dough into a 12 x 6-inch rectangle and position it so that a long side is facing you. Fold the 2 short ends onto the top so they meet in the middle. Starting with the closest end, roll dough away from you into a tight log.

- Place loaf in an oiled 9 x 5 x 4-inch loaf pan and cover with plastic wrap. Let proof at room temperature for 1 hour. Loaf will rise to slightly above the top of pan.

- While loaf is proofing, preheat oven to 385°F.

- Remove plastic and dust top of loaf with remaining tablespoon of whole-wheat flour. Place pan on center rack of oven and bake for approximately 50 minutes. Finished loaf will be medium brown on top. Let cool in the pan on a wire rack for at least 30 minutes, then run a sharp knife around the sides of the loaf to release it from the pan. Invert pan to remove loaf.

CHALLAH

The recipe for this traditional Jewish braid comes from our friend Andy Meltzer.
A former baker at Macrina, Andy is currently a baking instructor at the Culinary Institute
of America. The recipe was passed to Andy from family friends in upstate New York
and made its way to Seattle, where we bake it every Friday.

Makes 1 braided loaf

½ cup warm filtered water
2 tablespoons granulated sugar
1½ teaspoons dried yeast
¼ cup canola oil
1 tablespoon honey
2 eggs
2¼ cups unbleached all-purpose flour
1 teaspoon kosher salt
Egg wash made with 1 egg and 1 teaspoon water
1 tablespoon poppy seeds

- Place warm water and sugar in the bowl of your stand mixer. Sprinkle yeast on top and mix with a whisk until yeast is dissolved. (If mixing by hand, place water and yeast in a medium bowl and mix with a whisk.) Let rest for 5 minutes. Yeast will bloom and the mixture will look foamy. Add canola oil, honey, eggs, flour, and salt. Using the hook attachment, mix on low speed for about 2 minutes to bring ingredients together. Increase speed to medium and mix for another 10 to 12 minutes. (If mixing by hand, add oil, honey, eggs, flour, and salt and mix with a wooden spoon. Knead with your hands for about 15 minutes.) Dough will remain wet and will have good elasticity when stretched.

- Coat your hands with flour and pull dough from bowl onto a generously floured surface. Form dough into a ball. Place ball in an oiled, medium bowl and cover with plastic wrap. Set bowl in a warm room, 70 to 75°F, and let proof for 2 hours. Dough will almost double in size and will become much easier to handle.

- Place dough on a floured surface and flatten it with your hands to release excess air bubbles. Pat dough into a rectangle and divide it into 3 equal pieces. Roll each piece into a rope approximately 10 inches long. Line the ropes up side by side and, starting at either end, braid the ropes. Pinch ends together to form a seal and fold ends underneath.

- Line a rimmed baking sheet with parchment paper. Lift braid onto center of baking sheet and cover with plastic wrap. Let proof at room temperature for 40 to 45 minutes. Loaf will rise slightly and feel spongy to the touch.

- While loaf is proofing, preheat oven to 375°F.

- Remove plastic wrap and brush loaf with egg wash. Sprinkle poppy seeds over the top. Place baking sheet on center rack of oven and bake for approximately 30 minutes. Finished loaf will be a deep reddish brown on the top and bottom. Let cool on a wire rack for 30 minutes.

OATMEAL BUTTERMILK BREAD

This tasty loaf can easily be made in less than four hours. With its slightly nutty flavor, thin crust, and soft interior, it's ideal for kids' sandwiches such as peanut butter and jelly.

Makes 1 (9 x 5-inch) loaf

1½ cups rolled oats
1 cup boiling filtered water
¼ cup warm filtered water
2 teaspoons dried yeast
1½ cups buttermilk
½ cup canola oil
½ cup light brown sugar
1 cup coarse whole-wheat flour
3½ cups unbleached all-purpose flour
2 teaspoons kosher salt
1 spray bottle of water

- Set aside ¼ cup of rolled oats. Place the remaining 1¼ cups of oats in a medium bowl and cover with 1 cup of boiling water. Mix with a spoon to moisten all oats. Let bowl sit, uncovered, for 10 minutes, stirring frequently, while water is absorbed.

- Place ¼ cup of warm water in the bowl of your stand mixer and sprinkle yeast on top. Mix with a whisk to dissolve yeast. (If mixing by hand, combine warm water and yeast in a medium bowl and mix with a whisk.) Let rest for 5 minutes. Add soaked oats, buttermilk, canola oil, brown sugar, whole-wheat flour, all-purpose flour, and kosher salt. Using the hook attachment, mix on low speed for 1 or 2 minutes to combine ingredients. Increase speed to medium and mix for about 10 minutes. (If mixing by hand, add soaked oats, buttermilk, oil, sugar, flours, and salt and mix with a wooden spoon. Knead with your hands for 10 to 12 minutes.) Dough will be wet at first, but will eventually form a ball. Ball will have a satiny finish and will bounce back quickly when poked with a finger.

- Place dough in an oiled, medium bowl and cover with plastic wrap. Proof in a warm room, 70 to 75°F, for about 1 hour. Dough will almost double in size.

- Pull dough from bowl onto a floured surface and flatten it with your hands, releasing excess air bubbles. Form dough into a 12 x 6-inch rectangle and position it so that a long side is facing you. Fold the 2 short ends onto the top so they meet in the middle. Starting with the closest end, roll dough away from you into a log. Let loaf rest on its seam for a few minutes.

- Transfer dough to an oiled 9 x 5 x 4-inch loaf pan, seam side down. Using your hands, push down on dough to make sure it extends to all corners of the pan. Cover with plastic wrap and let proof in a warm room for 35 to 45 minutes. Loaf will rise to slightly above the top of the pan.

- While loaf is proofing, preheat oven to 385°F.

- Remove plastic and mist top of loaf with a spray bottle of water. Sprinkle with remaining oats. Place pan on center rack of oven and bake for approximately 1 hour. Top and sides of finished loaf will be deep golden brown. Let cool in the pan on a wire rack for at least 30 minutes, then run a sharp knife around sides of loaf to release it from the pan. Invert pan to remove loaf.

Chapter 4

SWEET BREADS

Classic Brioche Loaf

Raisin Brioche Twist

Apple Cinnamon Monkey Bread

Guatemalan Hot Chocolate Bread

S tarting a bakery is a tremendous amount of exhilarating work. During the first months after Macrina opened in August of 1993, I was working sixteen-hour days, as most new businesses require. But after a year or so, I was able to take a long weekend to attend a bread seminar in Berkeley, California. The seminar, "French Traditional Breads," was sponsored by the Bread Baker's Guild of America and hosted by the Acme Bread Company.

Our instructor was Professor Raymond Calvel, the revered French baking master. He was a true delight. In his white lab coat, and speaking through an interpreter, he had a presence and charisma similar to that of the amazing Julia Child (herself a former student of Calvel). The professor taught us how to mix and form a variety of traditional French breads, including *pain au levain* and a *poolish baguette*. I was fascinated by the entire lesson, but I was most taken by *La Mouna*, a loaf similar to brioche and flavored with a hint of orange. We were not yet making sweet breads like this at Macrina, and I was suddenly inspired to introduce a few.

The loaves in this chapter are what we call enriched breads. Unlike most of our daily breads, enriched loaves generally include the added ingredients of eggs, sugar, or butter. And, as you'll see, we sometimes throw in a little something extra. Who can resist, for example, a warm slice of Apple Cinnamon Monkey Bread oozing with sweet apple butter or brioche that's studded with raisins and coated in cinnamon sugar?

Our retail bakery provides us with endless opportunities to be creative, and we can count on our customers for instant feedback. The following recipes were developed at different times in Macrina's history, and all have become popular weekly standards at our store. I think you'll enjoy returning to these recipes again and again, whether you eat a whole loaf by yourself or share it with friends and family.

CLASSIC BRIOCHE LOAF

This buttery French breakfast bread is traditionally baked in fluted brioche molds.
The molds can be found in specialty kitchen shops and are available in every size imaginable.
Personally, I like to bake brioche in a loaf pan so it can be sliced for toast or croutons.
For best results, I recommend mixing this dough in a stand mixer.

Makes 1 (9 x 5-inch) loaf

¼ cup warm filtered water
½ cup granulated sugar
1½ teaspoons dried yeast
1 teaspoon pure vanilla extract
2 eggs
¾ cup whole milk
3½ cups unbleached all-purpose flour
1 teaspoon kosher salt
8 tablespoons unsalted butter (1 stick), at room temperature,
cut into dime-sized pieces
Egg wash made with 1 egg and 1 teaspoon water

- Place warm water and 2 teaspoons of the sugar in the bowl of your stand mixer. Sprinkle yeast on top and mix with a whisk until yeast is dissolved. Let stand for 5 minutes while yeast blooms.

- Add remaining sugar, vanilla extract, eggs, milk, flour, and salt. Using the hook attachment, mix on low speed for 3 minutes to start bringing dough together. Switch to medium speed and slowly drop pieces of butter into dough. Mix for 10 to 12 minutes. Dough will be wet and sticky and will have good elasticity when stretched.

- Pull dough from bowl onto a floured surface. Using extra flour on your hands, form dough into a ball. Place dough in an oiled, medium bowl and cover with plastic wrap. Proof in a warm room, 70 to 75°F, for about 2½ hours. Dough will almost double in size.

- Pull dough from bowl onto a floured surface and flatten it with your hands, releasing excess air bubbles. Form dough into a 12 x 6-inch rectangle and position it so that a long side is facing you. Fold the 2 short ends onto the top so they meet in the center. Starting with the closest end, roll dough away from you into a tight log.

- Lift loaf into an oiled 9 x 5 x 4-inch loaf pan, seam side down. Using your hands, push down on the dough to make sure it extends to all corners of the pan. Cover with plastic wrap and let proof in a warm room for about 1½ hours. Loaf will rise to top of pan.

- While loaf is proofing, preheat oven to 360°F.

- Remove plastic and brush top of loaf with egg wash. Place pan on center rack of oven and bake for approximately 40 minutes. Loaf will be golden brown on top and sides. Let cool in pan on a wire rack for at least 30 minutes, then run a sharp knife around sides of loaf to release it from the pan. Invert pan to remove loaf.

RAISIN BRIOCHE TWIST

This braid is a sweeter version of our Classic Brioche Loaf recipe. With the addition of plump raisins, cinnamon sugar, and butter, it's as satisfying as a gooey cinnamon roll.

Makes 1 (9 x 5-inch) braided loaf

¾ cup seedless raisins
1 recipe Classic Brioche Loaf dough *(page 43)*
1 cup Cinnamon Sugar Mixture *(recipe follows)*
4 tablespoons unsalted butter, melted

- Place raisins in a small bowl and cover with hot tap water. Let sit for 10 minutes while raisins plump, then drain and set aside.

- Prepare Classic Brioche dough through the mixing process as instructed, and let rest in the bowl for 5 minutes as instructed.

- Pull dough from bowl onto a floured surface and flatten into a rectangle. Sprinkle plumped raisins over entire surface of dough. Starting with a narrow end, roll dough away from you into a log. Fold ends underneath to form a loosely shaped ball. Place ball in an oiled, medium bowl and cover with plastic wrap. Let proof in a warm room, 70 to 75°F, for approximately 2½ hours. Dough will almost double in size.

- Line bottom and sides of a 9 x 5 x 4-inch loaf pan with parchment paper and spread Cinnamon Sugar Mixture evenly on a rimmed baking sheet.

- Place dough on a floured work surface and pat it into a 6 x 12-inch rectangle. Divide dough into 3 equal pieces and roll each piece into a rope approximately 10 inches long. Brush the strands of dough with melted butter, making sure they are thoroughly coated. One at a time, roll the coated strands of dough in the cinnamon mixture. Line the strands up side by side and, starting at either end, braid the pieces (see photos, next page). Pinch ends together to form a seal and fold ends underneath. Lift braid into lined loaf pan. Brush with melted butter and sprinkle with remaining

cinnamon sugar. Cover with plastic wrap and let proof in a warm room for 1 hour, or until loaf rises to fill three-quarters of the pan.

- While loaf is proofing, preheat oven to 360°F.

- Remove plastic and place loaf on center rack of preheated oven. Bake for about 45 minutes. Top and sides of loaf will be dark golden brown. The hot loaf will be very fragile, so let cool on wire rack for 20 minutes before removing from the pan. After 20 minutes, lift loaf out of pan and continue cooling on a wire rack. If needed, run a sharp knife around the sides of loaf and invert pan to remove it. (It's important to remove the loaf from the pan before the sugars cool and stick to the sides.)

CINNAMON SUGAR MIXTURE

This is the cinnamon sugar recipe we use at the bakery. It can be made up in advance and stored in an airtight container for weeks at a time. You'll see this recipe referred to throughout this book.

Makes 1 cup

½ cup granulated sugar
½ cup light brown sugar
1 tablespoon cinnamon
½ teaspoon freshly ground nutmeg

- Combine ingredients in a small bowl and mix well.

APPLE CINNAMON MONKEY BREAD

Motivated by childhood memories of sweet, pull-apart monkey bread from my neighborhood supermarket, I decided to create an updated version for Macrina. This loaf has a different appearance than the original, but it's even more satisfying.

Makes 1 loaf

FOR THE DOUGH:
½ cup whole milk
1½ teaspoons dried yeast
1 tablespoon granulated sugar
2 eggs
1¾ cups unbleached all-purpose flour
¼ cup barley flour*
1 teaspoon kosher salt
2 tablespoons unsalted butter, melted

FOR THE APPLE BUTTER:
1 medium Granny Smith apple
3 tablespoons unsalted butter
1 teaspoon cinnamon
2 tablespoons granulated sugar

FOR FINISHING THE LOAF:
½ cup Cinnamon Sugar Mixture *(page 45)*
Egg wash made with 1 egg and 1 teaspoon water
1 tablespoon raw sesame seeds
available in specialty shops and some supermarkets

PREPARING THE DOUGH:

● Warm milk slightly in a small saucepan and pour into the bowl of your stand mixer. Sprinkle yeast and sugar on top and mix with a whisk to dissolve yeast. (If mixing by hand, place warm milk, yeast, and sugar in a medium bowl and mix with a whisk.) Let stand for 5 minutes while yeast blooms.

● Add eggs, all-purpose flour, barley flour, salt, and melted butter. Using the hook attachment, mix on low speed for 1 minute to combine ingredients. Increase speed to medium and mix for approximately 12 minutes. (If mixing by hand, add eggs, flours, salt, and butter and mix with a wooden spoon. Knead with your hands for 12 to 15 minutes.) Dough will have a satiny sheen and will stretch easily.

• Transfer dough to an oiled, medium bowl and cover with plastic wrap. Proof in a warm room, 70 to 75°F, for 1 hour. Dough will double in size.

PREPARING THE APPLE BUTTER:

• Peel and core apple. Cut into ½-inch pieces and set aside.

• Melt butter in a medium saucepan over low heat. Add cut apples, cinnamon, and sugar and cook over medium heat until apples are fork tender, about 5 minutes. Remove from heat and mash apples with a fork until texture resembles coarse applesauce. Let cool.

ASSEMBLING THE LOAF:

• Pull dough from bowl onto a floured surface and flatten with your hands. Form dough into a 6 x 14-inch rectangle, approximately ¼ inch thick. Spread apple butter over entire surface of rectangle and sprinkle evenly with Cinnamon Sugar Mixture. Roll each of the 6-inch sides inwards until they meet in center, then carefully flip loaf over so the smooth side is on top.

• Line bottom and sides of a 9 x 5 x 4-inch loaf pan with parchment paper. Place loaf in the lined pan, seam side down, and cover with plastic wrap. Let proof in a warm room for 1 hour. Loaf will rise to fill approximately three-quarters of the pan.

• While loaf is proofing, preheat oven to 375°F.

• Remove plastic. Brush top of loaf with egg wash and sprinkle with sesame seeds. Place pan on center rack of oven and bake for 35 to 40 minutes. Loaf will be golden brown on top and sides. Let cool in the pan on a wire rack for 10 minutes. Grab ends of parchment paper and lift Monkey Bread from the pan before sugars cool and loaf sticks to the sides. The apple butter will still be hot, so let the bread cool on a wire rack a little longer before eating. Any leftovers can be wrapped in plastic wrap and stored for up to 2 days.

GUATEMALAN HOT CHOCOLATE BREAD

*The bakers at Macrina first baked this bread in an effort to raise funds
for a fire-damaged library in Panajachel, Guatemala. Slightly sweet, with chunks
of bittersweet chocolate, toasted almonds, and a hint of cinnamon, the loaves sold out
as fast as we could bake them. Our customers were eager to help rebuild another
neighborhood's gathering place, and a new loaf was added to my list of favorites.
For best results, this recipe should be prepared in a stand mixer.*

Makes 1 round loaf

⅓ cup whole almonds
4 tablespoons unsalted butter, chilled
½ cup whole milk
2 teaspoons dried yeast
¼ cup granulated sugar
1 teaspoon pure vanilla extract
¼ teaspoon pure almond extract
2 eggs
¼ cup dark cocoa powder, sifted
2¼ cups unbleached all-purpose flour
1 teaspoon kosher salt
3 ounces bittersweet chocolate, coarsely chopped
2 tablespoons Cinnamon Sugar Mixture *(page 45)*
Spray bottle of water

- Preheat oven to 350°F. Place almonds on a rimmed baking sheet and toast for 15 minutes, or until golden brown. Let cool. Coarsely chop and set aside.

- Cut butter into dime-sized pieces and set aside to reach room temperature.

- Warm milk slightly in a small saucepan and pour into bowl of your stand mixer. Add yeast, 1 tablespoon of the sugar, and vanilla extract. Mix with a whisk to dissolve yeast, then let bowl sit for 5 minutes while yeast blooms.

- Add remaining sugar, almond extract, eggs, cocoa powder, flour, and salt. Using the hook attachment, mix on low speed for about 2 minutes to bring ingredients together. Switch to medium speed and start dropping pieces of butter into dough. Continue mixing for 12 to 14 minutes. Dough will look satiny and stringy. Let dough rest for 5 minutes, then add chopped almonds and bittersweet chocolate and mix 2 minutes more to incorporate.

- Pull dough from bowl onto a floured work surface and form into a ball. Place ball in an oiled, medium bowl and cover with plastic wrap. Let proof in a warm room, 70 to 75°F, for 2 hours. Dough will almost double in size.

- Remove cover and place dough back on floured work surface. Flatten dough with your hands to release excess air bubbles. Pull edges of dough onto the top, repeating this action until you have formed a tight ball. Line a rimmed baking sheet with parchment paper and place ball in the center. Cover with plastic wrap and let proof in a warm room for 1 hour. Loaf will almost double in size.

- While loaf is proofing, preheat oven to 350°F.

- Remove cover and lightly mist top of loaf with a spray bottle of water. Sprinkle Cinnamon Sugar Mixture on top. Place baking sheet on center rack of oven and bake for 1 hour. The finished loaf with be deep brown and sound hollow when tapped on the bottom. Let cool on a wire rack for 30 minutes.

MORNINGS AT MACRINA

Mornings at Macrina

I t's morning at Macrina Bakery. By the time the doors open at seven, a small crowd of regulars has lined up outside. The first thing that every one notices when they walk in is the aroma—it's hard to resist. Then they see the display case, a feast for the eyes, overflowing with all kinds of breakfast pastries. "I'll take one of each!" is a comment we never tire of hearing.

Preparations for some breakfast pastries start as early as two days in advance, such as the mixing of croissant dough. Then, apples need to be peeled, cored, and baked with cinnamon sugar. Nuts and seeds are sorted, toasted, and chopped. Afternoon bakers measure out dry ingredients for the next morning's muffins, biscuits, scones, and coffee cakes. Every night the croissant dough is formed into a wide variety of pastries, which are then chilled until they are ready to be baked the next morning.

The morning crew arrives by five o'clock, switching on the lights and ovens. Then the rush begins. Raw croissant pastries are pulled from the refrigerator and set on top of the ovens to proof, and all kinds of fresh fruits are chopped for muffins and the daily coffee cake special. Fruit compote simmers on the stove, waiting to be served with steaming bowls of bread pudding. Eggs are cracked and buttermilk is measured for mixing biscuits, muffins, and scones. In a matter of minutes the ovens are filled and another round is being readied.

Steaming pastries are coming out of the ovens, and now it's time for the retail staff to take over. They line baskets with linen napkins and carefully fill them with warm muffins. Biscuits and scones are stacked on decorative plates. There's a lot of work to do in the final minutes, but it's also exciting. "Is the coffee brewed? Is the ice water out? Where's your apron?" Then the doors open and it's "Good Morning! Welcome to Macrina."

This section is full of the most requested recipes from Macrina's morning menu. Some of the recipes are a little challenging and some take only minutes to prepare. Try the tart and sweet Cherry Almond Scones, baked to a golden brown. Topped with homemade preserves, the buttermilk biscuits are perfect alongside your morning coffee. The buttery Croissant Dough may seem intimidating at first, but with patience and practice you'll find it easy to prepare. Soon you'll know the rewards of baking your own sweet Morning Rolls and golden Hazelnut Orange Pinwheels. The Fresh Fruit Muffins are so easy even a toddler can help—my daughter likes to stir in the berries. Use the best ingredients available, from butter and eggs to the freshest ripe fruits, and you'll be thrilled with the results.

Chapter 5

MUFFINS, SCONES & BISCUITS

Fresh Fruit Muffins

Cornmeal Raspberry Muffins

Rocket Muffins

Lemon Lavender Scones

Citrus Oat Scones

Cherry Almond Scones

Currant Anise Scones

Old-Fashioned Buttermilk Biscuits with Fresh Preserves

Cream Biscuits with Black Forest Ham and Romano Cheese

Ricotta Biscuits with Dried Cherries, Apricots & Raspberries

T his chapter is filled with recipes for Macrina's most popular muffins, scones, and biscuits. You'll find instructions for making our popular Rocket Muffins, a perfect morning pick-me-up, and the delicious Fresh Fruit Muffins, studded with ripe berries. I've also included the recipe for a personal favorite, the Citrus Oat Scones, which were the first scones ever made at the bakery. Follow a few basic rules, and soon you'll be waking the whole house with the tantalizing aroma of freshly baked breakfast pastries.

Use the freshest fruits and preserves available. Grab pints of ripe blueberries at the local farmer's market, or pick up some seasonal organic fruit from your supermarket. Whether you blend the fruit into Fresh Fruit Muffins or make preserves for topping buttermilk biscuits, you won't be disappointed. Because ripe fruit is naturally sweet, these recipes use less sugar than a lot of store-bought pastries.

Sift the ingredients. All of the recipes in this chapter call for the sifting of dry ingredients. Sifting ingredients like flour, salt, and sugar breaks down any lumps and helps mix the ingredients together evenly. The result is lighter and fluffier baked goods. If you haven't bothered sifting dry ingredients before, you'll be amazed at the difference it makes.

Pay attention to the butter. If a recipe calls for melted butter, I recommend melting it over medium heat, then letting it cool slightly for about two minutes. It's best if the melted butter is warmer than room temperature but not hot to the touch. If, on the other hand, a recipe calls for chilled butter, make sure the butter really is chilled. Sometimes a recipe will call for blending chilled butter into dry ingredients with a pastry cutter (although a fork can work as well). In these cases, cut the butter into the dry ingredients until the mixture is coarse and crumbly. If a recipe asks you to cream butter with sugar, be patient. It will take five to eight minutes of mixing in a stand mixer until the butter is smooth and pale in color.

Don't overmix. Unlike bread doughs, which are mixed longer and slower to develop gluten, muffins, scones, and biscuits should be mixed just until the batter comes together. Once all of the dry ingredients are incorporated into the wet, stop mixing. Overmixing will result in rubbery pastries, a sorry state of affairs. Biscuit and scone batters may require a little additional kneading or folding by hand; this is basically just a gentle continuation of the mixing process. Keep your hands well coated with flour and knead only until the mixtures become moldable.

Work quickly. Baking soda is the key leavening agent in many of these recipes. It's what will help your baked goods rise when they are in the oven. Once baking soda hits an acid such as buttermilk or yogurt, it starts to react, but the action doesn't last long. Bake these pastries as soon as they are ready for the oven.

Know your oven. We use convection ovens at the bakery, but the recipes in this chapter were designed for baking in a conventional home oven. If you are lucky enough to have a convection oven in your home, reduce the baking temperature by 25°F.

FRESH FRUIT MUFFINS

This muffin is a perfect showcase for fresh summer berries, succulent peaches, or winter cranberries. The batter is only slightly sweet, allowing the fruit flavors to speak for themselves.

Makes 6 to 8 muffins

3 cups unbleached all-purpose flour
¾ cup granulated sugar
¾ cup light brown sugar
1½ tablespoons baking powder
1½ teaspoons salt
4 eggs
1 tablespoon pure vanilla extract
1 teaspoon freshly grated lemon zest
1½ cups whole milk
8 tablespoons (1 stick) unsalted butter, melted and slightly cooled
2 cups ripe fruit (whole berries or fruit cut into ½-inch pieces)
½ cup coarse raw sugar

- Preheat oven to 375°F. Brush the insides of a muffin tin with canola oil.

- Sift flour, granulated sugar, brown sugar, baking powder, and salt into a medium bowl. Mix gently with a wooden spoon and set aside.

- In a separate medium bowl, combine eggs, vanilla extract, lemon zest, and milk, and mix with a whisk until combined. Add to the bowl of dry ingredients and stir with a wooden spoon just until all the dry ingredients are moistened. (It's important not to overmix.) Slowly add melted butter and continue mixing until batter is smooth and there are no visible streaks of butter. Gently fold fruit into batter, taking care to avoid crushing the fruit.

- Scoop batter into oiled muffin tin, filling the cups to the top. Sprinkle coarse raw sugar on tops of muffins and bake on center rack of oven for 25 to 30 minutes. Finished muffins will be golden brown. Let cool for at least 10 minutes, then slide a fork down the side of each muffin and gently lift it from the pan.

Cornmeal Raspberry Muffins

Topped with your favorite raspberry preserves, these golden muffins are a beautiful addition to any breakfast table. We like to use fresh pineapple in this recipe when it's available, but unsweetened, canned fruit is a fine alternative.

Makes 6 to 8 muffins

2 cups Pastry Flour *(recipe follows)*
½ cup granulated sugar
1 tablespoon baking powder
1½ teaspoons salt
1½ cups cornmeal
4 eggs
1 cup diced pineapple
1 cup pineapple juice
½ cup whole milk
8 tablespoons (1 stick) unsalted butter, melted and slightly cooled
½ cup raspberry preserves

- Preheat oven to 375°F. Brush the insides of a muffin tin with canola oil.

- Sift flour, sugar, baking powder, salt, and cornmeal into a medium bowl and mix with a wooden spoon. Set aside.

- Crack eggs into a medium bowl and mix with a whisk, then stir in the diced pineapple, pineapple juice, and milk. Add egg mixture to the bowl of dry ingredients and stir with a wooden spoon just until batter starts to come together, about halfway mixed. Slowly add melted butter and continue mixing until batter is smooth and there are no visible streaks of butter, about 1 minute.

- Scoop batter into oiled muffin tins, slightly over-filling them. Bake for 25 to 30 minutes, or until muffins are peaked and golden brown. Test the center of 1 muffin with a skewer. The skewer will come out clean if the muffins are done. Let cool for 10 minutes, then gently dent each muffin top with a spoon. Crown with a generous dollop of raspberry preserves. Slide a fork down the side of each muffin and gently lift it from the pan.

PASTRY FLOUR

Supermarkets are carrying more specialty foods than ever, which is particularly good news for home bakers. However, pastry flour is one of those ingredients that still isn't available in every grocery store. If you have trouble finding it, here is a simple alternative that you can make yourself.

Makes 4 cups of pastry flour

3 cups unbleached all-purpose flour
1 cup cake flour

- Sift flours into a medium bowl and toss until thoroughly mixed. Store in a dry airtight container.

ROCKET MUFFINS

This moist morning treat is a delicious alternative to the standard bran muffin. It's packed with goodness and is guaranteed to start you off on the right foot.

Makes 6 to 8 muffins

¾ cup hazelnuts
¾ cup all-purpose unbleached flour
¾ cup whole-wheat flour
2 tablespoons light brown sugar
1 tablespoon baking powder
2½ teaspoons baking soda
¼ teaspoon salt
1½ cups rolled oats
3 medium carrots, grated
1 small, ripe banana, mashed or puréed
2 eggs
½ cup canola oil
½ cup molasses
½ cup buttermilk
½ cup raspberry preserves

- Preheat oven to 350°F. Brush the insides of a muffin tin with canola oil.

- Place hazelnuts on a rimmed baking sheet and toast for 15 to 20 minutes, or until golden brown. Let cool, then remove as much of the loose skins as possible by rubbing the hazelnuts between the palms of your hands. Chop nuts medium-fine and set aside. Increase oven temperature to 375°F.

- Sift flours, brown sugar, baking powder, baking soda, and salt into a medium bowl. Add oats, chopped hazelnuts, and grated carrots. Toss with your hands until ingredients are combined.

- In a separate medium bowl, combine banana, eggs, canola oil, molasses, and buttermilk. Mix fully with a whisk. Add mixture to the bowl of dry ingredients and stir just until batter comes together, taking care not to overmix.

- Scoop batter into oiled muffin tins, filling them to the top. Bake on center rack of oven for about 25 minutes, or until tops are deep brown. Let cool for 10 minutes, then dent each muffin with a spoon and top with a dollop of raspberry preserves. Slide a fork down the side of each muffin and gently lift it from the pan.

Lemon Lavender Scones

These scones are perfect for breakfast or as part of a traditional afternoon tea.
I like to serve them with fresh summer berries and clotted cream.

Makes 6 triangle scones

2 cups unbleached all-purpose flour
⅓ cup granulated sugar
1 teaspoon salt
1 teaspoon baking powder
1 teaspoon baking soda
2 tablespoons freshly grated lemon zest
2 teaspoons finely chopped dried lavender*
4 tablespoons unsalted butter, chilled
½ cup nonfat yogurt
½ cup buttermilk
¾ cup powdered sugar
2 tablespoons freshly squeezed lemon juice
available in specialty shops and some supermarkets

- Preheat oven to 400°F. Line a rimmed baking sheet with parchment paper.

- Sift flour, granulated sugar, salt, baking powder, and baking soda into a medium bowl. Add lemon zest and 1½ teaspoons of the dried lavender. Mix with a wooden spoon.

- Cut chilled butter into 6 equal pieces and drop into bowl of dry ingredients. Using a pastry cutter or fork, cut butter into the mixture until it is evenly distributed and no large pieces of butter are visible. Combine yogurt and buttermilk in a small bowl and mix with a whisk. Add to dry ingredients and mix with a wooden spoon until dough comes together.

- Coat your hands with flour and pull dough from bowl onto a floured work surface. Knead the dough for a few minutes, folding and flattening it several times. It will remain quite moist. Pat the dough into a 9 x 4-inch rectangle, approximately 1 inch thick. Using a floured bench scraper or knife, divide the dough into 6 equal triangles. Lift scones onto the prepared baking sheet and bake on center rack of oven for 18 to 20 minutes. Finished scones will be golden brown. Let scones cool on the baking sheet for 10 minutes.

- In a medium bowl, combine the remaining lavender, powdered sugar, and lemon juice. Mix with a spoon until smooth. Drizzle glaze over warm scones.

CITRUS OAT SCONES

We've been baking these popular scones since day one. One of my favorite customers drives from forty-five miles away to get her hair cut at a nearby salon, and she always stops by the bakery afterwards for a sweet and a cup of coffee. She calls two days in advance to place an order for a dozen of these scones, which she likes to freeze and reheat for breakfast.

Makes 6 triangle scones

½ cup golden raisins

1½ cups unbleached all-purpose flour

1 teaspoon baking powder

1 teaspoon baking soda

½ teaspoon salt

¾ cup rolled oats

2 tablespoons freshly grated orange zest

⅓ cup granulated sugar

8 tablespoons (1 stick) unsalted butter, at room temperature
1 egg
⅓ cup buttermilk, plus extra for brushing on scones
¼ cup Cinnamon Sugar Mixture *(page 45)*

- Preheat oven to 375°F. Line a rimmed baking sheet with parchment paper.

- Place golden raisins in a small bowl and cover with warm water. Set aside to plump for about 15 minutes.

- Sift flour, baking powder, baking soda, and salt into a medium bowl. Add ½ cup of the oats and orange zest. Toss ingredients with your hands until thoroughly mixed. Set aside.

- Combine sugar and butter in the bowl of standing mixer. Using the paddle attachment, mix on medium speed for about 7 minutes to cream butter. The mixture will become smooth and pale in color and will increase slightly in volume. Scrape down the sides of the bowl with a rubber spatula. Add egg and continue mixing until egg is incorporated into butter.

- Drain raisins well and toss into the bowl of dry ingredients.

- Add dry ingredients and buttermilk to the bowl of creamed butter in 3 additions, alternating between small amounts of both. After each addition, pulse with the paddle attachment just until ingredients are combined.

- Using a plastic spatula, scrape the dough from the bowl onto a floured work surface. Coat your hands with flour and pat the dough into a 3 x 8-inch rectangle, approximately 1 inch thick. Using a floured bench scraper or knife, divide dough into 6 equal triangles. Place scones on the prepared baking sheet and brush with a little buttermilk. Sprinkle remaining oats and Cinnamon Sugar Mixture on top. Bake on center rack of oven for 20 to 25 minutes, or until scones are golden brown on top and bottom. Let scones cool on baking sheet for 10 minutes.

CHERRY ALMOND SCONES

These are Andrew's favorite breakfast snacks. They're not overly sweet and have a more biscuit-like texture than most other scones. Enjoy them on their own or perhaps alongside eggs scrambled with fontina and apple pork sausage.

Makes 8 to 10 round scones

½ cup dried tart cherries

½ cup whole almonds

3 cups unbleached all-purpose flour

½ cup granulated sugar

2 teaspoons baking powder

I teaspoon baking soda

12 tablespoons (1½ sticks) unsalted butter, chilled

I egg

¾ cup buttermilk

I teaspoon pure vanilla extract

¼ teaspoon pure almond extract

Egg wash made with I egg and I teaspoon water

¼ cup coarse raw sugar

- Preheat oven to 350°F.

- Place dried cherries in a small bowl and cover with warm water. Let soak for 10 minutes. Drain the plumped cherries, coarsely chop (check for pits), and set aside.

- Place almonds on a rimmed baking sheet and toast for approximately 15 minutes, or until golden brown. Let cool, then coarsely chop and set aside.

- Line a rimmed baking sheet with parchment paper.

- Sift flour, granulated sugar, baking powder, and baking soda into a medium bowl and toss with your hands to combine.

- Divide chilled butter into ¼-inch pieces and drop into bowl of dry ingredients. Using a pastry cutter or fork, cut butter into mixture until texture is coarse and crumbly. Add the chopped cherries and almonds and mix with a wooden spoon.

- Combine egg, buttermilk, vanilla extract, and almond extract in a small bowl and mix with a whisk. Add to dry ingredients and mix gently with a wooden spoon just until dough comes together. Take care not to overmix the dough.

- Coat your hands with flour and pull dough from bowl onto a floured surface. Knead the dough for a few minutes, folding and flattening it several times, until dough becomes moldable. Dust the work surface with a little more flour and roll dough out 1 inch thick. Using a round biscuit cutter (about 3 inches across), cut 8 to 10 scones from the dough. Place scones on the prepared baking sheet, brush with egg wash, and sprinkle coarse raw sugar over the tops. Bake on center rack of oven for 20 to 25 minutes, or until golden brown. Let scones cool on baking sheet for 10 minutes.

CURRANT ANISE SCONES

One of my pastry chefs originally created this scone solely for our wholesale customers. We had no intention of selling it at our retail bakery, but once in a while a few of the leftovers made their way to the pastry case. A couple of our regular customers started asking for the scones by name, and we now bake them every morning.

Makes 10 to 12 triangle scones

1 cup dried currants
1 teaspoon anise seeds
3½ cups unbleached all-purpose flour
¾ cup granulated sugar
2 tablespoons baking powder
1 teaspoon salt
2½ cups heavy cream
Egg wash made with 1 egg and 1 teaspoon water
Powdered sugar

- Preheat oven to 350°F. Line a rimmed baking sheet with parchment paper.

- Place currants in a medium bowl and cover with warm water. Set aside to soak and plump for about 10 minutes.

- In a small sauté pan, toast anise seeds over medium heat until fragrant, about 1 minute. Let cool, then chop finely and set aside.

- Sift flour, granulated sugar, baking powder, and salt into a medium bowl. Add chopped anise seeds and drained currants and toss ingredients until they are evenly distributed.

- Pour heavy cream into a medium bowl and whip with a whisk or hand-held mixer until medium-soft. Using a rubber spatula, gently fold half of the whipped cream into the dry ingredients, then fold in the remaining half. Scrape dough from bowl onto a floured work surface. Coat your hands with flour, then fold and flatten dough several times, until it becomes moldable. Next, form dough into a 3 x 16-inch rectangle. Coat a bench scraper or knife with flour and cut dough into 10 to 12 equal triangles.

- Lift scones onto the prepared baking sheet and brush tops with egg wash. Bake on center rack of oven for 20 to 25 minutes, or until scones are golden brown. Let scones cool on baking sheet for 15 minutes, then dust tops with powdered sugar.

OLD-FASHIONED BUTTERMILK BISCUITS WITH FRESH PRESERVES

You can't go wrong with these biscuits. They're terrific straight from the oven, and they also freeze incredibly well. For a fast breakfast treat, pop a frozen biscuit in a preheated 350-degree oven and bake for ten to fifteen minutes.

Makes 6 biscuits

2 tablespoons warm water
1 teaspoon dried yeast
3 cups Pastry Flour *(page 57)*
2 tablespoons granulated sugar
1½ teaspoons baking powder
½ teaspoon baking soda
¾ teaspoon salt
¾ cup vegetable shortening, cut into ½-inch pieces
1 cup buttermilk
Egg wash made with 1 egg and 1 teaspoon water
Coarse raw sugar
½ cup fresh preserves

- Preheat oven to 350°F. Line a rimmed baking sheet with parchment paper.

- In a small bowl, combine warm water and yeast. Mix with a whisk to dissolve yeast, then let sit for 5 minutes while yeast blooms.

- Sift flour, granulated sugar, baking powder, baking soda, and salt into a medium bowl. Toss with your hands to combine. Drop pieces of shortening into the bowl. Using a pastry cutter or fork, cut in shortening until it's evenly distributed and the mixture is coarse and crumbly. Add the yeast water and buttermilk and mix with a wooden spoon just until dough comes together. Take care not to overmix.

- Coat your hands with flour and pull dough from bowl onto a floured work surface. Pat dough into a rectangle, approximately 9 x 5 inches, positioning dough so that a long side is facing you. The dough will be sticky at first, so keep flouring your hands and the work surface as needed. To achieve the flaky, layered texture of these biscuits, it's important to give the dough a series of *tri-folds*: Fold the dough into thirds, as you would a letter, folding the left third over the center third first and then folding the right third on top. Sprinkle the work surface with a little more flour and flatten the folded dough into another 9 x 5-inch rectangle. Follow the same folding and flattening procedure 2 more times (for a total of 3 *tri-folds*), ending with a rectangle ¾ to 1 inch thick.

- Cut dough into 6 equal (2½ x 3-inch) rectangles and place on the prepared baking sheet. Brush biscuits with egg wash and sprinkle with coarse raw sugar. Bake on center rack of oven for 20 to 25 minutes, or until golden brown on top and bottom. Let cool on baking sheet for 10 minutes, then dent the top of each biscuit with a spoon. Top with heaping dollops of your favorite preserves.

CREAM BISCUITS WITH BLACK FOREST HAM AND ROMANO CHEESE

This recipe was inspired by my work experience in the pastry kitchen of the Bostonian Hotel in Boston. There, we used the plain biscuit as a base for all kinds of breakfast and lunch items. At Macrina, we add ham and cheese to create a savory breakfast alternative for our customers.

Makes 8 biscuits

4 cups Pastry Flour *(page 57)*
4 teaspoons baking powder
1 tablespoon salt
2 cups grated Romano cheese
1 cup diced Black Forest ham
3 cups heavy cream

- Preheat oven to 385°F. Line a rimmed baking sheet with parchment paper.

- Sift the flour, baking powder, and salt into a medium bowl. Add the grated cheese and diced ham and stir with a wooden spoon until ingredients are combined. Using your hands, push ingredients to the sides, creating a well in the middle of the bowl. Pour the cream into the well. With a wooden spoon, slowly pull the dry ingredients into the cream, mixing just until the dough comes together. The finished dough will remain sticky.

- Pull dough from bowl onto a floured work surface. Lightly coat your hands with flour and form the dough into a 10 x 5-inch rectangle. Fold the dough in half and press it down lightly with your fingertips. Repeat this process 2 more times, gently kneading the dough but not over-working it. Sprinkle a little more flour on the work surface and again form dough into a 10 x 5-inch rectangle, about 1 inch thick. Cut dough into 8 equal squares. Lift biscuits onto the prepared baking sheet.

- Bake on center rack of oven for about 30 minutes, or until biscuits are golden brown on top and bottom. Let cool on baking sheet for 10 minutes.

RICOTTA BISCUITS WITH DRIED CHERRIES, APRICOTS & RASPBERRIES

I recommend serving these fruit-studded biscuits with mild breakfast cheeses from your local farmer's market. If fresh raspberries aren't available, frozen berries can be substituted.

Makes 8 biscuits

½ cup dried tart cherries, coarsely chopped
½ cup unsulfured dried apricots, diced
4 cups Pastry Flour *(page 57)*
1 tablespoon baking powder
1 teaspoon baking soda
¼ cup granulated sugar
1½ teaspoons salt
8 tablespoons (1 stick) unsalted butter, chilled
1 cup ricotta cheese
1 cup buttermilk, plus extra for brushing on biscuits
1 cup fresh raspberries
Coarse raw sugar

- Preheat oven to 385°F. Line a rimmed baking sheet with parchment paper.

- Place cherries and apricots in a medium bowl and cover with hot water. Let soak for 10 minutes, then drain well and set aside.

- Sift flour, baking powder, baking soda, granulated sugar, and salt into a medium bowl. Toss with your hands to combine.

- Cut butter into ¼-inch pieces and drop into bowl of dry ingredients. Using a pastry cutter or fork, cut in butter until it's evenly distributed and the mixture is coarse and crumbly. Add the drained cherries and apricots and mix with a wooden spoon.

- In a separate medium bowl, combine ricotta and buttermilk and mix well with a wooden spoon. Fold one third of the ricotta mixture into the bowl of dry ingredients, then fold in another third. Add the final third of ricotta mixture along with the fresh raspberries and continue mixing just until ingredients are combined and dough starts coming together.

- Pull dough from bowl onto a floured work surface. Lightly coat your hands with flour and form the dough into a 9 x 5-inch rectangle. Fold the dough in half and press it down lightly with your fingertips. Repeat this process 2 more times, gently kneading the dough but not over-working it. Sprinkle a little more flour on the work surface and again form dough into a 9 x 5-inch rectangle, about 1 inch thick. Cut dough into 8 equal squares. Lift biscuits onto the prepared baking sheet.

- Brush biscuits with buttermilk and sprinkle a little coarse raw sugar on top. Bake on center rack of oven for 25 to 30 minutes, or until golden brown. Let cool on baking sheet for 10 minutes.

Chapter 6

CROISSANT PASTRIES

Croissant Dough

Morning Rolls

Hazelnut Orange Pinwheels

Macringle

Cinnamon Rolls with Coconut, Raisins & Walnuts

Several years ago I had the pleasure of visiting Clear Flour Bakery in Brook-line, Massachusetts. It was a wonderful experience. Even though the bakery's shelves were overflowing with tempting, fresh-baked loaves, it was a basket of golden pecan cinnamon rolls that caught my eye. Instead of the usual Danish dough that most cinnamon rolls are made with, these rolls were formed from light, buttery croissant dough. They were outstanding, and also very popular, which I learned the next morning when I returned to buy more for the journey home. Sorry, sold out.

Croissant dough is the most frequently made and well known laminated (layered) dough. It can also be one of the most challenging to prepare. Cold butter, the key ingredient, is enclosed inside a layer of dough and taken through a repetitive process of rolling out and folding. With so much butter in the dough, the biggest obstacle to success is heat. Keeping the ingredients and the room at a cool temperature makes the dough easier to handle. Also, when rolling the dough, try to keep the thickness as even as possible. If your first attempts don't turn out as well as expected, don't give up hope. Preparing your own croissant dough requires practice and patience, but the results are definitely worth it.

The croissant dough we make at Macrina (recipe included in this chapter) was the result of much experimentation. Slightly sweet, it's perfect for forming into creations such as our popular Morning Rolls, filled with vanilla sugar and baked golden brown with a crispy exterior. There is also a recipe for Macringle, where sweet almond cream is encased in yeasty croissant dough, a classic combination. Several of our regular customers have threatened me, saying that this book would not be complete without the recipe for their favorite pastry—Hazelnut Orange Pinwheels—so I've included that one as well. These are breakfast pastries at their best!

CROISSANT DOUGH

This recipe was inspired by an article I read in Cuisine *magazine back in 1983.
In the article, the talented chef Nick Malgieri shared his secrets for making great croissants.
My staff and I started experimenting on our own, and after adding a-little-of-this and taking
out a-little-of-that, we came up with what I think is a great recipe. At the bakery, we use
this dough as the base for a wide range of sweet and savory breakfast pastries. The key
to this recipe is keeping the butter and dough cool while you work with them.*

Makes approximately 2½ pounds of dough

1½ cups whole milk
1½ tablespoons dried yeast
3 tablespoons granulated sugar
2 tablespoons pure vanilla extract
1½ teaspoons kosher salt
3 cups and 3 tablespoons all-purpose unbleached flour
12 ounces (3 sticks) unsalted butter, chilled

- Pour milk into a saucepan and warm over medium heat. Remove from stove when
  milk is warm to the touch, taking care not to over-heat. Transfer to a large bowl and
  sprinkle yeast over the top. Add sugar and vanilla extract and mix with a whisk until
  dry ingredients are dissolved. Let sit for 5 minutes while yeast blooms.

- In a separate medium bowl, combine salt and 3 cups of the flour and mix with a
  wooden spoon. Add flour mixture to the bowl of milk and stir until all ingredients
  are incorporated. It's important not to over-mix the dough. Cover bowl with plastic
  wrap and place in refrigerator for at least 8 hours or overnight. While in the refrigerator, the dough will almost double in size.

- The next day, remove bowl of dough from the refrigerator and set on a counter.

- Cut cold butter into 12 equal pieces. Place butter and remaining 3 tablespoons flour
  in the bowl of a standing mixer. Using the paddle attachment, mix on low speed for
  about 2 minutes, until butter is completely smooth.

- Using a plastic scraper, scoop the butter mixture onto a floured work surface and
  pat into a 6-inch square. (At the bakery we refer to this as a *butter-block.*) Lightly flour
  the top and bottom of the butter-block to make it easier to handle, then lift it onto
  a piece of plastic wrap and set aside.

- Note: *Before going on to the next step, it's important to make sure that the butter-block and the
  bowl of dough are the same cool temperature. If the butter gets too warm and soft, place it in
  the refrigerator until it is thoroughly chilled. If necessary, do the same with the dough.*

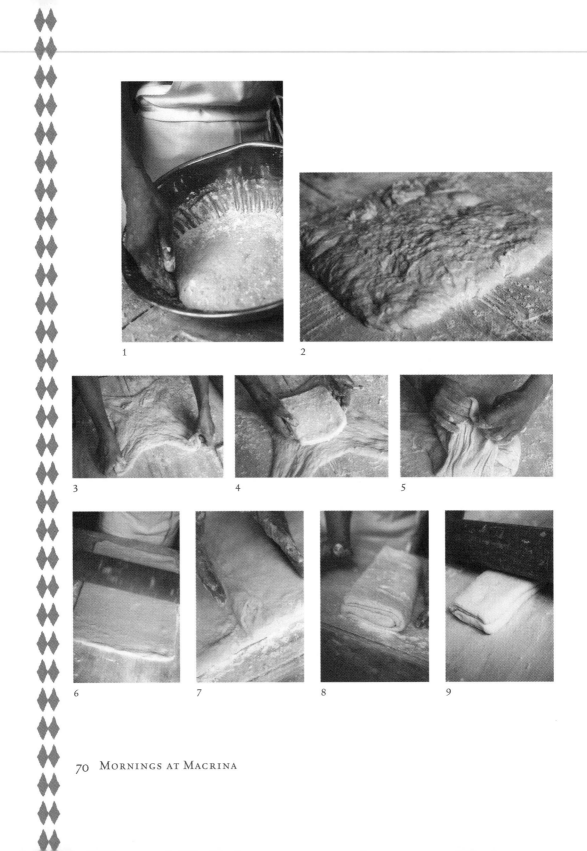

1

2

3

4

5

6

7

8

9

- The next step is incorporating the butter into the dough. Remove the plastic wrap from the bowl of dough and lightly sprinkle flour over the top. The spongy dough will be sticking to the bowl, so coat your fingers with a little flour and gently release the dough from the sides (photo 1). Pull dough onto a lightly floured work surface and gently pat into a square (photo 2). Stretch each of the corners outwards about 4 inches, creating an x shape and leaving a 7-inch square of dough in the center (photo 3). Place the cold butter-block in the center of the dough (photo 4) and fold the stretched corners on top, overlapping them slightly. Pinch all the seams of dough together, completely sealing the butter in dough (photo 5). Sprinkle a little more flour on your work surface and moving quickly to keep butter from softening, gently roll dough into a 12 x 20-inch rectangle, about ½ inch thick (photo 6). If the dough cracks open and butter starts to peek through, pinch the dough to re-seal it.

- Once the dough has been rolled out, it's time to start the *book-folds*. This process distributes the butter and dough into alternating layers, resulting in the wonderful flaky dough we all love. Note: *If the butter gets too soft it will start to seep through the dough. If this happens, place dough on a rimmed baking sheet lined with parchment paper, wrap well with plastic, and place in the refrigerator to chill for 30 minutes.* Position the rectangle so that a long side is facing you and fold the left and right sides on top, meeting in the center. Crease the seam gently with your fingers to make the next fold easier. Next, fold the dough in half, bringing the left side over the right so that it resembles a book (photos 7 & 8). Lift the folded dough onto a lined, rimmed baking sheet and cover with plastic wrap. Chill dough in the refrigerator for 30 minutes.

- After 30 minutes, remove dough from the refrigerator and let sit for 15 minutes. Remove plastic wrap and lift dough onto a floured surface, positioning dough so that the open side of the fold is in front of you. Roll dough, from left to right, into another 12 x 20-inch rectangle (photo 9). Moving quickly, follow the above book-fold instructions a second time. Lift folded dough back onto the lined, rimmed baking sheet, cover with plastic wrap, and chill in the refrigerator for another 30 minutes.

- The dough still needs one more fold. Remove dough from the refrigerator, let sit for 15 minutes, then follow the above book-fold instructions a third time. Cover the folded dough and let chill in the refrigerator for 30 minutes.

- Unlike pie dough, Croissant Dough really doesn't keep well. I recommend forming the dough into pastries right away. Once the pastries have been formed, they should be baked within 24 hours, or wrapped with plastic wrap and frozen.

MORNING ROLLS

We offer dozens of different breakfast pastries at the bakery, but Morning Rolls are hands-down the most popular item we make. A few customers are so attached to them that they have a standing daily order. I recommend forming these pastries the night before you want to serve them.

Makes 12 rolls

1 recipe Croissant Dough *(page 69)*
1½ cups granulated sugar
1½ tablespoons pure vanilla extract
Spray bottle of water

- Complete the Croissant Dough recipe as instructed and chill in the refrigerator for 30 minutes.

- In a medium bowl, combine sugar and vanilla extract and mix with a spoon until all sugar is coated. Set aside.

- Take Croissant Dough from refrigerator and remove plastic. Cut dough in half and place 1 piece on a lightly floured work surface. (Cover remaining dough with plastic wrap and return to the refrigerator.) Roll dough into a rectangle, approximately 12 x 20-inches. Gently brush top of dough to remove any extra flour, then mist with spray bottle of water. This will help the sugar mixture stick to the dough. Spread half of the sugar mixture over the entire surface. Starting with one of the long sides, roll dough away from you into a log. The finished log should be about 2½ to 3 inches in diameter. Repeat process with second piece of dough.

- Using a sharp chef's knife, cut each log into 6 equal rolls. Tuck the loose end of each roll underneath (see photos below). Place the rolls, tuck-sides-down, into oiled muffin tins and cover with plastic wrap. Let proof in a warm room, about 70°F, for 1 hour.

Rolls will rise slightly. Transfer to refrigerator for at least 8 hours or overnight. The dough will continue to ferment while it's in the refrigerator, developing a slightly sour flavor that contrasts perfectly with the sweetness of the vanilla sugar.

- The next morning, remove rolls from refrigerator and let sit, still covered, at room temperature for 1 hour.

- Preheat oven to 385°F.

- Remove plastic wrap and bake rolls on center rack of oven for 40 to 45 minutes. Finished rolls will be deep golden brown. Let cool for about 5 minutes, then turn pans over and gently remove the rolls with your fingers. Don't let the rolls cool for too long in the pans or the sugar will harden and the rolls will stick.

HAZELNUT ORANGE PINWHEELS

A very talented pastry chef of ours, Katie Fuller, created this recipe after a vacation in Italy. She returned with lots of ideas, and this was one of our favorites. I recommend forming these pastries the night before you want to serve them. Enjoy them with a cup of hot, strong coffee.

Makes 12 pinwheels

1 recipe Croissant Dough *(page 69)*
1 cup hazelnuts
½ cup granulated sugar
1 cup powdered sugar
1 tablespoon freshly grated orange zest
4 teaspoons fresh orange juice
Spray bottle of water

- Complete the Croissant Dough recipe as instructed and chill in the refrigerator for 30 minutes.

- Preheat oven to 350°F.

- Place hazelnuts on a rimmed baking sheet and toast for 15 to 20 minutes, or until golden brown. Let cool, then remove as much of the loose skins as possible by rubbing the hazelnuts between the palms of your hands. Chop nuts medium-fine and set aside.

- Place hazelnuts and granulated sugar in the bowl of a food processor and blend for about 30 seconds, until mixture is finely chopped. Set aside.

- Take Croissant Dough from refrigerator and remove plastic. Cut dough in half and place one piece on a lightly floured work surface. (Cover remaining dough with plastic wrap and return to the refrigerator.) Roll dough into a rectangle, approximately 12 x 20-inches. Gently brush top of dough to remove any extra flour, then mist with spray bottle of water. Spread half of the hazelnut mixture over the surface of the dough. Start-

ing with one of the 12-inch sides, roll dough away from you into a log. The finished log should be about 4 inches in diameter. Repeat process with second piece of dough.

- Using a sharp chef's knife, divide each log into 6 equal pinwheels. Place the pinwheels on a rimmed baking sheet lined with parchment paper and cover with plastic wrap. Let proof in a warm room, about 70°F, for 1 hour. Pinwheels will rise slightly. Transfer to refrigerator for at least 8 hours or overnight. The dough will continue to ferment while it's in the refrigerator, developing a slightly sour flavor that contrasts perfectly with the sweetness of the filling.

- The next morning, remove pinwheels from refrigerator and let sit, still covered, at room temperature for 1½ hours.

- Preheat oven to 375°F.

- In a medium bowl, combine powdered sugar, orange zest, and orange juice. Mix with a wooden spoon until sugar is dissolved and glaze is smooth. Set aside.

- Remove plastic from pinwheels and bake for 25 to 30 minutes, or until golden brown. Let cool on baking sheet for 10 minutes, then drizzle a small amount of glaze over each pinwheel.

MACRINGLE

*This is Macrina's version of Kringle, the traditional Scandinavian breakfast pastry.
The classic version is made with Danish dough and filled with almond paste, but I like
to use our flaky Croissant Dough and a light almond cream. It makes a beautiful
presentation for brunch or a holiday table.*

Serves 10–12

1 recipe Croissant Dough *(page 69)*
1 cup whole almonds
8 tablespoons (1 stick) unsalted butter, at room temperature
½ cup granulated sugar
1 egg
3 tablespoons pure vanilla extract
1½ tablespoons all-purpose unbleached flour
Egg wash made with 1 egg and 1 teaspoon water
Coarse raw sugar
Powdered sugar

- Complete the Croissant Dough recipe as instructed and chill in the refrigerator for 30 minutes.

- Preheat oven to 350°F. Place almonds on a rimmed baking sheet and toast for about 20 minutes, or until golden brown. Let cool.

- Place cooled almonds in the bowl of a food processor and blend until medium fine. Add butter, granulated sugar, egg, vanilla extract, and flour and blend for about 3 minutes, or until smooth. Scrape almond cream into a small bowl and set aside.

- Take Croissant Dough from refrigerator and remove plastic. Cut dough in half and place 1 piece on a lightly floured work surface. Set second piece aside. Gently roll dough into a 12 x 20-inch rectangle, taking care not to tear the dough. If the dough resists being rolled, let it sit for a few minutes to relax, then try again. Lift rolled dough onto a rimmed baking sheet lined with parchment paper. Repeat process with second piece of dough.

- Scoop half of the almond cream onto the center of each rectangle and spread it out to approximately 4 x 16 inches. Fold the long sides of each rectangle on top of the almond cream, leaving a 1-inch opening down the center. Fold 1 inch of dough underneath each of the ends and pinch to seal. This creates a double-thick crust that will keep the almond cream from oozing out during baking. Brush the top of the dough with egg wash and sprinkle with coarse raw sugar. (Avoid brushing the almond cream with egg wash.)

- Note: *At this point, the pastries can be baked or wrapped well with plastic wrap and frozen for up to 2 weeks. Make sure that the frozen pastries are completely defrosted before baking.*

- Preheat oven to 385°F.

- Let the pastries sit at room temperature for 30 minutes. Dough will rise slightly and become soft to the touch. Bake for about 30 minutes, or until a deep golden brown on top and bottom. Let cool on baking sheet for about 10 minutes, then cut into slices. Dust with powdered sugar before serving.

CINNAMON ROLLS WITH COCONUT, RAISINS & WALNUTS

My Grandmother Bakke made the most incredible cinnamon rolls I've ever tasted. One day, always open to improving on a good thing, she decided to add two of her favorite ingredients—coconut and walnuts. The results were spectacular. I recommend forming these pastries the night before you want to serve them.

Makes 12 cinnamon rolls

1 recipe Croissant Dough *(page 69)*
½ cup seedless raisins
1 cup walnut halves
½ cup granulated sugar
½ cup light brown sugar
1 teaspoon pure vanilla extract
2 teaspoons cinnamon
½ cup shredded, unsweetened coconut
Spray bottle of water

- Complete the Croissant Dough recipe as instructed and chill in the refrigerator for 30 minutes.

- Place raisins in a small bowl and cover with hot tap water. Let soak for 10 minutes, then drain and squeeze with your hands to remove excess liquid. Set aside.

- Preheat oven to 350°F. Place walnuts on a rimmed baking sheet and toast for 15 minutes, or until golden brown. Let cool 10 minutes. Chop coarsely and set aside.

- In a medium bowl, combine sugars, vanilla extract, and cinnamon. Mix well with a wooden spoon and set aside.

- Take Croissant Dough from refrigerator and remove plastic. Cut dough in half and place 1 piece on a lightly floured work surface. (Cover remaining dough with plastic wrap and return to the refrigerator.) Roll dough into a 12 x 20-inch rectangle and lightly mist dough with a spray bottle of water. Spread half of the cinnamon-sugar mixture over the entire surface. Sprinkle half of the raisins, half of the walnuts, and half of the shredded coconut on top. Starting with one of the long sides, roll dough away from you into a log. The finished log should be about 3 inches in diameter. Repeat process with second piece of dough.

- Using a sharp chef's knife, cut each log into 6 equal rolls. Tuck the loose end of each roll underneath (see photos, page 72). Place the rolls, tuck sides down, into oiled muffin tins and cover with plastic wrap. Let proof in a warm room, about 70°F, for 1½ hours. Rolls will rise slightly. Transfer to refrigerator for at least 8 hours or overnight. The dough will continue to ferment while it's in the refrigerator, developing a slightly sour flavor that contrasts perfectly with the sweetness of the filling.

- The next morning, remove the cinnamon rolls from the refrigerator and let sit, still covered, at room temperature for 1 hour.

- Preheat oven to 385°F.

- Remove plastic and bake for 40 to 45 minutes. Finished rolls will be a deep, golden brown. Let cool for about 5 minutes, then turn pan over and gently remove the rolls. Don't let them cool for too long in the pan or the sugars will harden and the rolls will stick.

Chapter 7

COFFEE CAKES

Brown Sugar & Almond Coffee Cake

Apple Anadama Coffee Cake

Squash Harvest Loaf

Lemon–Sour Cherry Coffee Cake

Ginger Pear Upside-Down Cake

My favorite thing to do on a free morning is go out to breakfast, and here in Seattle we're lucky to have many bakeries and cafes to choose from. The first thing I do when I walk into one of these places is look for the "specials" board. What kind of coffee cake are they serving today? Baked fresh and loaded with dried or fresh fruits, coffee cakes are irresistible. I love the rich, buttery flavor, the creamy textures, and the sugary toppings. What a treat!

Coffee cakes are one of the easiest breakfast pastries to prepare. Using fresh, carefully measured ingredients will help ensure success, as will following a few simple rules. I think the most important step is the creaming of the butter and sugar. Beating the ingredients until the sugar is fully dissolved and the butter is oxygenated, giving it a pale color, will result in lighter and fluffier coffee cakes. This process can take up to eight minutes, depending on whether you use a stand mixer or mix by hand, but I think it's important to take the time.

While it's essential that you take your time creaming the butter, it is equally important not to overmix the final batters. Gently fold the ingredients together and stop mixing as soon as the last of the dry ingredients are absorbed into the wet. Overmixing will result in rubbery coffee cakes.

This chapter contains recipes for some of our most popular coffee cakes. We are always changing our offerings at the café, sometimes to reflect the season and other times just to have fun. The Brown Sugar & Almond Coffee Cake is ideal for showcasing fresh summer berries, and the Ginger Pear Upside-Down Cake, loaded with fresh ginger, makes a wonderful winter warmer. I hope you'll enjoy them as much as I do.

Brown Sugar & Almond
Coffee Cake

This coffee cake is a stand-out favorite among our brunch customers. I like to use fresh berries whenever possible, but frozen fruit will also work well in this recipe.

Makes 1 (9-inch square) cake

4 cups all-purpose unbleached flour
2½ teaspoons baking powder
1 teaspoon baking soda
1 teaspoon salt
10 ounces (2½ sticks) unsalted butter, at room temperature
1¾ cups light brown sugar
5 eggs
½ cup whole milk
2 teaspoons pure almond extract
2 teaspoons pure vanilla extract
1 cup buttermilk
2 cups fresh or frozen raspberries
1 cup whole almonds, coarsely chopped
Powdered sugar

- Preheat oven to 325°F. Oil a 9-inch square baking pan.

- Sift flour, baking powder, baking soda, and salt into a large bowl. Toss with your hands and set aside

- Combine butter and sugar in the bowl of a stand mixer. Using the paddle attachment, mix on medium speed for 5 to 8 minutes to cream the butter. The mixture should be smooth and pale in color.

- In a medium bowl, combine eggs, milk, and almond and vanilla extracts and mix with a whisk. Add a small amount of egg mixture to the bowl of creamed butter and mix on medium speed until fully incorporated. Continue adding small amounts until all of the egg mixture is mixed into the butter. Scrape down the sides of the bowl with a rubber spatula and mix for another 30 seconds.

- Remove the bowl from your stand mixer. Alternately add small amounts of the flour mixture and the buttermilk to the bowl, mixing with a wooden spoon just until all the ingredients are incorporated. Fold in the raspberries, taking care not to smash the fruit. Pour the batter into the prepared baking pan and spread evenly. Sprinkle chopped almonds over the top.

• Bake on center rack of oven for about 1 hour, or until golden brown. Test center of cake with a skewer. It will come out clean when the cake is finished. Let cool for 20 minutes on a wire rack, then dust with powdered sugar and cut into pieces. This coffee cake will be fragile until it has completely cooled, so remove the warm pieces carefully, using a pie server to lift the pieces out of the pan.

APPLE ANADAMA COFFEE CAKE

This dense New England–style coffee cake is a wonderful autumn harvest treat. I'm not sure where the name Anadama originated, but Americans have been baking versions of this coffee cake for generations. Try it alongside scrambled eggs and smoky bacon.

Makes 1 (9-inch square) cake

FOR THE BATTER:
1 cup all-purpose unbleached flour
½ cup semolina flour*
½ cup fine whole-wheat flour
¼ cup cornmeal
2 teaspoons baking powder
1 teaspoon baking soda
1 teaspoon cinnamon
½ teaspoon ground cloves
¼ teaspoon freshly ground nutmeg
1 teaspoon kosher salt
8 tablespoons (1 stick) unsalted butter, at room temperature
½ cup light brown sugar
⅓ cup molasses
3 eggs
1 teaspoon pure vanilla extract
2 Granny Smith apples, peeled and grated
⅔ cup buttermilk
available in specialty shops and some supermarkets

FOR THE TOPPING:

2 tablespoons unsalted butter, chilled

3 tablespoons cornmeal

3 tablespoons light brown sugar

1 tablespoon all-purpose unbleached flour

⅓ cup pecans, coarsely chopped

- Preheat oven to 325°F. Oil a 9-inch square baking pan

PREPARING THE BATTER:

- Combine flours, cornmeal, baking powder, baking soda, cinnamon, cloves, nutmeg, and salt in a medium bowl. Mix with a wooden spoon and set aside.

- Place butter and brown sugar in the bowl of a stand mixer and using the paddle attachment, mix on medium speed for 5 to 8 minutes. The creamed butter will become smooth and pale in color.

- In a medium bowl, combine molasses, eggs, and vanilla extract and mix with a whisk. With the stand mixer on low speed, slowly pour the molasses mixture into the creamed butter and mix with the paddle attachment for about 2 minutes. At first the batter will look like it's separating, but don't worry. Add the grated apples and continue mixing on low speed for 30 seconds.

- Remove bowl from the stand mixer. Alternately add small amounts of the flour mixture and the buttermilk to the bowl, mixing with a wooden spoon just until the batter comes together. Pour batter into the prepared baking pan and spread evenly. Set aside.

TOPPING THE COFFEE CAKE:

- Place all topping ingredients in the bowl of a stand mixer and mix with the paddle attachment on low speed for 1 to 2 minutes. The topping will become coarse and crumbly.

- Spread topping evenly over coffee cake batter and bake for 40 to 45 minutes. Test center with a skewer. It will come out clean when the cake is finished. Let cool for 20 minutes on a wire rack, then run a sharp knife around the sides of the cake to release it from the baking pan. Invert pan to remove the coffee cake, then place it, topping side up, on a serving plate. Leftovers can be wrapped in plastic and stored at room temperature for up to 3 days.

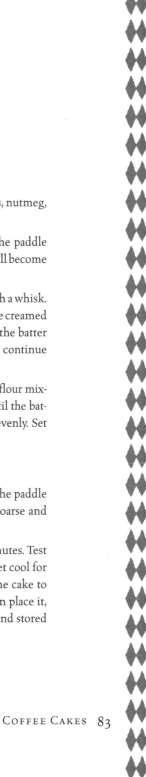

SQUASH HARVEST LOAF

*I developed this recipe with the help of Macrina's first pastry chef, Lynn Upson.
While it can be prepared with canned pumpkin, I prefer to use fresh Roasted Butternut
Squash, which gives the loaf a rich color and natural sweetness.*

Makes 2 (9 x 5 x 3-inch) loaves

½ cup walnut halves
½ cup pecan halves
1 cup pumpkin seeds
3½ cups unbleached all-purpose flour
2 teaspoons baking powder
2 teaspoons baking soda
½ teaspoon freshly ground nutmeg
1½ teaspoons cinnamon
1½ teaspoons salt
1 cup canola oil
1½ cups granulated sugar
1½ cups light brown sugar
2 cups Roasted Butternut Squash *(recipe follows)*,
or 2 cups canned pumpkin purée
4 eggs
¾ cup buttermilk

- Preheat oven to 375°F. Oil two 9 x 5 x 3-inch loaf pans.

- Spread walnuts and pecans on a rimmed baking sheet. Spread pumpkin seeds on another rimmed baking sheet. Toast nuts and seeds for 15 minutes, then remove the nuts. Toast pumpkin seeds for another 5 minutes. Let cool. Chop nuts and seeds medium-fine and combine in a small bowl. Reduce oven temperature to 325°F.

- Sift flour, baking powder, baking soda, nutmeg, cinnamon, and salt into a medium bowl. Set aside ¼ cup of chopped nuts and seeds for garnish and add the remainder to the flour mixture. Mix with a wooden spoon.

- Combine oil and sugars in the bowl of a stand mixer. Using the paddle attachment, mix on medium speed for about 4 minutes. Add 2 cups of puréed Roasted Butternut Squash and mix for another 2 minutes. Add eggs, one at a time, making sure each egg is fully incorporated before adding another.

- Remove bowl from the stand mixer. Alternately add small amounts of the flour mixture and the buttermilk to the bowl, mixing with a wooden spoon just until all dry ingredients are incorporated into the batter. Pour batter into the prepared baking pans, filling each two-thirds full. Sprinkle remaining nuts and seeds lengthwise down center of each loaf.

- Bake loaves on center rack of oven for 1 hour and 10 minutes, or until golden brown, then test centers with a skewer. It will come out clean when the loaves are finished. Let cool in the pans for 20 minutes on a wire rack, then run a sharp knife around the sides of the loaves to release them from the pans. Invert pans to remove the loaves. Let them finish cooling on a wire rack.

Roasted Butternut Squash

We use a lot of roasted squash at Macrina. The roasting process intensifies the natural sweetness of the squash and reduces its water content. I recommend keeping some in the freezer for last-minute baking.

Makes about 2 cups of puréed squash

1 medium (1½ pounds) butternut squash

- Preheat oven to 375°F.

- Wash squash, then cut it in half lengthwise and remove the seeds with a spoon. Place squash, cut sides down, on a rimmed baking sheet or roasting pan. Pour 1½ cups of water into the baking sheet, surrounding the squash. Bake for about 1 hour, or until skin is dark brown and flesh is fork tender. Remove from oven and let cool for about 20 minutes. Scoop cooled squash out of its skin and purée in a food processor until smooth. Let the puréed squash cool completely, uncovered, then store it in an airtight container. The squash will last for up to 3 days in the refrigerator or for up to 1 month in the freezer.

LEMON–SOUR CHERRY COFFEE CAKE

This glazed loaf makes a perfect family breakfast or afternoon tea cake.
It has a rich, dense texture that's similar to pound cake. Wrapped in cellophane and tied with
a festive ribbon, it also makes a great hostess gift at weekend brunches.

Makes 1 bundt cake

FOR THE BATTER:
1½ cups dried tart cherries
4 cups unbleached all-purpose flour
1 tablespoon baking powder
½ teaspoon baking soda
½ teaspoon salt
8 ounces (2 sticks) unsalted butter, at room temperature
2¼ cups granulated sugar
3 tablespoons freshly grated lemon zest
5 eggs
¼ cup freshly squeezed lemon juice
1 cup plain yogurt

FOR THE GLAZE:
1 cup powdered sugar
2 teaspoons freshly grated lemon zest
2 tablespoons freshly squeezed lemon juice

- Preheat oven to 325°F. Oil a 12-cup bundt pan.

PREPARING THE BATTER:

- Place dried cherries in a medium bowl and cover with hot tap water. Let soak and plump for 10 minutes, then drain thoroughly and check for pits.

- Sift flour, baking powder, baking soda, and salt into a large bowl Toss with your hands and set aside.

- Combine butter, sugar, and lemon zest in the bowl of a stand mixer. Using the paddle attachment, mix on medium speed for 5 to 8 minutes. The mixture will become smooth and pale in color. Add eggs, one at a time, making sure each egg is fully mixed into the butter before adding another. After the last egg is incorporated, slowly add the lemon juice and mix for 1 more minute. Scrape down the sides of the bowl and mix for 30 seconds to make sure all of the ingredients are fully incorporated. Remove the bowl from the mixer.

- Alternately add small amounts of the flour mixture and the yogurt to the batter, mixing with a wooden spoon just until all dry ingredients are incorporated into the batter. Set aside 10 or 12 cherries for garnish and gently fold the remainder into the batter, taking care not to overmix. Pour batter into the prepared bundt pan, filling two thirds of the pan. Bake on center rack of oven for 1 hour and 10 minutes, or until the top is golden brown. Check the center of the coffee cake with a skewer. It will come out clean when the cake is finished. Let cool in the pan on a wire rack for at least 20 minutes.

- Loosen the sides of the cake with a sharp knife. Place a serving plate, upside down, on top of the cooled bundt pan and invert the pan to remove the cake. Let cake cool completely.

GLAZING THE CAKE:

- Sift powdered sugar into medium bowl, then add lemon zest and lemon juice. Mix with a spoon until smooth. Drizzle glaze over the cooled coffee cake and top with the reserved plumped cherries.

GINGER PEAR UPSIDE-DOWN CAKE

Topped with caramelized fruit, this cake is spectacular. We call for pears in this recipe, but you can substitute ripe plums, nectarines, or apples. I recommend serving this cake warm, with whipped cream.

Makes 1 (9-inch) cake

FOR THE TOPPING:
3 tablespoons unsalted butter, at room temperature
½ cup light brown sugar
1½ teaspoons cinnamon
4 to 5 ripe pears, peeled, cored, and quartered lengthwise

FOR THE BATTER:
8 ounces (2 sticks) unsalted butter, at room temperature
¾ cup light brown sugar
2 tablespoons peeled, grated ginger
3 eggs
⅔ cup molasses
3 cups all-purpose unbleached flour
1½ teaspoons baking powder
1½ teaspoons baking soda
½ teaspoon salt
1½ cups buttermilk

● Preheat oven to 325°F. Oil a 9-inch springform pan and line the bottom with a 10-inch circle of parchment paper (see page xvi).

PREPARING THE TOPPING:

● In a medium saucepan, combine butter, brown sugar, and cinnamon. Melt butter over medium heat for about 1 minute, then pour into the springform pan, completely coating the parchment paper. Place the quartered pears on top of the butter and sugar mixture, lining the pieces up tightly so that none of the pan's bottom shows through. I like to fan the slices into a decorative circle. Set pan in center of a rimmed baking sheet and set aside.

PREPARING THE BATTER:

- Cut butter into 1-inch pieces and place in the bowl of a stand mixer. Add brown sugar and using the paddle attachment, cream the mixture on medium speed for 5 to 8 minutes. Butter will become smooth and pale in color. Add the grated ginger and mix for 1 minute. Scrape down the sides of the bowl with a rubber spatula. Switch to low speed and add the eggs, one at a time, making sure each egg is fully incorporated before adding another. After the last egg has been added, slowly pour in molasses and continue mixing until fully distributed. The mixture will look like it's breaking up but will come together after the dry ingredients are added. Remove bowl from stand mixer.

- Sift flour, baking powder, baking soda, and salt into a separate medium bowl, and toss together with your hands.

- Alternately add small amounts of the flour mixture and buttermilk to the batter, mixing with a rubber spatula just until all of the dry ingredients are absorbed. Take care not to overmix the batter. Pour batter into the pear-lined springform pan, filling it to just below the top. If necessary, use a rubber spatula to smooth out the surface.

- Carefully transfer the baking sheet to the center rack of the oven and bake for just under 2 hours, or until golden brown. Test center with a skewer. It will come out clean when the cake is finished. Let cool in the pan for 10 minutes on a wire rack. Cover the springform pan with an upside-down serving plate, then carefully turn them over. Release the sides of the pan and lift. Gently lift the pan's base off the cake and peel away the parchment paper.

Chapter 8

BREAKFAST BREAD PUDDINGS

Honey Lemon Bread Pudding with Blueberry Compote

Raspberry Cinnamon-Sugar Bread Pudding with Nectarine Compote

Savory Bread Pudding with Cranberries, Sausage & Chèvre

I am proud to say that I still love Macrina's bread pudding. And when you've seen it every day for a decade, being able to say that means something! Bread puddings are the ultimate comfort food: creamy, rich, and satisfying. Like crostini and bread salads, they are also an ideal way to use up day-old bread. Whenever you have leftovers from a favorite loaf, save them in the freezer. From fruit-filled breakfast puddings to savory brunch varieties, the possibilities are almost endless.

The most important ingredient in any bread pudding is, obviously, the bread. In addition to providing texture and flavor, bread makes up most of a pudding's volume. If a loaf isn't delicious enough to eat with dinner, it shouldn't be used in a bread pudding either. To prepare bread cubes for bread pudding, first remove the crusts from day-old or defrosted loaves, then cut the loaves into 1-inch cubes and toast them lightly in a 350°F oven to dry them out. About 10 minutes will usually do the trick. The drier the bread cubes, the more easily they will absorb the custard, which will give the final pudding a lighter texture.

Aside from quality, there really are no rules when it comes to choosing which breads to use in bread puddings. Using scraps from sweet breads, such as our Apple Cinnamon Monkey Bread, can have delicious results, though puddings made with these breads will be denser than those made with lighter loaves. Personally, I like to use rustic European breads, such as Ciabatta or Classic Italian Loaf, in these recipes. Occasionally, when making savory bread puddings, for instance, I'll use a darker, nutty loaf. Experiment and find your own favorite combinations.

HONEY LEMON BREAD PUDDING
WITH BLUEBERRY COMPOTE

This pudding is great for breakfast, as part of a brunch buffet, or as the centerpiece of a Sunday picnic. Using sourdough bread for the cubes, combined with the tangy flavor of lemon zest, provides a great balance to the sweet blueberry compote.

Serves 9–12

2 cups whole milk

2 cups half-and-half

¾ cup honey

1 teaspoon pure vanilla extract

3 egg yolks

2 eggs

8 cups oven-dried white bread cubes (about 1½ loaves, cut into 1-inch cubes)

3 tablespoons freshly grated lemon zest

6 tablespoons unsalted butter, melted

Blueberry Compote *(recipe follows)*

- Preheat oven to 325°F. Oil a 9-inch square baking pan.

- Combine milk, half-and-half, honey, vanilla extract, egg yolks, and eggs in a medium bowl. Whisk until thoroughly blended and set aside.

- Place bread cubes in a medium bowl, then add lemon zest and melted butter. Toss until cubes are evenly coated. Transfer bread cubes to the prepared baking pan and pour milk mixture over the top, not quite filling the pan. Stir slightly with a wooden spoon to make sure all the cubes are coated. Place a plate on top of the bread cubes to weigh them down and help them absorb all of the moisture. Set aside for 20 minutes.

- Remove the plate and wrap the baking pan tightly with aluminum foil. Poke 2 small vent holes in opposite corners of the foil. Place pan in the center of a large roasting pan, at least 2 inches deep, and place roasting pan on center rack of oven. Pour hot water into the pan to reach halfway up the sides of the baking pan. (This water bath helps the bread pudding to cook more evenly.) Bake for 1 hour and 15 minutes, then carefully remove the foil and bake for another 15 minutes to brown the top and set the custard. Lift the pudding out of the roasting pan and let cool for 20 minutes on a wire rack.

- Wrapped in plastic wrap, this bread pudding will last for up to 3 days in the refrigerator. (Wait for the pudding to cool completely before wrapping it.) To refresh the pudding, simply wrap it in foil and warm it in a 350°F oven for 10 minutes.

BLUEBERRY COMPOTE

If you can't find fresh blueberries for this recipe, feel free to substitute quality frozen berries.

3 cups (1½ pints) fresh blueberries
¾ cup granulated sugar
2 teaspoons freshly grated lemon zest
1 teaspoon cornstarch

- Combine 2 cups of the blueberries, sugar, lemon zest, and cornstarch in a medium bowl. Toss gently to coat blueberries. Pour into a medium saucepan and simmer over medium heat, stirring occasionally, until liquid thickens and blueberries start to burst, about 5 minutes. Remove from heat and stir in the remaining cup of blueberries. Ladle compote over generous servings of warm bread pudding.

RASPBERRY CINNAMON-SUGAR BREAD PUDDING WITH NECTARINE COMPOTE

Ripe summer fruit and a crunchy topping make this a memorable breakfast offering. I recommend using day-old white breads such as our Classic Italian Loaf, Ciabatta, or Macrina Casera for this recipe. When fresh fruit is not available, frozen is a fine alternative.

Serves 9–12

FOR THE BREAD PUDDING:
3 cups whole milk
1 cup heavy cream
¾ cup honey
3 teaspoons cinnamon
3 egg yolks
2 eggs
8 cups oven-dried white bread cubes (about 1½ loaves,
cut into 1-inch cubes; see pages 93 and 96)
6 tablespoons unsalted butter, melted
2 cups (1 pint) fresh raspberries
½ cup coarsely chopped walnuts

½ cup rolled oats
3 tablespoons granulated sugar
3 tablespoons light brown sugar
½ teaspoon freshly ground nutmeg
Nectarine Compote (*recipe follows*)

PREPARING THE BREAD PUDDING:

- Preheat oven to 325°F. Oil a 9-inch square baking pan.

- Combine milk, cream, honey, 1 teaspoon of the cinnamon, egg yolks, and eggs in a medium bowl. Whisk until thoroughly blended and set aside.

- Place bread cubes in a medium bowl and pour melted butter over the top. Toss until cubes are evenly coated. Pour about half of the bread cubes into the prepared baking pan, just covering the bottom of the pan. Add half of the raspberries, then add the remaining bread cubes, followed by the rest of the berries. Pour milk mixture over the top of the cubes, not quite filling the pan. Stir slightly with a wooden spoon to make sure all the cubes are coated. Place a plate on top of the bread cubes to weigh them down and help them absorb all of the moisture. Set aside for 20 minutes. This is a good time to prepare the topping.

- Combine walnuts, oats, granulated sugar, brown sugar, remaining cinnamon, and nutmeg. Mix with a wooden spoon and set aside.

- Remove plate from bread pudding and sprinkle topping over the cubes. Wrap the baking pan tightly with aluminum foil. Poke 2 small vent holes in opposite corners of the foil. Place pan in the center of a large roasting pan, at least 2 inches deep, and place roasting pan on center rack of oven. Pour hot water into the pan to reach about 1 inch up the sides of the baking pan. (This water bath helps the bread pudding to cook evenly.) Bake for 1 hour and 15 minutes, then carefully remove the foil and bake for another 15 minutes to brown the top and set the custard. Poke center of pudding with a knife to make sure custard has set. Lift the pudding out of the roasting pan and let cool for 20 minutes on a wire rack.

- Wrapped in plastic wrap, this bread pudding will last for up to 3 days in the refrigerator. (Wait for the pudding to cool completely before wrapping it.) To refresh the pudding, simply wrap it in foil and warm it in a 350°F oven for 10 minutes.

NECTARINE COMPOTE

4 nectarines, pitted and cut into ¾-inch pieces
¾ cup granulated sugar
1½ tablespoons all-purpose unbleached flour
¼ teaspoon cinnamon
¼ teaspoon freshly grated lemon zest

- Combine half of the nectarines, and the sugar, flour, cinnamon, and lemon zest in a medium bowl. Toss gently to coat the fruit. Pour into a medium saucepan and simmer over medium heat, stirring occasionally, until fruit juices are exuded and the liquid thickens, 5 to 8 minutes. Remove from heat and stir in the remaining nectarines. Spoon warm compote over bowls of bread pudding.

SAVORY BREAD PUDDING WITH CRANBERRIES, SAUSAGE & CHÈVRE

This savory pudding is best made with a blend of light and dark bread cubes. The Cracked Wheat Walnut Cider loaf works well with our Macrina Casera. Serve warm with fresh seasonal fruit.

Serves 9–12

2 cups whole milk
2 cups half-and-half
½ cup light brown sugar
½ teaspoon cinnamon
2 tablespoons freshly grated orange zest
1 tablespoon coarsely chopped fresh sage
3 egg yolks
2 eggs
4 cups oven-dried white bread cubes (about ¾ loaf, cut into 1-inch cubes)
4 cups oven-dried dark bread cubes (about ¾ loaf, cut into 1-inch cubes)
2 cups fresh or frozen cranberries
6 ounces (about 4 links) pork sausage, fully cooked and cut into ¼-inch pieces

6 tablespoons unsalted butter, melted
6 ounces goat cheese

- Preheat oven to 325°F. Oil a 9-inch square baking pan.

- Combine milk, half-and-half, brown sugar, cinnamon, orange zest, sage, egg yolks, and eggs in a medium bowl. Whisk until thoroughly blended and set aside.

- Place bread cubes in a large bowl and add cranberries, cooked sausage, and melted butter. Toss until evenly distributed then transfer to the prepared baking pan. Pour milk mixture over the top, not quite filling the pan, and stir slightly with a wooden spoon. Crumble goat cheese on top of bread cubes. Place a plate on top of the bread cubes to weigh them down and help them absorb all of the moisture. Set aside for 20 minutes.

- Remove the plate and wrap the baking pan tightly with aluminum foil. Poke 2 small vent holes in opposite corners of the foil. Place pan in the center of a large roasting pan, at least 2 inches deep, and place the roasting pan on center rack of oven. Pour hot water into the pan to reach halfway up the sides of the baking pan. (This water bath will help the bread pudding cook evenly.) Bake for 1 hour and 15 minutes, then carefully remove the foil and bake for another 15 minutes to brown the top and set the custard. Lift the pudding out of the roasting pan and let cool for 20 to 30 minutes on a wire rack.

- Wrapped in plastic wrap, this bread pudding will last for up to 2 days in the refrigerator. (Wait for the pudding to cool completely before wrapping it.) To refresh the pudding, simply wrap it in foil and warm it in a 350°F oven for 10 minutes.

FROM OUR PASTRY CASE

FROM OUR PASTRY CASE

When we first opened our retail shop back in 1993, our antique pastry case proudly displayed three kinds of tarts, two different cookies, and one type of biscotti. It was a simple beginning. As new customers discovered the store, we started selling out of desserts and often needed to whip up some last-minute offerings. My pastry chef, Lynn Upson, and I would talk about our favorite childhood desserts and about what we were baking at home. Then, if we happened to have the ingredients, we would create versions that worked for Macrina and our clientele. Today our customers know a very different bakery. The pastry crew bakes dozens and dozens of daily desserts, filling the five-foot display case, six window shelves, and every inch of counter space. It's a sight to behold.

This section of the book contains dozens of my favorite dessert recipes. They've been adapted from a wide range of sources and are now daily and weekly standards at the bakery. One thing almost all of them have in common is that they originated in someone's home kitchen. Many of them are cherished family traditions, handed down through generations of home bakers. The Coconut Cake, for example, is a version of my grandmother's recipe, and the Fresh Strawberry Tartlets were inspired by my mother's baking. The recipe for Classic Ricotta Pie was inspired by my visits to Boston's Italian bakeries. I've enjoyed poring through classic pastry books and old cooking magazines, and pastry cooks are encouraged to bring in recipes they've found on their own. The sources are endless, and our list of recipes continues to grow.

Regardless of how a recipe reaches our kitchen, we work to make it our own, just as you do at home. One of my goals for the bakery has been to create a consistent, recognizable style, while continuing to experiment with new ideas. I think we've achieved that goal. Two characteristics that unite all of our desserts are the quality of the ingredients and the care taken in preparation. After all, if you are going to spend an afternoon baking a cake, you want it to be as delicious and as beautiful as possible. Taking the time to toast nuts and seeds before incorporating them into batters, making sure that fruits and berries are at their peak, or patiently sifting dry ingredients will help any baker achieve success.

It's convenient and fun to pick up dessert from your neighborhood bakery—I'm certainly glad that people do!—but it's not that difficult to make many of these desserts at home. It just takes a little practice and planning. For example, keeping small batches of Flaky Pie Dough in the freezer, or even pre-formed pastry shells, will help make last-minute baking easier. When summer arrives, and your local markets are filled with cherries, raspberries, nectarines, and peaches, fill a bag with your favorites and make a Fresh Fruit Crostata, a double-crusted Classic Blueberry Pie, or an Apple & Bing Cherry Galette. In fact, make two or three. Tarts freeze well and can be baked later, when the season has changed and the fruits are no longer available. Pull a frozen layer of Almond Cake from the freezer and serve it with sweet, plump blackberries and Mascarpone Cream. What's most important is that you have fun with these recipes, and that you enjoy sharing them with your friends and family.

Chapter 9

CAKES

Bittersweet Chocolate Gâteau
Lemon Butter Cake with Fresh Strawberries & Lemon Cream
Semolina Pound Cake with Fresh Preserves
Mom's Chocolate Cake
Coconut Cake with Raspberries & Lemon Cream
Chocolate Cherry Pound Cake
Mascarpone Cheesecake
Almond Cake with Mascarpone Cream & Fresh Blackberries

When I was a child my favorite cakes were those made by my grandmother Bakke, the home baker in our family. Each spring I would ask her to make me the same birthday cake, her famous Banana Coconut Whipped Cream Layer Cake. I remember that her cakes were denser than the ones from our local bakery, and I loved the way she sweetened the whipped cream with sugar and vanilla. But my favorite thing about the cake was that the entire thing was coated in *green* toasted coconut. What kid could resist? This is the kind of baking I love to celebrate at Macrina Bakery, as well as at home. I like to make traditional family recipes prepared with the highest quality ingredients. And while none of the recipes in this chapter call for green food coloring, they're all decorated in a simple style that makes a statement.

There's no need to be afraid of making cakes. They do take time to put together, but with the right ingredients and equipment, as well as a little practice and preparation, you will have stunning success. One of the most important tools is a stand mixer. Of course you can always use a hand-held electric mixer, but using a stand mixer makes the process much easier, and ultimately more satisfying. Most of the recipes in this chapter, like the Mom's Chocolate Cake, are American classics, and are quite simple to make. The way we enhance most of these cakes is by brushing the layers with flavored syrups, which moisten the layers and add a little extra flavor. You'll find tips like these throughout the recipes.

As with all cooking, it's important to remember balance of flavors. I like to use sweet and tart berries to contrast with rich frostings. I also recommend using heavier frostings only on the outside of cakes, layering the insides with lighter options such as lemon cream, fresh fruit, or your favorite preserves. Another thing to keep in mind is portion size. A light dessert such as the Almond Cake with Mascarpone Cream and Fresh Blackberries can be served in generous slices, while the rich Chocolate Cherry Pound Cake should be probably be enjoyed in moderation. I would rather have a guest ask for another slice of dessert than push the plate away saying "That was so rich."

There are a lot of cake recipes in this chapter—one for every occasion. Serve the easy-to-prepare Bittersweet Chocolate Gâteau for a simple (and sexy) evening dessert. The Semolina Pound Cake is perfect for a light afternoon treat. And, of course, the Coconut Cake is always a big hit at children's birthday parties.

Bittersweet Chocolate Gâteau

This velvety cake is easy to prepare and makes an elegant presentation. It's also flourless, which makes it perfect for entertaining guests with wheat allergies. I like to add plump, ripe raspberries and garnish the slices with Lightly Sweetened Whipped Cream.

Makes 1 (9-inch) cake

10 ounces bittersweet chocolate
9 eggs
12 tablespoons (1½ sticks) unsalted butter, at room temperature
¾ cup granulated sugar
¼ cup dark cocoa powder, sifted
2 cups (1 pint) fresh raspberries
Lightly Sweetened Whipped Cream *(recipe follows)*
Powdered sugar

- Preheat oven to 350°F. Oil a 9 x 3-inch springform pan. Set aside.

- Chop chocolate into small pieces and place in a small stainless steel bowl. Place bowl on top of a saucepan filled with 2 inches of simmering water, making sure that the bottom of the bowl does not come in contact with the water. It's important that the water be just simmering; if it's too hot it will scorch the chocolate. Stir chocolate with a rubber spatula until all of the pieces have melted and reached a smooth consistency. Remove the bowl from the heat and set it on the stovetop to keep it slightly warm.

- Separate eggs, placing yolks in a small bowl and whites in a medium bowl. Set bowls aside.

- Combine butter and sugar in the bowl of a stand mixer and using the paddle attachment, mix on low speed for 1 to 2 minutes. Increase speed to medium and mix for about 5 minutes more to cream the butter. The mixture will become smooth and pale in color. Start adding the egg yolks, 2 at a time, taking care to mix each addition fully before adding more yolks. Scrape down the sides of the bowl with a rubber spatula as needed. After all of the yolks are incorporated, add the sifted cocoa powder and continue mixing until combined.

- Remove the bowl from the stand mixer and fold in the melted chocolate with a rubber spatula. The batter will thicken. Using a whisk or hand-held mixer, whip egg whites until medium-stiff peaks form. Gently fold the whipped egg whites into the batter, one third at a time. Continue folding the batter until there are no visible white streaks; it's important that the whites be fully incorporated into the batter. The final mixture should have a sponge-like texture. Pour the batter into the prepared springform pan and scatter half of the raspberries over the top. Poke the berries down with your fingers until they are just below the surface.

- Place pan on center rack of oven and bake for 45 to 50 minutes, or until the center is set. Let cool on a wire rack for 30 minutes. Release the sides of the pan and lift, leaving the cake on the pan bottom. Dust the top of the cake with powdered sugar and garnish with the remaining raspberries. Serve with Lightly Sweetened Whipped Cream. It's best to enjoy this cake the day it's baked, but it can be stored at room temperature for up to one day. It will become very dense and fudge-like if kept in the refrigerator.

LIGHTLY SWEETENED WHIPPED CREAM

This is my favorite recipe for whipped cream. It's perfect with just about any tart or layered in a cake with fresh fruit. Use the freshest cream you can find.

2 cups heavy cream
2 tablespoons granulated sugar
1 teaspoon pure vanilla extract
¼ cup powdered sugar

- Combine ingredients in a medium bowl and mix with a whisk or hand-held mixer until the cream reaches the desired consistency. I usually stop whisking as soon as the cream starts to form soft peaks.

LEMON BUTTER CAKE WITH FRESH STRAWBERRIES & LEMON CREAM

Enhanced with fresh lemon juice and zest, this light butter cake was inspired by a recipe in Rose Levy's outstanding book The Cake Bible. *It's one of our bakery's most popular birthday cakes, and it is often requested for wedding celebrations.*

Makes 1 (9-inch) layer cake

FOR THE CAKE LAYERS:
2¾ cups cake flour
2¼ cups granulated sugar
1 tablespoon plus 1 teaspoon baking powder
¾ teaspoon salt
5 teaspoons freshly grated lemon zest
8 egg yolks

1 tablespoon pure vanilla extract
1 cup plus 3 tablespoons whole milk
8 ounces (2 sticks) unsalted butter, at room temperature

FOR THE STRAWBERRIES:
2 cups (1 pint) fresh strawberries, washed and stemmed
1 teaspoon fresh lemon zest
3 tablespoons granulated sugar
Lemon Syrup (*recipe follows*)
Lemon Cream (*recipe follows*)

PREPARING THE CAKE LAYERS:

- Preheat oven to 325°F. Prepare a (9 x 3-inch) springform pan by brushing it with oil and lining the bottom and sides with pieces of parchment paper (see page xvi). For this recipe, the parchment paper should extend 1½ inches above the sides of the pan. Set aside.

- Sift flour, sugar, baking powder, and salt into a medium bowl. Add lemon zest and toss with your hands to evenly distribute the ingredients. Set aside. In a separate medium bowl, combine egg yolks, vanilla extract, and ¼ cup of the milk. Mix with a whisk and set aside.

- Place butter in the bowl of a stand mixer. Using the paddle attachment, mix on low speed for 1 to 2 minutes. Increase speed to medium and mix for 5 minutes more, or until butter is smooth and pale in color. Add the flour mixture and pulse a few times to start bring the ingredients together, then mix on low until the flour mix- ture is fully incorporated into the butter. Keep the mixer on low speed and pour in the remaining milk in a slow stream. Increase speed to medium and mix for about 30 seconds more, then lower the bowl and scrape down the sides with a rubber spatula. Add one third of the egg mixture and mix on medium speed for 20 to 30 seconds, then lower the bowl and scrape down the batter with a rubber spatula. Repeat this process 2 more times, or until all of the egg mixture is incorporated.

- Pour the batter into the prepared springform pan and place it on center rack of oven. Bake for approximately 1 hour and 25 minutes, or until top is golden brown. Test center with a skewer to make sure it's done. Remove the cake from the oven and let it cool completely in the pan on a wire rack, at least 1 hour.

PREPARING THE STRAWBERRIES:

- Set aside a few strawberries to use for garnish. Thinly slice the remaining berries about ⅛ inch thick and place in a medium bowl with lemon zest and sugar. Toss well and set aside.

ASSEMBLING THE CAKE:

- After the cake has cooled, release the sides of the pan and lift. Peel the parchment paper from the sides of the cake, then carefully turn the cake over. Lift the pan's base off of the cake and remove the remaining parchment paper. Turn the cake back over, setting it bottom side down on a counter or cutting board. Using a sharp bread knife, trim off a thin layer of the darkened sides and top of the cake. Next, cut the cake horizontally into 3 equal layers.

- Place the top layer of cake upside down on a plate or cardboard cake circle and brush with one third of the Lemon Syrup. Cover the cake with half of the sliced strawberries and spread a generous dollop of Lemon Cream over the berries with a rubber spatula. Place another layer of cake on top of the cream and repeat the same procedure. Add the final cake layer, and frost the top and sides with the remaining cream. Top the cake with a few whole strawberries or flowers from your garden and store it in the refrigerator. This cake is best served at room temperature, so remove it from the refrigerator 30 minutes before serving. Leftovers can be stored in the refrigerator for 1 to 2 days.

LEMON SYRUP

This recipe makes a simple syrup that can be used to moisten many different cakes.

Makes enough syrup for 1 (9-inch) layer cake

½ cup water
⅓ cup granulated sugar
½ cup freshly squeezed lemon juice

- Combine water and sugar in a medium saucepan and bring to a boil over medium-high heat. Stirring frequently, cook until sugar is dissolved and the liquid is syrupy, 10 to 12 minutes. Remove from heat and add lemon juice. Set aside to cool.

LEMON CREAM

This recipe makes a great, slightly sweet alternative to heavy frostings.
Try serving it also alongside ripe summer berries.

Makes enough cream for 1 (9-inch) layer cake

6 egg yolks
1 cup granulated sugar
⅔ cup fresh lemon juice
6 tablespoons unsalted butter, at room temperature and cut into dime-sized pieces
3 cups heavy cream

- Combine egg yolks, sugar, and lemon juice in medium stainless steel bowl and mix well with a whisk. Place bowl on top of a saucepan filled with 2 inches of simmering water, making sure that the bottom of the bowl does not come in contact with the water. It's important that the water be just simmering; if it's too hot it will scorch the ingredients and scramble the eggs. Whisking constantly, cook the mixture for about 10 minutes, or until it has thickened considerably. (It should be thick enough to stick to the back of a spoon.) Add butter and continue whisking until melted and fully incorporated.

- Remove bowl from stovetop and strain the mixture through a medium-fine sieve into a clean medium bowl. At this point the mixture is a curd. Stir with a whisk for about 2 minutes to speed up the cooling process. Cover the bowl with plastic wrap, placing the plastic directly on the surface of the curd to keep a skin from forming, and transfer to the refrigerator for 20 to 30 minutes to finish cooling.

- Pour heavy cream into a medium bowl. Using a whisk or hand-held mixer, whip cream until medium-stiff peaks form. Remove the cooled curd from the refrigerator and fold in the whipped cream with a rubber spatula, mixing until cream is evenly distributed. Frost your cake or cover bowl with plastic wrap and store in the refrigerator for up to 10 hours. Once the Lemon Cream has been stored in the refrigerator it will need to be re-whipped with a whisk until medium-stiff peaks form.

SEMOLINA POUND CAKE WITH FRESH PRESERVES

This rustic dessert is similar to classic European country cakes.
Layered with quality preserves, it has a rich, buttery flavor and requires no frosting at all.
Try it with a cup of your favorite tea.

Makes 1 (9-inch) layer cake

10 eggs
2½ cups unbleached all-purpose flour
1 cup semolina flour
1 tablespoon plus 1 teaspoon baking powder
1 tablespoon freshly grated lemon zest
10 ounces (2½ sticks) unsalted butter, at room temperature
2½ cups granulated sugar
2 teaspoons brandy
½ teaspoon salt
1 recipe Lemon Syrup *(page 108)*
½ cup high-quality blackberry preserves
½ cup high-quality strawberry preserves
1 cup cookie crumbs, preferably crumbled biscotti or butter cookies
Powdered sugar

- Preheat oven to 325°F. Prepare a 9 x 3-inch springform pan by brushing it with oil and lining the bottom and sides with pieces of parchment paper (see page xvi). Set aside.

- Separate the eggs, placing yolks in a small bowl and whites in a medium bowl. Set aside.

- Combine the flours and baking powder in a medium bowl. Add lemon zest and mix well with a wooden spoon. Set aside.

- Combine butter and sugar in the bowl of a stand mixer and using the paddle attachment, mix on low speed for 1 to 2 minutes. Increase speed to medium and mix for about 5 minutes more to cream the butter. The mixture will become smooth and pale in color. Add brandy, and then egg yolks, 2 at a time, mixing each addition fully before adding more yolks. Scrape down the sides of the bowl with a rubber spatula as needed.

- Add one third of the dry ingredients to the bowl of the stand mixer and mix on low speed just until incorporated. Repeat 2 times with the remaining dry ingredients, taking care not to overmix the batter. Remove bowl from the mixer and scrape down the sides. Add salt to the bowl of egg whites and whip with a whisk or hand-held mixer until medium-stiff peaks form. Gently fold the whipped egg whites into the batter with a rubber spatula, mixing until the whites are completely incorporated and there are no visible streaks.

- Pour the batter into the prepared springform pan and place it on the center rack of oven. Bake for about 1½ hours, or until top is golden brown. Test center with a skewer to make sure it's done. Remove the cake from the oven and let it cool in the pan on a wire rack for at least 30 minutes.

- After the cake has cooled, release the sides of the pan and lift. Peel the parchment paper from the sides of the cake, then carefully turn the cake over. Lift the pan's base off the cake and remove the remaining parchment paper. Turn the cake back over, setting it bottom side down on a counter or cutting board. Cut the cake horizontally into 3 equal layers.

- Place the bottom layer of cake on a serving plate or cardboard cake circle and brush it with a little Lemon Syrup. Spread blackberry preserves over the surface and top with another layer of cake. Brush with more syrup and spread raspberry preserves on top. Add the top layer of cake. Brush the outer edges of the cake with syrup and press cookie crumbs all around the sides. Dust powdered sugar over the top of the pound cake.

Mom's Chocolate Cake

*This dessert is named in honor of those homemade chocolate cakes that moms are famous for.
I like to apply the frosting in big swirls.*

Makes 1 (9-inch) layer cake

FOR THE CAKE LAYERS:

2 eggs
¾ cup whole milk
⅓ cup canola oil
2 teaspoons pure vanilla extract
1¾ cups granulated sugar
1½ cups unbleached all-purpose flour
¼ cup dark cocoa powder, sifted
1 teaspoon baking powder
1 teaspoon baking soda
¾ teaspoon salt
¾ cup boiling water

FOR THE VANILLA SYRUP:
¼ cup pure vanilla extract
¼ cup granulated sugar
¼ cup water

FOR THE CHOCOLATE FROSTING:
12 ounces unsweetened chocolate, coarsely chopped
1 pound (4 sticks) unsalted butter, at room temperature
3½ cups powdered sugar, sifted
2 tablespoons pure vanilla extract

PREPARING THE CAKE LAYERS:

- Preheat oven to 325°F. Prepare a 9 x 3-inch cake pan by brushing the inside with oil, then lining the bottom with a 9-inch circle of parchment paper. Set aside.

- Combine eggs, milk, canola oil, and vanilla extract in a medium bowl and mix well with a whisk. Set aside.

- Sift sugar, flour, cocoa powder, baking powder, baking soda, and salt into the bowl of a stand mixer. Toss with your hands to combine. Attach the bowl to the stand mixer. Add the wet ingredients to the bowl of dry ingredients and using the whisk attachment, mix on medium speed until combined, about 2 minutes. Keep mixing as you add the boiling water in a slow stream, mixing just until the water is incorporated, about 30 seconds.

- Pour the batter into the prepared cake pan. Place pan on center rack of oven and bake for 55 to 60 minutes, or until cake is set in the center. Test center with a skewer to make sure the cake is done. Remove from the oven and let cool in the pan on a wire rack for at least 30 minutes.

PREPARING THE VANILLA SYRUP:

- Combine ingredients in a small saucepan and bring to a boil over medium-high heat. Stirring frequently, cook until sugar is dissolved and the liquid is syrupy, 2 to 3 minutes. Remove from heat and let cool.

PREPARING THE CHOCOLATE FROSTING:

- Place chocolate in a medium stainless steel bowl. Place bowl on top of a saucepan filled with 2 inches of simmering water, making sure that the bottom of the bowl does not come in contact with the water. It's important that the water be just simmering; if it's too hot it will scorch the chocolate. Stir chocolate with a rubber spatula until all of the pieces have melted and reached a smooth consistency. Remove the bowl from the heat and let cool to room temperature.

- Combine butter and powdered sugar in the bowl of your stand mixer and using the paddle attachment, mix for 5 to 8 minutes to cream the butter. Start on low speed and gradually increase to medium. Starting out on a higher speed will likely result in a snow storm of powdered sugar—a real mess. When the butter mixture is light and fluffy, add the melted chocolate and mix until incorporated. Add the vanilla extract and continue mixing until the frosting is thick enough to spread, a few more minutes. If the frosting gets too soft, simply chill it in the refrigerator to firm it up. If it stays in the refrigerator for too long, let it sit out for a few minutes and then re-whip it.

ASSEMBLING THE CAKE:

- Invert the cooled cake to remove it from the pan. If it sticks, run a sharp knife around the sides of the cake to release it from the pan. Peel the parchment paper off the bottom of the cake. Using a sharp bread knife, carefully cut the cake horizontally into 3 equal layers. Place the bottom layer on a serving plate or cardboard cake circle and brush it with a little vanilla syrup. Spread a generous amount of chocolate frosting (about ¼ inch) over the cake. Top it with another layer of cake and repeat the process. Add the final cake layer. Place a dollop of frosting on top of the cake and spread it ⅛ inch thick, spreading any excess frosting down onto the sides. Spread a little more frosting on the sides until the entire cake has what bakers call a crumb coat: a thin underlayer of frosting that keeps crumbs out of the final layer of frosting. Crumbs will be clearly visible through the frosting. Chill the cake in the refrigerator for 20 to 30 minutes. The remaining frosting can stay at room temperature while the cake chills.

- Remove the cake from the refrigerator and add the final layer of frosting. I like to create a swirl pattern in the frosting, just like the cakes I remember from childhood. Store in the refrigerator for up to 2 days. This cake is best served at room temperature, so remove it from the refrigerator 1 hour before serving.

Coconut Cake with Raspberries & Lemon Cream

This cake looks so inviting that it never lasts long in our pastry case. Covered with toasted coconut, it has a fuzzy-bunny look to it that always grabs attention. It tastes great, too!

Makes 1 (9-inch) layer cake

3 cups shredded, unsweetened coconut
1 cup coconut milk
5 egg whites
1 teaspoon pure almond extract
1 teaspoon pure vanilla extract
2¼ cups cake flour
1¾ cups granulated sugar
1 tablespoon plus 1 teaspoon baking powder
1 teaspoon salt
12 tablespoons (1½ sticks) unsalted butter, at room temperature
1 recipe Lemon Syrup *(page 108)*
½ recipe Lemon Cream *(page 109)*
2 cups (1 pint) fresh raspberries
White Chocolate Frosting *(recipe follows)*

- Preheat oven to 325°F. Prepare a 9 x 3-inch springform pan by brushing it with oil and lining the bottom and sides with pieces of parchment paper (see page xvi). Set aside.

- Place coconut on a rimmed baking sheet and spread it into an even layer. Toast on center rack of oven for 3 minutes. To make sure coconut toasts evenly, remove the baking sheet from the oven and toss coconut with tongs or spoons. Spread it out evenly again and toast for another 3 minutes, or until coconut is lightly toasted. Pour toasted coconut into a medium bowl and set aside.

- In a medium bowl, combine coconut milk, egg whites, almond extract, and vanilla extract. Mix with a whisk and set aside.

- Sift flour, sugar, baking powder, and salt into the bowl of a stand mixer. Add 1 cup of the toasted coconut and using the paddle attachment, mix on low speed for about 30 seconds. Cut butter into 8 pieces and scatter the pieces over the surface of the flour mixture. Mix on low speed until the mixture is coarse and crumbly and there are no visible pieces of butter, 1 to 2 minutes. Add half of the wet ingredients and mix on medium speed for 30 seconds. Scrape down the sides of the bowl with a rubber spatula and add the remaining wet ingredients. Mix until combined, another 30 seconds or so, and scrape down the sides of the bowl again.

- Pour the batter into the prepared springform pan. Bake on center rack of oven for about 1 hour, or until top is golden brown. Test the center with a skewer to make sure it's done. Remove the cake from the oven and let it cool on a wire rack for at least 1 hour.

- After the cake has cooled, release the sides of the pan and lift. Peel the parchment paper from the sides of the cake, then carefully turn the cake over. Lift the pan's base off the cake and remove the remaining parchment paper. Turn the cake back over, setting it bottom side down on a counter or cutting board. Next, cut the cake horizontally into 3 equal layers.

- Place the top layer of cake upside down on a plate or cardboard circle and brush it with a little Lemon Syrup. Spread a ¼-inch layer of Lemon Cream over the cake and sprinkle half of the raspberries over the top. Place another layer of cake on top of the raspberries and repeat the same procedure. Add the final layer of cake. Place a dollop of White Chocolate Frosting on top of the cake and spread it ⅛ inch thick, spreading any excess frosting down onto the sides. Spread a little more frosting on the sides until the entire cake has a crumb coat: a thin underlayer of frosting that keeps crumbs out of the final layer of frosting. Crumbs will be clearly visible through the frosting. Chill the cake in the refrigerator for 20 to 30 minutes. The remaining frosting can stay at room temperature while the cake chills.

- Remove the cake from the refrigerator and add a final layer of frosting. Next, carefully press the remaining toasted coconut onto the frosting, covering the sides and top of the cake evenly. (Placing the cake on a piece of parchment paper or on baking sheet before coating it with coconut will make the job less messy.) Store in the refrigerator for up to 2 days. This cake is best served at room temperature, so remove it from the refrigerator one hour before serving.

WHITE CHOCOLATE FROSTING

This simple, not-too-sweet frosting is easy to prepare and can be used on a wide range of desserts. Try topping chocolate cupcakes with heaping spoonfuls.

Makes enough frosting for 1 (9-inch) layer cake, with some to spare

12 ounces white chocolate, coarsely chopped
8 ounces (2 sticks) unsalted butter, at room temperature
1 pound cream cheese, at room temperature
2 tablespoons freshly squeezed lemon juice, at room temperature

- Place chocolate in a medium, stainless steel bowl. Place bowl on top of a saucepan filled with 2 inches of simmering water, making sure that the bottom of the bowl does not come in contact with the water. It's important that the water be just simmering; if it's too hot it will scorch the chocolate. Stir chocolate with a rubber spatula until all of the pieces have melted and reached a smooth consistency. Remove the bowl from the heat and let cool to room temperature.

- Make sure that all of the ingredients, including the melted chocolate, are at room temperature.

- Place butter in the bowl of a stand mixer and using the paddle attachment, beat butter until it is smooth, 3 to 5 minutes. Add cream cheese and beat for another 3 to 5 minutes, until mixture is light and fluffy and there are no visible lumps. Add lemon juice and continue mixing until incorporated. Finally, add the melted chocolate and continue mixing until the frosting has a smooth and light texture, about 2 minutes. If the frosting gets too soft to work with, simply chill it in the refrigerator until it firms up a little bit.

- This frosting can be made in advance and stored for up to 1 week in the refrigerator. If the frosting has been kept in the refrigerator for more than a couple of hours it will need to be refreshed before using: Bring the frosting to room temperature and place it in the bowl of stand mixer, then whip it with the paddle attachment for about 3 minutes.

CHOCOLATE CHERRY POUND CAKE

Suzanne De Galan, the editor of this book, personally requested that this recipe be included. It's as decadent a dessert as you'll find, so I recommend serving small portions.

Makes 1 bundt cake

2 cups dried tart cherries
2 cups dark cocoa powder
2 cups unbleached all-purpose flour
½ teaspoon baking powder
1 teaspoon salt
12 ounces (3 sticks) unsalted butter, at room temperature
3¼ cups granulated sugar
5 eggs
1¼ cups buttermilk
1 cup semi-sweet chocolate chips
Chocolate Glaze *(recipe follows)*

- Cover dried cherries with warm water and set aside to plump.

- Preheat oven to 325°F. Prepare a 12-cup bundt pan by thoroughly brushing the insides with canola oil.

- Sift cocoa powder, flour, baking powder, and salt into a medium bowl. Toss with your hands to evenly distribute the ingredients and set aside.

- Combine butter and sugar in the bowl of a stand mixer and using the paddle attachment, mix on low for 1 to 2 minutes. Increase speed to medium and mix for about 5 minutes more to cream the butter. The mixture will become smooth and pale in color. Add eggs, one at a time, mixing each one fully before adding another. Scrape down sides of the bowl with a rubber spatula as needed. Next, add alternating portions of the dry ingredients and buttermilk, one quarter at a time. Remove bowl from the mixer and scrape down the sides.

- Drain the plumped cherries and set aside 8 for garnish. Add the remainder to the batter. Pour in the chocolate chips and fold the ingredients in with a rubber spatula. Spread the batter evenly into the prepared bundt pan. Bake cake on center rack of oven for 1¾ to 2 hours, then test the center with a skewer to make sure it's done. Let cool on a wire rack for about 1 hour. This is a good time to prepare the Chocolate Glaze.

- Run a sharp knife around the sides of the pan to release the cake. Place a serving plate, upside down, on top of the cooled bundt pan, and invert the pan to remove the cake. Let the cake cool completely. Drizzle Chocolate Glaze all over the top, allowing the glaze to run down the sides. Top with the remaining plumped cherries and serve. This cake will last for 2 days in an airtight container or wrapped with plastic wrap. I recommend storing it at room temperature, as it will become very dense and fudge-like if kept in the refrigerator.

CHOCOLATE GLAZE

In addition to making the Chocolate Cherry Pound Cake even more delectable, this simple glaze is also great for topping cupcakes or drizzling over tarts.

Makes enough glaze to top 1 bundt cake

1 cup heavy cream
2 cups semi-sweet chocolate chips

● Pour cream into a medium saucepan and place over medium heat. As soon as cream begins to boil, turn off the heat and add chocolate chips. Mix constantly with a whisk until chocolate has melted. Let cool slightly. It's best to use this glaze while it's still warm, as it will harden quickly.

MASCARPONE CHEESECAKE

This recipe was a gift from Lisa Snider, the mother of our pastry chef, Karra Wise. She made it as a special in our cafe one day, and it was so popular that we've been making it ever since. If you prefer, Chocolate Glaze (above) can be substituted for the White Chocolate Frosting.

Makes 1 (9-inch) cheesecake

2¼ cups cookie crumbs, preferably vanilla wafers or graham crackers
9 tablespoons unsalted butter, melted and cooled to room temperature
¼ cup heavy cream
1 tablespoon pure vanilla extract
2 tablespoons freshly grated lemon zest
1¼ cups granulated sugar
1½ pounds cream cheese, at room temperature
8 ounces mascarpone cheese, at room temperature
5 eggs
1 egg yolk
½ cup White Chocolate Frosting *(page 117)*
1 cup mixed ripe berries
Powdered sugar

- Preheat oven to 325°F. Butter a 9 x 3-inch springform pan and line the bottom and sides with pieces of parchment paper (see page xvi). For this recipe, the parchment paper should extend about ½ inch above the top of the pan's sides. Set aside.

- In a medium bowl, combine cookie crumbs and melted butter. Toss until crumbs are evenly coated. Using your hands, press crumbs into the prepared springform pan, first covering the bottom, then covering the lower 1½ inches of the sides. Set aside.

- In a small bowl, combine cream, vanilla extract, and lemon zest. Mix lightly with a fork and set aside.

- Combine sugar, cream cheese, and mascarpone in the bowl of a stand mixer. Using the paddle attachment, mix on medium speed for 5 to 8 minutes, until mixture is creamy and there are no visible lumps. Scrape down the sides of the bowl with a rubber spatula. Add eggs and egg yolk, one at a time, making sure each egg is fully incorporated before adding another. Scrape down the sides of the bowl before adding each egg. Add the cream mixture and continue mixing until evenly distributed, 1 to 2 minutes.

- Pour the filling into the crumb-lined springform pan. Place the pan on a rimmed baking sheet. (This will make the pan easier to handle and will also capture any

leakage that occurs during baking.) Place baking sheet on center rack of oven and bake for about 1 hour and 20 minutes. The center will still appear soft and jelly-like, but will set as it cools. Remove from oven and let cool completely on a wire rack, about 1 hour.

- Release the sides of the pan and peel away the parchment paper. Place a cake circle or flat plate, upside down, on top of the cheesecake. Carefully invert the cake and remove the pan bottom and remaining parchment paper. Invert the cake back onto a serving plate. Using an offset spatula, cover the top of the cooled cake with White Chocolate Frosting. Top with fresh berries and store in the refrigerator up to 3 days. This cake is best served at room temperature, so remove it from the refrigerator 30 minutes before eating. I like to dust each serving with a little powdered sugar.

Almond Cake with Mascarpone Cream & Fresh Blackberries

Macrina's Operations Manager, Kimberly Johnson, says that this is her favorite cake. She recommends it to everyone who'll listen. The dense, moist cake is just perfect for layering with berries and cream.

Makes 1 (9-inch) layer cake

FOR THE CAKE LAYERS:
3 eggs
¾ cup plain low-fat yogurt
2 teaspoons pure almond extract
½ teaspoon pure vanilla extract
1½ cups cake flour
1¾ cups granulated sugar
¾ teaspoon baking soda
¾ teaspoon baking powder
½ teaspoon salt
1½ cups finely ground almonds
8 ounces (2 sticks) unsalted butter, at room temperature

FOR THE ALMOND SYRUP:
1 cup granulated sugar
½ cup filtered water
2 teaspoons pure almond extract

FOR THE MASCARPONE CREAM:
1 cup heavy cream
¼ cup powdered sugar, sifted
8 ounces mascarpone cheese, at room temperature

FOR FINISHING THE CAKE:
4 cups (2 pints) fresh blackberries
1 teaspoon freshly grated lemon zest
Powdered sugar

PREPARING THE CAKE LAYERS:

- Preheat oven to 325°F. Prepare a 9 x 3-inch springform pan by brushing it with oil and lining the bottom and sides with pieces of parchment paper (see page xvi). Set aside.

- Combine eggs, ¼ cup of the yogurt, almond extract, and vanilla extract in a medium bowl. Mix well with a whisk and set aside. Sift flour, sugar, baking soda, baking powder, and salt into a separate medium bowl. Add almonds and mix with a spoon. Set aside.

- Place butter in the bowl of your stand mixer and using the paddle attachment, cream the butter on medium speed for 5 to 8 minutes. The butter will be light and fluffy. Add the dry ingredients and the remaining ½ cup of yogurt. Turn the switch on and off a few times to start bringing the ingredients together, then increase speed to medium and mix for 1 to 2 minutes. Add one third of the egg mixture and mix for about 30 seconds, then lower the bowl and scrape down the sides with a rubber spatula. Repeat this process 2 more times, until all of the wet ingredients are incorporated.

- Pour the batter into the prepared cake pan and bake on center rack of oven for about 1 hour and 10 minutes, or until top is golden brown. Test center with a skewer to make sure it's done. Remove the cake from the oven and let it cool on a wire rack for at least 1 hour.

PREPARING THE ALMOND SYRUP:

● Combine sugar and water in a medium saucepan and mix with a whisk to dissolve the sugar. Cook over medium heat for 2 to 3 minutes, stirring frequently, then remove from the heat and add almond extract. Let cool slightly before using.

PREPARING THE MASCARPONE CREAM:

● Combine cream and sugar in a medium bowl and whip with a whisk or hand-held mixer until medium-soft peaks form. Set aside. Place mascarpone in a medium bowl and whip with a whisk for 1 to 2 minutes, until it thickens a little. Using a rubber spatula, gently fold the whipped cream into the whipped mascarpone until evenly distributed.

ASSEMBLING THE CAKE:

● Combine 3 cups (1½ pints) of blackberries, lemon zest, and ¼ cup of almond syrup in a medium bowl. Mix gently with a spoon and set aside to marinate for a few minutes.

● After the cake has cooled, release the sides of the pan and lift. Peel the parchment paper from the sides of the cake, then carefully turn the cake over. Lift the pan's base off the cake and remove the remaining parchment paper. Turn the cake back over, setting it bottom side down, on a counter or cutting board. Next, cut the cake horizontally into 3 equal layers. The layers will be fragile, so handle them with care. I recommend using the removable bottom from a tart pan to move the layers around.

● Place the bottom layer of cake on a plate or cardboard cake circle and brush it with a little almond syrup. Spread slightly more than one third of the mascarpone cream over the cake and top it with half of the marinated blackberries. Place another layer of cake on top of the berries and repeat the same process. Add the final cake layer and place a dollop of mascarpone cream in the center. Spread it into a 5-inch circle, leaving the outer edge of the cake unfrosted. Pile the remaining blackberries onto the cream and dust powdered sugar over the whole cake. Store in the refrigerator for up to 3 days. This cake is best served at room temperature, so remove it from the refrigerator 30 minutes before serving.

Chapter 10

PIES & TARTS

Flaky Pie Dough

Sweet Almond Dough

Pasta Frolla

Sesame Almond Dough

Mom's Fresh Strawberry Tartlets

Classic Blueberry Pie

Fresh Fruit Crostata

Lemon Chess Tart

Apple & Bing Cherry Galette

Chocolate & Brandied Cherry Tart

Pear & Honey Custard Tart

Apricot Frangipane Tart

Champagne Grape Tart

Huckleberry & Crème Fraîche Tart

Plum & Almond Crumb Tart

Classic Ricotta Pie

Florentine Tart with Nectarines & Pine Nuts

One of my favorite things about living in the Pacific Northwest is the abundance of local fruit, from apples and pears to cherries, raspberries, huckleberries, and more. And I can't think of a better way to eat this bounty than in a simple tart or pie. Tarts and pies are one of the easiest desserts to prepare and are the perfect vehicle for showcasing the natural sweetness of ripe fruit. A slice of Classic Blueberry Pie, topped with vanilla ice cream, for instance, is the ideal way to highlight these summer berries, and it's as satisfying as anything I can imagine.

One of the first steps in preparing any tart or pie is deciding which kind of crust you want to use. This chapter begins with four very different crust recipes, all of which are used daily at our bakery. Once you've mastered the Flaky Pie Dough you'll never want to use another store-bought crust again. The dough is used in a wide range of recipes, from Lemon Chess Tart to Chocolate & Brandied Cherry Tart. Also included is a recipe for our variation of the classic Italian Pasta Frolla, as well as one of my personal favorites, the cookie-like Sweet Almond Dough. All these doughs are easy to prepare and can be stored in your freezer, making last-minute baking more approachable.

In this chapter you'll find more than a dozen recipes from Macrina Bakery as well as helpful hints and professional secrets for preparing out-of-this-world pies and tarts at home. For example, it's best to chill or even freeze a tart shell before baking it. This helps keep the dough from shrinking in the pan, and assures a flakier crust. This chapter also has step-by-step instructions for pre-baking pastry shells, often the most important part of successful tart and pie baking. Work your way through these recipes, and before long you'll be a tart fanatic like me.

FLAKY PIE DOUGH

*Hands down, this is the most frequently prepared recipe in our pastry shop.
We've been using it nonstop since the day we opened our doors. The dough is perfect for
all kinds of baking, from savory quiche to deep-dish pies and classic tarts.*

Makes enough dough for 2 double-crusted (9-inch) pies,
or 2 (10-inch) rustic galettes or tarts

5¼ cups unbleached all-purpose flour
1 tablespoon kosher salt
12 tablespoons (1½ sticks) unsalted butter, chilled and cut into ¼-inch pieces
1¾ cups solid vegetable shortening, chilled
1 cup ice water

- Combine flour and salt in a large bowl and toss together. Add butter and cut it into the flour until the texture is coarse and crumbly. You can use a pastry cutter or your fingers, but I like to use 2 forks. Break up the shortening and add it in small

pieces. Cut in the shortening until the dough is crumbly again. Add ice water and mix just until the water is incorporated and the dough sticks together when pinched. This dough is quite sticky, so dust your hands with flour before handling it. Pull dough from bowl onto a lightly floured work surface (chilled marble is ideal) and pat it into a block. Wrap the dough tightly in plastic wrap and chill in the refrigerator for at least 1 hour before using. Since this recipe makes enough dough for 2 pies or tarts, I recommend cutting it in half before chilling.

- Flaky Pie Dough will last for up to 4 days in the refrigerator and for up to 1 month in the freezer. If you freeze half or all of the dough, it's a good idea to double wrap it. Frozen dough needs to be fully defrosted before it's used, and my preferred method is to transfer the dough to the refrigerator 1 day before I plan on baking with it. The dough can also be defrosted at room temperature, but it needs to be re-chilled in the refrigerator for 1 hour prior to using.

Tips for Perfect Pie Dough & Crusts

The following are a few tips that will help you make the best pie dough and crusts possible.

- If you want to make a perfect batch of pie dough, mix it by hand.

- Make sure the butter, shortening, and water are all well chilled before you get started. If you are working in a very warm room (over 80°F), I recommend chilling the mixing bowl as well. Working with cold ingredients helps create a flakier crust.

- Cut the butter and shortening into small pieces, about ¼-inch cubes, before adding them to the flour. This will help you cut them into the flour quicker, keeping the fats from getting warm. Make sure that the butter and shortening are fully incorporated into the dough—any large chunks will dissolve when the dough is baked, resulting in a cracked crust.

- Add all of the ice water at once, and mix just until it's incorporated into the dough. At that point, I pat the dough into a block, wrap it in plastic wrap, and chill it in the refrigerator or freeze it for later use.

- Make sure the dough is fully chilled before working with it.

- Form the dough into a ball before rolling it out. This makes it easier to maintain a circular shape as you are rolling.

- Make sure your rolling surface is clean and coated with a light dusting of flour. A chilled piece of marble is the ultimate surface for keeping the dough cold.

- Once you have placed the rolled-out dough into a tart pan, chill the shell in the refrigerator or freezer for at least 30 minutes before baking it.

- Make sure your oven is preheated before baking. If the temperature is too low, the dough will shrink in the pan.

PRE-BAKED TART SHELL

When I had the honor of making tarts with Julia Child for her Baking With Julia *series, we joked together about not wanting soggy bottoms—on our tarts, that is. Nothing ruins a tart like a wet, chewy crust, and the best way to prevent this from happening is to pre-bake (or blind bake) the shells. This is a step that professional bakers never skip.*

Half of a Flaky Pie Dough recipe will provide enough dough to line 1 (8- to 10-inch) tart pan, with some to spare.

Note: I always use tart pans with removable bottoms.

- Coat your hands with flour and shape the chilled piece of dough into a ball. Working on a floured surface, flatten the ball slightly and roll it into a 14-inch circle, about ⅛ inch thick. Turn the dough occasionally and toss a little flour underneath to keep it from sticking to the work surface. Fold the dough in quarters to make it easier to handle and lift it into your tart pan. Unfold the dough and press it into the pan, then trim away all but ¾ inch of the overhanging edge. Fold the overhanging edge into the tart pan and press the dough together, creating a double-thick crust around the edge of the tart shell. Chill in the refrigerator or freezer for at least 30 minutes. (Chilling the dough relaxes the gluten and keeps the butter cold. This helps prevent the tart shell from shrinking in the pan while it bakes.) Once the crust is chilled it can be pre-baked or wrapped tightly with plastic and kept frozen for up to 1 month.

- Preheat oven to 375°F.

- Line the chilled tart shell with an oversized piece of parchment paper and fill it with dried beans or baking weights (see photo, page 127). At the bakery we use dried pinto beans, which can be used over and over again. Press the beans down to make sure there are no air pockets between the crust and the parchment paper. Bake on center rack of oven for 25 to 30 minutes, until edges are golden brown. (Baking time will vary slightly depending on the size of the tart shell.) Remove the shell from the oven and let it sit for 15 to 20 minutes before removing the paper and beans. Check to see if the bottom of the shell is done. If the bottom still looks wet, return it to the oven for 2 to 3 minutes. If bubbles appear on the bottom of the crust, carefully depress them with a dishtowel, taking care to avoid the escaping steam. The entire tart shell should have a light, golden brown color. Let cool before filling.

- It's important to inspect pre-baked tart shells for cracks before using them. Cracks will allow fillings to seep out during the baking process, creating a sticky mess and a broken crust. A tart shell that is full of cracks really can't be fixed, but a few small cracks can easily be repaired. Using your thumb or forefinger, simply spread a thin layer of raw pie dough over the cracks just before filling the shells. (Use just enough raw dough to fill the cracks.)

SWEET ALMOND DOUGH

This cookie-like dough is easy to make and even easier to work with. Rather than rolling out the dough, you simply press it into the tart pans by hand.

Makes enough dough for 1 (10-inch) tart

¼ cup whole almonds
½ cup granulated sugar
1½ cups unbleached all-purpose flour
½ teaspoon pure vanilla extract
½ teaspoon pure almond extract
8 tablespoons (1 stick) unsalted butter, melted and slightly cooled

● Preheat oven to 350°F.

● Spread almonds on rimmed baking sheet and toast for about 10 minutes, or until golden brown. Let cool, then finely grind in a food processor. Measure out 2 tablespoons of ground almonds and set aside. (The remaining ground almonds will not be needed.)

● Combine 2 tablespoons of the ground almonds, sugar, and flour in a medium bowl and mix with a wooden spoon. In a separate bowl, mix together vanilla extract, almond extract, and melted butter. Add butter mixture to the bowl of dry ingredients and mix until coarse and crumbly, using your hands to break up any large lumps. The finished dough will stick together when squeezed between your thumb and forefinger.

● At this point, the dough is ready to be pressed into a tart ring. It doesn't need to be chilled. If you're not ready to bake with the dough, pack it into a ball and wrap it tightly in plastic wrap. The wrapped dough can be stored in the refrigerator for 1 or 2 days, or frozen for up to 1 month. It's a good idea to double wrap the dough before freezing it.

● Frozen Sweet Almond Dough needs to be fully defrosted before it's used. My preferred method is to transfer the dough to the refrigerator 1 day in advance. Generally this crumbly dough is pressed into tart pans by hand rather than rolled out, but once it has been frozen the dough will be quite firm. In this case, roll the dough out ⅛ inch thick and fit it into the desired tart pan. The dough will probably crack when you lift it, but don't worry. Simply pinch the cracks together with your fingers to repair.

PASTA FROLLA

Pasta Frolla, a slightly sweet Italian pastry dough, is perfect for a wide range of tarts and pies, such as our Classic Ricotta Pie and Apricot Frangipane Tart. This is the recipe we use at the bakery, a version enriched with eggs, vanilla, citrus zest, and a hint of anise.

Makes enough dough for 1 double-crusted (9-inch) pie or 1 (10-inch) tart

4⅔ cups unbleached all-purpose flour

⅔ cup granulated sugar

1 teaspoon salt

½ teaspoon ground anise seed

1 tablespoon freshly grated lemon zest

1 tablespoon freshly grated orange zest

10 ounces (2½ sticks) unsalted butter, chilled and cut into ¼-inch pieces

2 eggs

2 egg yolks

2 teaspoons pure vanilla extract

- Sift flour, sugar, and salt into a medium bowl. Add anise seed, lemon zest, and orange zest and toss together. Add butter and using 2 forks (you can also use a pastry cutter or your fingers), cut butter into the mixture until the texture is coarse and crumbly.

- Combine eggs, egg yolks, and vanilla extract in a small bowl and mix with a whisk. Add to dough and mix with a fork just until ingredients are combined and evenly moistened. Pull dough from bowl onto a lightly floured work surface and knead briefly, working it into a ball. The finished dough will remain quite dry and crumbly. Wrap the dough tightly in plastic wrap and chill in the refrigerator for at least 1 hour before using. The wrapped dough can be stored in the refrigerator for up to 4 days or frozen for up to 1 month. It's a good idea to double wrap the dough before freezing it.

- Frozen Pasta Frolla needs to be fully defrosted before it's used, and my preferred method is to transfer the dough to the refrigerator 1 day before I plan on baking with it. The dough can also be defrosted at room temperature, but it needs to be re-chilled in the refrigerator for 1 hour prior to using.

SESAME ALMOND DOUGH

This is the dough we use for the popular Fresh Fruit Crostata, as well as our
annual Harvest Pie. The not-too-sweet dough has a texture similar to shortbread
cookies, and it's a perfect companion for a wide range of seasonal fruits. It may break when
you are rolling it or lining a tart pan, but don't worry. This dough is easy to work with.
Simply pinch cracks together, or press small pieces of dough into holes in the crust.
I recommend preparing this dough in a stand mixer.

Makes enough dough for 1 (10-inch) lattice-topped tart

1 cup whole almonds
¾ cup sesame seeds
3 cups unbleached all-purpose flour
¾ cup granulated sugar
¼ teaspoon salt
1 teaspoon cinnamon
¼ teaspoon freshly grated lemon zest
10 ounces (2½ sticks) unsalted butter, chilled and cut into ½-inch pieces
3 eggs
1 teaspoon pure vanilla extract

- Preheat oven to 350°F.

- Spread almonds and sesame seeds on separate rimmed baking sheets and place on center rack of oven. Toast until golden brown, about 10 minutes (almonds may take a few minutes more than sesame seeds). Remove from oven and set aside to cool.

- Combine cooled almonds and sesame seeds and 1 cup of the flour in the bowl of a food processor and pulse to a fine texture. (The flour helps absorb oils from the nuts and seeds and keeps the mixture from becoming a paste.) Pour the mixture into the bowl of your stand mixer and add the remaining flour, sugar, salt, cinnamon, and lemon zest. Using the paddle attachment, briefly mix on low speed to distribute the ingredients. Add the butter and continue mixing on low speed until the mixture is coarse and crumbly, 3 to 5 minutes.

- Combine eggs and vanilla extract in a small bowl and mix with a whisk. Add to the dough and, still using the paddle attachment, turn the switch on and off a few times, just until ingredients are combined and evenly moistened. Pull dough from bowl onto a lightly floured work surface and knead briefly, working it into a ball. Wrap the dough tightly in plastic wrap and chill in the refrigerator for at least 2 hours before using. The wrapped dough can be stored in the refrigerator for up to 4 days or frozen for up to 1 month. It's a good idea to double wrap the dough before freezing it.

- Frozen Sesame Almond Dough needs to be fully defrosted before it's used, and my preferred method is to transfer the dough into the refrigerator 1 day before I plan on baking with it. The dough can also be defrosted at room temperature, but it needs to be re-chilled in the refrigerator for 1 to 2 hours prior to using.

MOM'S FRESH STRAWBERRY TARTLETS

Every June the city of Portland, Oregon, holds its Rose Festival,
an annual event that for me will always be associated with strawberries. When I was growing
up in Portland, it was during the festival that roadside stalls, each with its stacked crates of
ripe, sweet berries, would appear in the city's East Side. I know everybody thinks their local
strawberries are the best, but Portland's really are amazing. We would eat them for breakfast,
dusted with powdered sugar, and my mom would always make her famous strawberry pie. At
Macrina, if the weather permits and the berries are ripe early
enough, we like to make these strawberry tartlets for Mother's Day.

Makes 4 (4-inch) tartlets

½ recipe Flaky Pie Dough (*page 127*), chilled
6 cups (3 pints) fresh ripe strawberries, washed and trimmed
½ cup granulated sugar
½ teaspoon freshly grated lemon zest
1 tablespoon cornstarch
1 teaspoon pure vanilla extract
4 ounces white chocolate, coarsely chopped
¼ cup honey
2 tablespoons filtered water

- Divide the chilled pie dough into 4 equal pieces and form each piece into a ball. Working on a floured surface, roll each ball into a 7½-inch circle, about ⅛ inch thick. Line 4 (4-inch) tart pans with the rolled crusts and trim away all but ¾ inch of overhanging dough from each crust. Fold the overhanging dough inside the pans, so that only ¼ inch of dough extends above the rim of each tart ring. Crimp the edges (see photos, page 136) and chill the tart shells in the refrigerator for at least 45 minutes.

- Preheat oven to 375°F.

- Place the chilled tart shells on a rimmed baking sheet. Line each tart shell with a piece of parchment paper and fill the shells with dried beans or baking weights. Bake tart shells on center rack of oven for 25 to 30 minutes, or until edges are golden brown. Carefully remove paper and beans and check to see if crusts are done. If the bottoms of the crusts are moist or wet looking, return them to the oven to continue baking (without the parchment paper or beans) for 2 to 3 minutes. Watch the shells carefully to make sure they don't burn. If bubbles appear on the bottom of the crusts, carefully depress them with a tea towel, taking care to avoid the escaping steam. Set the finished tart shells on a wire rack to cool.

- Divide the strawberries evenly between 2 bowls, with the most perfect-looking berries in 1 bowl and the imperfect berries in another. Set the prettier berries aside to decorate the tops of the tartlets.

- To the other bowl of strawberries, add sugar, lemon zest, cornstarch, and vanilla extract. Using a wooden spoon, mix the ingredients together and mash the berries slightly. Transfer to a medium saucepan and cook over medium heat for 7 to 10 minutes, stirring constantly. The berries will release their juices and the mixture will thicken. Remove from heat and return cooked berries to their original bowl. Set aside to cool.

- Place white chocolate in a medium stainless steel bowl. Place bowl on top of a saucepan filled with 2 inches of simmering water, making sure that the bottom of the pan does not come in contact with the water. It's important that the water be just simmering. If the water is too hot it will scorch the chocolate. Stir with a rubber spatula until chocolate is completely melted, then remove from heat and let cool slightly.

- Using a pastry brush, cover the bottom of each tart shell with the melted chocolate. (Not only will this taste delicious, but the chocolate will help keep the tart bottoms from getting soggy.) Allow the chocolate to cool and harden. Spoon a half-inch layer of the cooled (room temperature) strawberry filling into each of the tart shells. Top each tartlet with the whole berries, arranging them stem-side down and completely covering the strawberry filling.

- In a small saucepan, combine honey and water and whisk together. Heat briefly over medium heat to create a glaze for the tarts. Let cool slightly. Using a pastry brush, paint a little glaze over all of the strawberries and the outer edges of the tartlets, giving them a shiny finish.

- Gently remove the tart pans and arrange the tartlets on a decorative platter. It's best to serve these tarts within a few hours of preparation. The crusts will get soggy if they are stored for very long.

CLASSIC BLUEBERRY PIE

Few things in life are as wonderful as a homemade blueberry pie. It is heaven on earth!
I recommend using slightly tart organic blueberries whenever possible.

Makes 1 (9-inch) double-crusted pie

7 cups (3½ pints) organic blueberries
¾ cup granulated sugar
¼ cup light brown sugar
2 teaspoons freshly grated lemon zest
1 teaspoon cinnamon
1 teaspoon pure vanilla extract
3 tablespoons unbleached all-purpose flour
½ recipe Flaky Pie Dough *(page 127)*, chilled
1 tablespoon unsalted butter, cut into small pieces
Egg wash made with 1 egg and 1 teaspoon water
Coarse raw sugar
Vanilla ice cream, for serving

- Sort through the blueberries, removing any stems and leaves. Gently rinse the berries and lay them out on paper towels to air dry.

- Combine 3½ cups of the blueberries, granulated sugar, brown sugar, lemon zest, cinnamon, vanilla extract, and flour in a medium saucepan and mix with a spoon. Cook over medium heat until the fruit juices have been released and the mixture has thickened, 5 to 8 minutes, stirring frequently to keep the mixture from burning. Pour the cooked fruit into a large stainless steel bowl and add the remaining blueberries. Stir with a spoon and set aside until the fruit has cooled to room temperature.

- Divide the chilled pie dough into 2 pieces, making one piece slightly larger than the other. Coat your hands with flour and shape the larger piece of dough into a ball. Working on a floured surface, flatten the ball slightly, then roll it into a 12-inch circle, about ⅛ inch thick. Fit the rolled dough into a 9-inch pie pan, then trim the edges of the dough to leave a 1-inch overhang around the pan. Roll out the remaining piece of dough ⅛ inch thick and trim it into a 10-inch circle. Set aside. This will be the top crust.

- Pour the cooled fruit into the pie shell and dot with butter. Brush the top side of the overhanging dough with a little egg wash. Lift the top crust onto the pie, folding it in half to make it easier to accurately position. Lift the overhanging dough onto the top crust and crimp with your fingers (see photos, below). Mark the crimped edges with a fork, then brush all of the crust with egg wash. Sprinkle with coarse raw sugar and chill in the refrigerator for at least 30 minutes.

- Preheat oven to 375°F. Line a rimmed baking sheet with parchment paper.

- Place the pie on the prepared baking sheet. Using a sharp knife, cut 4 slits in the center of the crust. Bake pie for 50 to 55 minutes. The crust will be golden brown and the fruit will be bubbling in the center of the pie. Let cool for 30 to 40 minutes, then serve with vanilla ice cream.

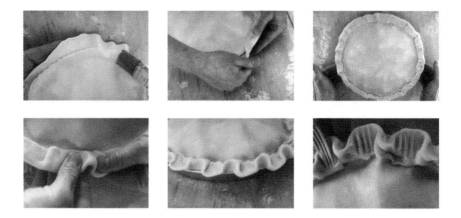

FRESH FRUIT CROSTATA

This Italian-style tart can be customized to suit any season. In the winter, it's delicious filled with pears, apples, and cranberries. In the summer, I like to mix ripe berries with sweet figs. One of my all-time favorites is the combination of blueberries and juicy nectarines, as in the recipe that follows. As always, use the freshest, ripest fruit you can find.

Makes 1 (10-inch) lattice-topped tart

3 cups (1½ pints) blueberries
5 ripe nectarines, washed, pitted, and cut into ¼-inch slices
1½ cups granulated sugar

2 tablespoons unbleached all-purpose flour
½ teaspoon freshly grated lemon zest
2 tablespoons unsalted butter, cut into small pieces
Freshly squeezed lemon juice *(optional)*
1 recipe Sesame Almond Dough *(page 132)*, chilled
Egg wash made with 1 egg and 1 teaspoon water
Coarse raw sugar

- Combine 1½ cups of the blueberries, half of the nectarines, and the sugar, flour, lemon zest, and butter in a medium saucepan. Stir with a wooden spoon. Cook over medium heat until the fruit juices have been released and the mixture has thickened, about 10 minutes, stirring frequently to keep the fruit from burning. Pour the cooked fruit into a large stainless steel bowl and add the remaining blueberries and nectarines. Stir with a wooden spoon and set aside to cool. After the fruit has cooled slightly, check the flavor. If needed, add a little freshly squeezed lemon juice to taste. Continue cooling fruit to room temperature.

- Divide the chilled Sesame Almond Dough into 2 pieces, making one piece slightly larger than the other. Place the larger piece of dough in the refrigerator to keep it chilled, and gently form the smaller piece of dough into a ball. Place the dough on a large piece of floured parchment or waxed paper and roll it into a 10-inch square, about ⅛ inch thick. Using a fluted pastry wheel or a sharp knife, cut dough into 1-inch-wide strips. Lift the paper onto a tray or cookie sheet and chill in the refrigerator until you're ready to top the tart.

- Remove the remaining piece of dough from the refrigerator. Working on a floured surface, gently shape the dough into a ball, then roll it into a 13-inch circle, about ⅛ inch thick. For best results, make sure the dough is very cold. This dough is fragile but resilient. If it cracks, simply press it together with your fingers.

- Using a long knife or offset spatula, gently release the rolled dough from the work surface. Fold the dough in half to make it easier to lift and fit it into a 10-inch tart pan with a removable bottom. Using your fingers, press the dough into the tart pan, evenly covering the bottom and sides. If the dough breaks, simply press it together. Once the crust is even, pinch away any excess dough around the rim of the tart pan to create a level edge.

- Pour the cooled fruit mixture into the tart shell, filling it to the top. Remove the strips of dough from the refrigerator. Brush the top edge of the crust with egg wash. Begin assembling the lattice top (see photos, page 138). Lay 1 strip of dough horizontally across the bottom of the tart, pinching the ends to seal it to the crust. Break away any overhanging dough, and lightly brush the strip with egg wash. Lay another strip of dough vertically up the left side of the tart, overlapping the horizontal strip. Seal it to the crust, break away any excess, and brush the strip with egg wash. Continue adding more strips in this fashion, leaving about ½ inch between each strip, until the crostata is covered. If any of the strips break while you're handling them, brush the ends with a little egg wash and pinch them back together again. Place the assembled crostata in the freezer and let chill for at least 30 minutes.

- Preheat oven to 350°F. Line a rimmed baking sheet with parchment paper.

- Remove the crostata from the freezer and place it on the prepared baking sheet. Brush it again with egg wash and sprinkle coarse raw sugar over the top. Bake on center rack of oven for 55 to 60 minutes, or until the crust is golden brown and the fruit is bubbling. Let the crostata cool on a wire rack for 20 to 30 minutes, then remove the outer ring of the tart pan. (If it cools any longer the sugars will harden and it will become very difficult to remove the crostata from the ring.) Serve at room temperature.

Baking with Julia

Few people are as recognizable and beloved as Julia Child. Just saying her name makes me smile. I've always found the baking life to be full of rewards, but the highlight of my career came when I was asked to take part in Julia's *Baking with Julia* project. A member of Julia's production team informed me that they would be filming a series of twenty-six television shows, along with a companion cookbook written by the award-winning Dorie Greenspan. The goal was to showcase bakers from all around the country, and to celebrate all forms of baking. Would I like to be involved? Of course I would.

I flew to Boston in July of 1995, excited to tape my episodes and meet one of my heroes. We would be filming in Julia's actual kitchen, a place I'd only dreamt of visiting. I arrived to find Julia's friendly staff ready and eager to get to work. They escorted me into the famous kitchen, and there she was. I know everyone says it, but what a presence Julia has! She was gracious, engaging, and inspiring. We spent that day planning and preparing for the next day's show, and I couldn't wait to get started.

The next morning began with makeup and hair styling (not my usual routine!) followed by tips for working in front of the cameras. Then the filming began. My initial camera shyness was gone as soon as Julia started speaking to me. I demonstrated four tart recipes, including a double-crusted pie and Macrina's Fresh Fruit Crostata, all of which I enjoyed. But what made the show magical was Julia. Her legendary style and her ability to ask exactly the right questions on behalf of home bakers carried the show. It was a hot day in Cambridge, the air conditioning was broken, and my pie dough was giving me some trouble, but Julia made the six-hour taping session a breeze.

Years later, the television series is in reruns, and the celebrated cookbook is in thousands of kitchens. Whenever the show airs in Seattle, customers stop by to tell me how much they enjoyed it and to ask what it was like to work with Julia. My answer stays the same. It was amazing, and a privilege I'll never forget.

LEMON CHESS TART

This version of a traditional English Chess Tart is one of Macrina Bakery's signature desserts. I got the original recipe from a food history class I took at the California Culinary Academy, and since then I've worked with the recipe to find the perfect balance between sweet and tart. For best results, I recommend having all of the ingredients at room temperature before you get started.

Makes 1 (10-inch) tart

2¼ cups granulated sugar
2 tablespoons white cornmeal
1½ tablespoons unbleached all-purpose flour
6 eggs
1 tablespoon freshly grated lemon zest
¾ cup freshly squeezed lemon juice
¼ cup whole milk
6 tablespoons unsalted butter, melted and slightly cooled
1 pre-baked (10-inch) Flaky Pie Dough tart shell *(page 129)*
Powdered sugar
White chocolate curls, fruit slices, or edible flowers for garnish *(optional)*
Lightly Sweetened Whipped Cream *(page 106)*

- Prepare all of the ingredients and let them sit at room temperature for 30 minutes. Preheat oven to 325°F.

- Sift sugar, cornmeal, and flour into a large bowl. Crack the eggs into the sugar mixture one at a time, whisking between each addition. Continue whisking as you add lemon zest, lemon juice, milk, and melted butter, making sure each ingredient is thoroughly blended before adding another.

- Make sure that your pre-baked tart shell is not cracked, then place it on a rimmed baking sheet. Pour the tart filling into the shell, filling it to just below the top. Bake the tart for 40 to 45 minutes, until center is set and the surface is golden brown. (Note: Check the tart after the first 15 minutes of baking to make sure it is browning evenly. If one side of the tart is browning more quickly than the other side, carefully rotate the baking sheet to even out the baking.)

- Let the tart cool on a wire rack for at least 1 hour, then remove the sides of the pan and dust the tart with powdered sugar. I like to pile white chocolate curls in the center of the tart, but you can also decorate it with your favorite ripe fruits or edible flowers like violets. Serve with a generous dollop of Lightly Sweetened Whipped Cream.

APPLE & BING CHERRY GALETTE

I have fond memories of the first time we made this dessert. My friend Kay Simon, winemaker and co-owner of Washington's Chinook Winery, had stopped by the café with some bottles of Merlot that we'd ordered. She also brought along a surprise gift—five pounds of sweet, sun-ripened cherries from her neighbor's farm in Prosser, Washington. We popped a few into our mouths and started daydreaming of all the wonderful pastries we could make with the fruit. The end result was one of my favorite summer desserts.

Serves 8 to 10

6 Granny Smith apples
½ tablespoon freshly squeezed lemon juice
¾ cup granulated sugar
3 tablespoons unbleached all-purpose flour
½ tablespoon cinnamon
2 tablespoons unsalted butter, cut into small pieces
2 cups fresh Bing cherries, stemmed and pitted
1 tablespoon pure vanilla extract
½ recipe Flaky Pie Dough *(page 127)*, chilled
Egg wash made with 1 egg and 1 teaspoon water
2 tablespoons coarse raw sugar
Vanilla ice cream, for serving

● Preheat oven to 375°F.

● Peel and core apples and cut into ½-inch slices (approximately 12 slices per apple). Place apple slices and lemon juice in a large bowl. Add sugar, flour, and cinnamon and toss until slices are evenly coated. Spread apples into a single layer on a rimmed baking sheet and dot with pieces of butter. Roast on center rack of oven for 15 minutes to release some of the juices and intensify the flavors. Set aside to cool. Increase oven temperature to 385°F.

● In a large bowl, combine cooled apples, cherries, and vanilla extract. Mix gently with a wooden spoon and set aside.

● Coat your hands with flour and shape the chilled piece of dough into a ball. Working on a floured surface, flatten the ball slightly and roll it into a 14-inch circle, about ⅛ inch thick. Gently transfer rolled dough onto a parchment-lined, rimmed baking sheet. Pile fruit onto center of the dough, leaving excess liquid in the bowl, and spread to cover about 8 inches, leaving a 3-inch border of dough around the filling. Lift border on top of the filling, tucking and folding the dough to create a gathered, or pleated, finish (see photos, page 204). Lift each of the folds up and brush underneath with egg wash to seal the crust. Brush all exposed dough with egg wash and sprinkle with coarse raw sugar. Chill in the freezer for at least 30 minutes.

- Place tart on center rack of oven and bake for 15 minutes. Reduce heat to 375°F and bake for 40 more minutes, or until crust is golden brown. If the apples start to burn before the crust is ready, cover them with a small piece of aluminum foil. Let cool on the baking sheet for 20 to 30 minutes. Serve warm with vanilla ice cream.

CHOCOLATE & BRANDIED CHERRY TART

This rich and oozing chocolate tart is simply irresistible. Long before warm chocolate cakes became fashionable, rustic bakeries like ours were preparing velvety just-set brownies and tortes, a tradition that inspired this recipe. We recommend serving the tart warm with Lightly Sweetened Whipped Cream.

Makes 1 (10-inch) tart

5 ounces unsweetened chocolate, coarsely chopped
12 tablespoons (1½ sticks) unsalted butter, at room temperature
1½ cups granulated sugar
1 tablespoon unbleached all-purpose flour
6 eggs
2 cups Brandied Cherries *(recipe follows)*
1 pre-baked (10-inch) Flaky Pie Dough tart shell *(page 129)*
Powdered sugar
Lightly Sweetened Whipped Cream *(page 106)*

- Preheat oven to 300°F.

- Combine chocolate and butter in a medium stainless steel bowl. Place bowl on top of a saucepan filled with 2 inches of simmering water, making sure that the bottom of the bowl does not come in contact with the water. It's important that the water be just simmering; if it's too hot it will scorch the ingredients. Stir chocolate and butter with a rubber spatula until they are completely melted and combined. Remove the bowl from heat and let cool to room temperature.

- In a separate medium bowl, combine granulated sugar, flour, and eggs. Mix well with a whisk. Add to the bowl of cooled chocolate and mix with a rubber spatula until all ingredients are thoroughly combined and the mixture has thickened.

- Place pre-baked tart shell on a rimmed baking sheet. Scatter 1 cup of drained Brandied Cherries over the bottom of the pastry shell, then pour the chocolate mixture over the cherries, filling the shell to just below the top. Place baking sheet on center rack of oven and bake for about 30 minutes, or until center is just set. Let cool on a wire rack for 30 minutes, then remove the sides of the pan and dust the tart lightly with powdered sugar. Serve the warm slices with a spoonful of the remaining Brandied Cherries and garnish with Lightly Sweetened Whipped Cream.

BRANDIED CHERRIES

This is one of my favorite ways to use fresh Bing cherries. In Washington State we have an abundance of the sweet fruit every summer, but when fresh cherries aren't available I recommend using the highest quality dried cherries you can find.

Makes approximately 2 cups

½ cup granulated sugar
½ cup brandy
1 tablespoon pure vanilla extract
¼ cup filtered water
2 cups Bing cherries, stemmed and pitted
2 tablespoons unsalted butter *(optional)*

- Combine sugar, brandy, vanilla extract, and water in a medium saucepan and bring to a simmer over medium heat. Add cherries and stir with a wooden spoon to make sure all the fruit is coated. Reduce heat to low and cook for 3 minutes, stirring frequently. Cover the pan and remove from heat. Let cherries steep for 1 hour. At this point the cherries are ready for using in cake or tart recipes. Store in an airtight container for up to 1 week in the refrigerator.

- To make a Brandied Cherry Sauce, reheat the cherries and stir in the 2 tablespoons of butter. The sauce is a nice accompaniment to tarts or cakes or spooned over ice cream. Try it on your favorite pancakes.

PEAR & HONEY CUSTARD TART

This tart is really easy to prepare, but it is so beautiful that your guests
will think it took you all day. We often feature it as our special in the café, where
the tart's sweet almond crust has a loyal following.

Makes 1 (10-inch) tart

¼ cup whole almonds
1 recipe Sweet Almond Dough *(page 130)*, at room temperature
3 cups white wine
¾ cup granulated sugar
3 pears, peeled, halved, and cored
1 cup heavy cream
½ cup honey
2 eggs
2 tablespoons unbleached all-purpose flour
½ teaspoon pure vanilla extract
½ teaspoon pure almond extract

- Preheat oven to 350°F.

- Spread almonds on rimmed baking sheet and toast for about 10 minutes, or until golden brown. Let cool, then finely grind in a food processor. Set aside for garnishing the tart.

- Using your fingers, press the Sweet Almond Dough into a 10-inch tart pan with a removable bottom. Form an even crust, about ⅛ inch thick, over the bottom and all the way up the sides of the pan. (It's important that the crust be the same thickness on the bottom and the sides.) Chill in the refrigerator for 30 minutes.

- Preheat oven to 350°F.

- Line the chilled tart shell with a piece of parchment paper and fill it with dried beans or baking weights (see photo, page 127). Bake on center rack of oven for 20 to 25 minutes, or until crust is golden brown. Carefully remove the paper and beans and set tart shell aside to cool. Leave the oven on.

- Combine wine and sugar in a medium, heavy-bottomed saucepan and bring to a boil. Reduce heat and simmer for 5 minutes, whisking occasionally. Gently place pears in the hot wine, rounded sides down, and poach for 7 to 10 minutes, or until pears are fork-tender. Remove pears with a slotted spoon and set aside to cool. Continue simmering the poaching liquid until it has reduced by half its volume, then set it aside to use as a glaze on the finished tart.

- Combine cream, honey, eggs, flour, vanilla extract, and almond extract in a medium bowl and mix well with a whisk.

- Place cooled, pre-baked tart shell on a rimmed baking sheet. Slice the poached pears in half again lengthwise and arrange them in the bottom of the tart shell. (At the bakery we like to spread the slices out in a fan-like pattern.) Pour the custard filling over the pears, filling the shell to just below the top. Place baking sheet on center rack of oven and bake for 50 to 55 minutes, or until custard is set and golden brown. Let the tart cool on a wire rack for 30 minutes, then remove the sides of the pan.

- Warm the reduced wine glaze over low heat until it thins, then brush the surface of the tart with a little glaze. Sprinkle ground toasted almonds around the outer edge.

APRICOT FRANGIPANE TART

This combination of roasted almond frangipane and Pasta Frolla is perfectly balanced by sweet-tart fruits such as apricots. You could also use plums, poached pears, figs, or cherries.

Makes 1 (10-inch) tart

½ recipe Pasta Frolla *(see page 131)*, chilled
½ cup slivered almonds
1 cup whole almonds
8 tablespoons (1 stick) unsalted butter, at room temperature
½ cup granulated sugar, plus additional for sprinkling
2 eggs
1½ tablespoons pure vanilla extract
1½ tablespoons unbleached all-purpose flour
10 to 12 ripe apricots, washed, pitted, and quartered
2 tablespoons unsalted butter, melted

- Place chilled Pasta Frolla on a floured work surface and form it into a ball. Flatten ball slightly, then roll it into a 14-inch circle, about ⅛ inch thick. At this point the dough is too fragile to be folded, so slide something flat, such as an extra tart pan bottom, under the dough. Lift the dough, center it over the 10-inch tart pan with a removable bottom, then ease the dough into the pan as you pull the extra tart pan bottom away. Press the dough into the tart pan with your fingers, pinching together any cracks that occur. Fold in the inch of overhanging dough, creating a double-thick crust around the edges of the tart. Chill in the refrigerator for at least 30 minutes.

- Preheat oven to 350°F.

- Line the chilled tart shell with a piece of parchment paper and fill it with dried beans or baking weights (see photo, page 127). Bake on center rack of oven for 20 to 25 minutes, or until crust is golden brown. Carefully remove the paper and beans and set tart shell aside to cool. Leave the oven on.

- Spread slivered almonds and whole almonds on rimmed baking sheets and toast until golden brown. (The slivered almonds will take 3 to 5 minutes, and the whole almonds will take 10 to 15 minutes.) Set aside to cool. Leave the oven on.

- Place cooled whole almonds in the bowl of a food processor and process until nuts are ground to a medium-fine consistency. Add butter, sugar, eggs, vanilla extract, and flour and blend for about 3 minutes. This is the frangipane.

- Using a rubber spatula, scrape the frangipane from the mixing bowl and spread it evenly, about ⅛ inch thick, onto the bottom of the cooled tart shell. Starting at the edge of the tart, cover the frangipane with concentric circles of apricot slices, laying the slices skin sides down. Brush the apricots with melted butter and sprinkle a little granulated sugar over the top. Place tart on a rimmed baking sheet and bake on center rack of oven for 35 to 40 minutes. The edges of the apricots will darken and the frangipane will be a deep, golden brown. Let cool on a wire rack for at least 30 minutes, then remove the sides of the tart pan. Place the finished tart on a serving plate and sprinkle slivered almonds around the outer edge of the tart.

CHAMPAGNE GRAPE TART

Walking through Seattle's Pike Place Market is a great way to get inspired about cooking. There always seems to be something new to see and taste. It's at the market that I usually find the summer's first batch of Champagne grapes, only available for a few weeks each year. They're great baked on focaccia with fresh herbs and Gorgonzola, but my favorite way to enjoy them is in this simple tart. Not only is it a perfect summer dessert but it also fits perfectly into a cheese course.

Makes 1 (10-inch) tart

5 cups champagne grapes, stemmed and washed
½ cup granulated sugar
1½ tablespoons cornstarch
1 tablespoon freshly squeezed lemon juice
½ teaspoon cinnamon
¼ teaspoon ground nutmeg
¼ recipe Flaky Pie Dough *(page 127)*, chilled
1 pre-baked (10-inch) Flaky Pie Dough tart shell *(page 129)*
2 tablespoons unsalted butter, cut into small pieces
Egg wash made with 1 egg and 1 teaspoon water
2 tablespoons coarse raw sugar

- Combine 2½ cups of the grapes, sugar, cornstarch, lemon juice, cinnamon, and nutmeg in a medium saucepan and mix with a spoon. Cook over medium heat until the fruit juices have been released and the mixture has thickened, 5 to 10 minutes, stirring frequently to keep it from burning. Pour the cooked fruit into a medium stainless steel bowl and add the remaining grapes. Stir with a spoon and set aside until the fruit has cooled to room temperature.

- Place chilled dough on a floured work surface and roll it out ⅛ inch thick. Using a cookie cutter or a small, sharp knife, cut about 20 (2-inch) leaves out of the dough and place them on a lined baking sheet. Chill in the refrigerator until needed.

- Preheat oven to 350°F.

- Place pre-baked tart shell on a rimmed baking sheet. Pour the cooled fruit into the shell, filling it to just below the top. Dot the surface with pieces of butter. Remove leaves from the refrigerator and set 3 of them aside. Arrange the rest of the leaves in a single circle around the outer edge of the tart. Each of the leaves should overlap by about ¼ inch and just touch the outer crust. Brush a little egg wash under each of the overlapping points to help seal the leaves together. Lay the remaining 3 leaves in the center of the tart. Finally, lightly brush all of the leaves with egg wash and sprinkle with coarse raw sugar.

- Bake on center rack of oven for 40 to 45 minutes, or until leaves are golden brown and the fruit is bubbling near the center. Let cool on a wire rack for 1 hour before serving.

HUCKLEBERRY & CRÈME FRAÎCHE TART

If you've ever picked huckleberries, you know what a long, tedious process it is. Luckily there are people like my friend Anna. Every October she picks pint after pint of the sought-after berries and offers them to markets and restaurants around Seattle. Her arrival at the bakery is eagerly anticipated, and our pastry cooks light up with all kinds of ideas for the berries. This recipe calls for a small blowtorch, which can be purchased at kitchen stores and most hardware stores.

Makes 1 (10-inch) tart

3 cups fresh huckleberries
1 recipe Sweet Almond Dough (*see page 130*), at room temperature
1½ cups crème fraîche*
3 eggs
¾ cup granulated sugar
1 tablespoon pure vanilla extract
2 teaspoons cinnamon
¼ teaspoon ground nutmeg
available in specialty shops and some supermarkets

- Sort through the huckleberries, removing any stems and leaves. Gently rinse the berries and lay them out on paper towels to air dry.

- Using your fingers, press the Sweet Almond Dough into a 10-inch tart pan with a removable bottom. Form an even crust, about ⅛ inch thick, over the bottom and all the way up the sides of the pan. (It's important that the crust be the same thickness on the bottom and the sides.) Chill in the refrigerator for 30 minutes.

- Preheat oven to 350°F.

- Line the chilled tart shell with a piece of parchment paper and fill it with dried beans or baking weights (see photo, page 127). Bake on center rack of oven for 20 to 25 minutes, or until crust is golden brown. Carefully remove the paper and beans and set aside to cool. Leave the oven on.

- Combine crème fraîche, eggs, ½ cup of the sugar, and vanilla extract in a medium stainless steel bowl. Mix well with a whisk until eggs are fully incorporated. Place bowl on top of a saucepan filled with 2 inches of simmering water, making sure that the bottom of the bowl does not come in contact with the water. It's important that the water be just simmering; if it's too hot it will scorch the ingredients. Stir constantly with a rubber spatula until the mixture is warmed through, approximately 95°F when tested with a candy thermometer. Warming the custard in this way will help the tart to bake faster and prevent the huckleberries from bursting.

- Place the cooled tart shell on a rimmed baking sheet and scatter the huckleberries evenly across the bottom of the shell. Pour the warmed custard over the berries, filling the shell to just below the top. Place baking sheet on center rack of oven and bake for 25 to 30 minutes, or until tart is just set. Let cool on a wire rack for 20 minutes.

- Combine remaining ¼ cup of sugar, cinnamon, and nutmeg in a small bowl. Toss ingredients together, then sprinkle evenly over the top of the tart. Using a small blowtorch, carefully caramelize the surface of the tart. The sugars will turn a deep, golden brown. (If you don't have a blowtorch, place the tart under a preheated broiler and turn frequently until the surface of the tart is evenly browned.) This tart is best served warm.

PLUM & ALMOND CRUMB TART

This easy-to-prepare tart is perfect with an afternoon cup of coffee or for the kids' after-school snack. The recipe calls for plums, but you can easily substitute ripe cherries, apricots, or nectarines.

Makes 1 (10-inch) tart

1 recipe Sweet Almond Dough *(page 130)*, at room temperature
¼ cup slivered almonds
8 ounces cream cheese, at room temperature
3 eggs

⅔ cup granulated sugar
½ teaspoon freshly grated lemon zest
4 tablespoons cornstarch, sifted
¼ teaspoon ground nutmeg
6 to 8 ripe plums, washed, pitted, and cut into 6 slices each
Crumb Topping (*recipe follows*)
Powdered Sugar

- Using your fingers, press the Sweet Almond Dough into a 10-inch tart pan with a removable bottom. Form an even crust, about ⅛ inch thick, over the bottom and all the way up the sides of the pan. (It's important that the crust be the same thickness on the bottom and the sides.) Chill in the refrigerator for 30 minutes.

- Preheat oven to 350°F.

- Spread slivered almonds on a rimmed baking sheets and toast until golden brown, 3 to 5 minutes. Set aside to cool. Leave the oven on.

- Line the chilled tart shell with a piece of parchment paper and fill it with dried beans or baking weights (see photo, page 127). Bake on center rack of oven for 20 to 25 minutes, or until crust is golden brown. Carefully remove the paper and beans and set aside to cool. Leave the oven on.

- Place cream cheese in the bowl of your stand mixer. Using the paddle attachment, mix on medium speed for about 5 minutes, scraping down the sides of the bowl frequently. Add the eggs, one at a time, making sure each egg is fully incorporated before adding another. Continue to frequently scrape down the sides of the bowl. Add sugar, lemon zest, cornstarch, and nutmeg and mix until ingredients are combined, about 1 minute.

- Place the cooled tart shell on a rimmed baking sheet. Spread the cream cheese filling onto the bottom of the shell, filling it half way. Starting at the edge of the tart, cover the cream cheese with concentric circles of plum slices, cut sides down. Sprinkle Crumb Topping evenly over the plums. Bake on center rack of oven for about 1¼ hours, or until topping is golden brown and the filling is set.

- Let the tart cool on a wire rack for 1 hour. If the fruit you use is particularly juicy, you may need to chill the tart in the refrigerator to help it set. Garnish slices with toasted slivered almonds and powdered sugar.

CRUMB TOPPING

Makes about 1½ cups of topping

1¼ cups unbleached all-purpose flour
½ cup granulated sugar
½ teaspoon cinnamon
8 tablespoons (1 stick) unsalted butter, chilled

- Combine flour, sugar, and cinnamon in a medium bowl and mix with a wooden spoon. Cut the butter into ¼-inch pieces and drop them into the bowl of dry ingredients. Mix with your fingers, working the butter into the flour until the mixture is coarse and crumbly.

CLASSIC RICOTTA PIE

During the 1980s, while I was working at the Bostonian Hotel,
I was lucky enough to live in Boston's North End neighborhood. Living in this
working-class Italian neighborhood, with its amazing cafes, delicatessens, vegetable
markets, and bakeries, was a delight. This pie, studded with raisins, bittersweet chocolate,
and hazelnuts, reminds me of the first ricotta tarts I enjoyed back in the North End.
This pie needs to set before it can be sliced, so bake it one day before you wish to serve it.

Makes 1 (9-inch) tart

⅓ cup raisins
¼ cup hazelnuts
1 recipe Pasta Frolla (*page 131*), chilled
2½ pounds ricotta
¾ cup granulated sugar
1 tablespoon unbleached all-purpose flour
½ teaspoon salt
1 tablespoon pure vanilla extract
2 teaspoons freshly grated orange zest
4 egg yolks
4 ounces finely chopped bittersweet chocolate
Egg wash made with 1 egg and 1 teaspoon water
Coarse raw sugar

- Preheat oven to 350°F.

- Place raisins in a small bowl and cover with warm water. Set aside to soak.

- Place hazelnuts on a rimmed baking sheet and toast for approximately 20 minutes, or until golden brown. Let cool, then remove as much of the loose skins as possible by rubbing the hazelnuts between the palms of your hands. Finely chop and set aside.

- Place chilled Pasta Frolla on a floured work surface. Cut off one-third of the dough and set this smaller piece of dough aside. Form the larger piece into a ball, then roll it into a 19-inch circle, about ⅛ inch thick. At this point the dough is too fragile to be folded, so slide something flat, such as an extra tart pan bottom, under the dough. Lift the dough, center it over a 9 x 4-inch springform pan, then ease the dough into the pan as you pull the extra tart pan bottom away. Press the dough into the springform pan with your fingers, pinching together any cracks that occur. Trim the edges of the dough to leave a 1-inch overhang around the pan. Set aside at room temperature.

- Form the remaining piece of dough into a ball and roll it out ⅛ inch thick, then trim it into a 9-inch circle. Cut a ½-inch hole in the center of the circle, which will act as a vent during baking. Lift the circle onto a piece of parchment paper and set aside.

- Combine ricotta, sugar, flour, salt, vanilla extract, and orange zest in the bowl of your stand mixer. Using the paddle attachment, mix on low speed until ingredients come together, 1 to 2 minutes. Remove the bowl from the mixer. Using a rubber spatula, fold in egg yolks, 2 at a time. Scrape down the sides of the bowl to make sure eggs are fully incorporated.

- Drain raisins and add them to the ricotta mixture. Add chocolate and hazelnuts and fold them in with a rubber spatula until evenly distributed.

- Pour the ricotta mixture into the crust, filling it to the top. Tap the pan on the counter a few times to make sure the filling is settled and to remove any air bubbles. Center the 9-inch crust on top of the filling and brush the outer edge (about 1½ inches) with a little egg wash. Lift the overhanging dough on top of the pie and seal the crusts together by pressing gently with your fingers. Create a ring of pleats around the edge by pinching the dough. Brush the entire surface with egg wash and sprinkle a little coarse raw sugar over the top. Chill in the refrigerator for 30 minutes.

- Preheat oven to 325°F.

- Place the chilled pie on a rimmed baking sheet and bake on center rack of oven for approximately 2 hours, or until the crust is golden brown and the ricotta is set in the center. (Poke a knife into the center of the pie; it will come out clean if the ricotta is set.) Cool the pie on a wire rack until it reaches room temperature, then chill it in the refrigerator overnight. Remove the sides of the pan and place the pie on a decorative serving platter. Wrapped in plastic wrap, this pie will last for up to 4 days in the refrigerator.

FLORENTINE TART WITH
NECTARINES & PINE NUTS

I found my inspiration for this recipe while attending classes at the California Culinary Academy. We were fortunate to have many guest chefs as teachers, one of whom was Carlo Middione, owner of San Francisco's Vivande restaurant. I loved his cooking style, which emphasized simplicity and making the most out of each ingredient's natural flavors. This tart is a variation on one of his recipes.

Makes 1 (10-inch) tart

1 cup candied orange peel
¼ cup pine nuts
1½ cups fine dry white bread crumbs
4 tablespoons unsalted butter, melted
8 tablespoons (1 stick) unsalted butter, at room temperature
1½ cups granulated sugar
3 eggs
¾ cup unbleached all-purpose flour
¼ cup whole milk
1 tablespoon freshly grated lemon zest
3 nectarines, pitted and cut into ⅛-inch slices
2 tablespoons Cinnamon Sugar Mixture *(page 45)*

- Preheat oven to 350°F. Prepare a 10-inch tart pan with a removable bottom by brushing it with oil. Set aside.

- Place orange peel in a small bowl and cover with hot tap water. Let soak for about 20 minutes. Drain and set aside.

- Spread pine nuts on a rimmed baking sheet and lightly toast on center rack of oven for 3 to 5 minutes. Set aside to cool. Leave the oven on.

- Combine bread crumbs and 3 tablespoons of the melted butter in a medium bowl. Toss with a spoon until bread crumbs are evenly coated. Press bread crumbs into the bottom of the prepared tart pan. Set aside.

- Combine the stick of room-temperature butter and sugar in the bowl of your stand mixer. Using the paddle attachment, mix on medium speed for 5 to 8 minutes to cream the butter. The finished mixture should be smooth and pale. Continue mixing as you add eggs, one at a time, making sure that each egg is fully incorporated before adding another. Gradually add flour and milk, alternating between small amounts of both until all is absorbed into the batter. Lower the bowl and scrape down the sides with a rubber spatula. Mix briefly to ensure that all of the ingredients are combined. Remove the bowl from the mixer and fold in pine nuts, orange peel, and lemon zest.

- Place the lined tart ring on a rimmed baking sheet, then pour in the batter. Starting at the outer edge of the tart, cover the batter with concentric circles of nectarine slices, overlapping each slice by about ½ inch. Gently brush nectarines with the remaining melted butter and sprinkle with Cinnamon Sugar Mixture.

- Bake on center rack of preheated oven for approximately 1 hour, or until golden brown. Test the center of the tart with a skewer to make sure it's done. Let cool on a wire rack for 30 minutes before removing the sides of the pan. I like to serve this tart slightly warm.

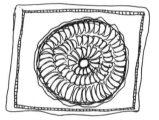

Chapter 11

THE COOKIE BASKET

There's something special about having a freshly baked cookie with a cold glass of milk. We all know the feeling. It is part cherished memory, part simple sensory satisfaction. For most of us, baking cookies is the first chance we ever have to bake, and the experience can lead to a happy lifetime of cooking. Cookies and brownies are probably the most frequently baked items in a home kitchen. The basic ingredients of flour, sugar, and butter are already in most homes, and the recipes are generally easy to follow. To make sure your cookies are as good as they can be, it helps to follow a few simple rules.

- **Cream the butter.** If a cookie recipe calls for butter and sugar, it's important to mix, or cream, the two together. Use a stand mixer to cream the ingredients with the paddle attachment for about five minutes. Start out on low speed for the first minute or so, then increase the speed to medium. This process aerates the butter, creating a light color and creamy texture, and ultimately gives the cookies more height.

- **Pay attention to the eggs.** As with all perishable ingredients, always use the freshest, highest quality eggs you can find. Add eggs to the cookie dough one at a time, making sure each egg is completely incorporated into the batter before adding another. I recommend scraping the sides and bottom of the mixing bowl frequently with a rubber spatula to make sure every bit of the egg is mixed into the dough.

- **Fold in the dry ingredients.** Rather than separately adding dry ingredients such as flour, baking soda, and salt to a cookie dough, combine them in one bowl and mix well with a whisk, so that they will be evenly distributed throughout the cookies. Then, when the instructions call for it, fold the dry ingredients into the wet ingredients with a rubber spatula. Add small amounts at a time, folding in each batch until all of the flour has been absorbed into the dough. Folding the dough helps avoid over-mixing, which could result in tough cookies.

- **Chill the dough.** It's tempting to form and bake your cookies as soon as you make the dough—waiting can be agony when there are hungry people around—but chilling the finished dough for one hour in the refrigerator will ensure thicker, chewier cookies. If the butter inside the dough is not chilled before baking, it will melt quickly when placed in the oven, resulting in flat cookies that burn around the edges but stay raw in the middle. It's worth waiting an hour to make the best cookies possible.

Simply put, a tray of fresh cookies or brownies is comfort food at its best. This chapter contains recipes for Macrina's most popular cookies, biscotti, and bar cookies. We've included the sought-after recipe for our Ginger & Molasses Cookies, crisp on the edges, chewy in the center, and filled with freshly grated ginger. It is easy to prepare and kids can help roll the balls of dough in sugar. The Caramel Pecan Brownies are decadent enough to satisfy even the most serious sweet tooth. You'll also find a recipe for Roasted Walnut & Anise Biscotti, which are light and crisp and which make a beautiful gift when piled in a decorative tin. Whatever your favorite recipes turn out to be, enjoy sharing the results with friends and family, and you can't go wrong.

PEANUT BUTTER COOKIES

Coated in sugar and scored with a fork, these dense and moist cookies are the real, old-fashioned favorites. For the best cookies, use the highest quality natural peanut butter you can find.

Makes 16 cookies

2¼ cups unbleached all-purpose flour
1 teaspoon baking powder
2 teaspoons baking soda
¼ teaspoon salt
10 tablespoons (1¼ sticks) unsalted butter, at room temperature
⅓ cup vegetable shortening, at room temperature
1 cup granulated sugar
¾ cup light brown sugar
1½ cups unsweetened chunky peanut butter
2 eggs
1 teaspoon pure vanilla extract
1 cup peanuts, coarsely chopped

- Combine flour, baking powder, baking soda, and salt in a medium bowl. Set aside.

- Combine butter, shortening, ½ cup of the granulated sugar, and brown sugar in the bowl of your stand mixer. Using the paddle attachment, mix briefly on low speed to start bringing the ingredients together. Increase speed to medium and mix for about 5 minutes, until the mixture is smooth and pale in color. Add peanut butter and mix until thoroughly combined, about 1 minute, scraping down the sides of the bowl as needed. Add 1 egg and mix until incorporated. Scrape down the sides, then add vanilla and the remaining egg. Mix until egg is fully absorbed, then remove the bowl from the mixer and scrape down the sides again.

- Using a rubber spatula, fold half of the flour mixture into the dough. After the flour is fully incorporated, fold in the rest of the flour mixture and continue folding until all of the flour has been absorbed.

- Cover your hands with a little flour and remove the cookie dough from the bowl. Place half of the dough on a sheet of parchment paper and form it into a 2-inch-thick log, about 8 inches long. Pour half of the peanuts onto the parchment paper and, using your hands, coat the log with the nuts. Tightly wrap the parchment paper around the log and twist the ends of the paper to seal the package. Repeat with remaining dough. Chill logs in the refrigerator for at least 1 hour. At this point the dough can be cut into cookies or stored in the refrigerator for up to 4 days.

- Preheat oven to 350°F. Line 2 rimmed baking sheets with parchment paper and pour the remaining ½ cup of granulated sugar into a pie pan or shallow bowl.

- Remove the chilled logs of dough from the refrigerator and carefully unwrap. Using a sharp knife, cut each of the logs into 8 (1-inch-thick) cookies. Dip one side of each cookie in sugar and place the cookies, sugar sides up, on the prepared baking sheets. Arrange 8 cookies on each baking sheet, leaving a 2-inch space between each cookie. Using a fork, score a crosshatch design in the center of each cookie. Place 1 sheet of cookies in the refrigerator while baking the other sheet.

- Bake cookies, 1 sheet at a time, on center rack of oven for 20 to 25 minutes each. To help the cookies bake evenly, rotate the baking sheet every 4 minutes or so. The finished cookies will be golden brown, and slightly puffed up. Let cool on the baking sheet for 10 minutes. The cooled cookies can be stored in an airtight container for up to 3 days.

GINGER & MOLASSES COOKIES

I think it's the fresh ginger that makes these cookies so special.
They also have the perfect balance of chewy and crisp.

Makes 16 cookies

2¼ cups unbleached all-purpose flour
1½ teaspoons baking soda
2 teaspoons cinnamon
1½ teaspoons ground cloves
1 teaspoon salt
½ cup vegetable shortening, at room temperature
6 tablespoons unsalted butter, at room temperature
1½ cups light brown sugar
2 eggs
2 teaspoons peeled and grated ginger
⅓ cup dark molasses
1 cup granulated sugar

- Combine flour, baking soda, cinnamon, ground cloves, and salt in a medium bowl. Mix with a whisk until evenly distributed and set aside.

- Combine shortening, butter, and brown sugar in the bowl of your stand mixer. Using the paddle attachment, mix on medium speed for about 5 minutes, until

the mixture is smooth and pale in color. Add
1 egg and mix until incorporated. Scrape
down the sides of the bowl. Add remaining
egg and scrape down the sides of the bowl
again. Add ginger and molasses and mix on
low speed for 1 minute. The mixture may
look as if it's separating, but have no fear. It
will come together once the dry ingredients
are added. Remove the bowl from the mixer
and scrape down the sides of the bowl again.

- Using a rubber spatula, fold half of the flour
  mixture into the dough. After the flour is fully
  incorporated, fold in the rest of the flour mixture and continue folding until all of the flour
  has been absorbed. Scrape down the sides of
  the bowl and cover it with plastic wrap. Chill
  in the refrigerator for at least 1 hour. At this
  point the dough can be formed into cookies
  or stored in the refrigerator for up to 4 days.

- Preheat oven to 350°F. Line 2 rimmed baking sheets with parchment paper and pour
  granulated sugar into a pie pan or shallow bowl.

- Scoop dough out of the bowl (I like to use a medium ice cream scoop) and roll the
  dough into 2-inch balls. Toss each of the balls in granulated sugar until evenly coated,
  then place 8 on each baking sheet, leaving 3 inches between each ball. Slightly flatten
  each ball of dough with the palm of your hand to keep the balls from rolling around.

- Place 1 sheet of cookies in the refrigerator while baking the other sheet.

- Bake cookies, 1 sheet at a time, on center rack of oven for 15 to 18 minutes each.
  To help the cookies bake evenly, rotate the baking sheet every 4 minutes or so. The
  finished cookies will be golden brown and slightly puffed up but will collapse while
  they cool. Let cool on the baking sheet for 15 minutes. The cooled cookies can be
  stored in an airtight container for up to 3 days.

CHOCOLATE & APRICOT COOKIES

This recipe originally came from Rick Katz, a talented pastry chef I've had the honor of working with on several occasions. We bake this cookie every day at the bakery and rarely have leftovers. I doubt you will either.

Makes 16 cookies

2¼ cups unbleached all-purpose flour
1 teaspoon baking soda
¼ teaspoon salt
½ teaspoon finely ground espresso beans
10 ounces bittersweet chocolate, coarsely chopped
¾ cup unsulfured dried apricots, diced
8 ounces (2 sticks) unsalted butter, at room temperature
¾ cup granulated sugar
¾ cup light brown sugar
2 eggs
2 teaspoons pure vanilla extract

• Combine flour, baking soda, salt, and espresso in a medium bowl. Mix with a whisk until evenly distributed. Add chocolate and apricots and mix well with a spoon. Set aside.

• Combine butter, granulated sugar, and brown sugar in the bowl of your stand mixer. Using the paddle attachment, mix on medium speed for about 5 minutes, until the mixture is smooth and pale in color. Add 1 egg and mix until incorporated. Scrape down the sides of the bowl, then add the remaining egg and vanilla extract. Continue mixing until incorporated, about 1 minute. Remove the bowl from the mixer and scrape down the sides of the bowl again.

• Using a rubber spatula, fold half of the dry ingredients into the dough. After the first batch is fully incorporated, fold in the rest of the dry ingredients and continue folding until all of the flour has been absorbed. Scrape down the sides of the bowl and cover it with plastic wrap. Chill in the refrigerator for at least 1 hour. At this point the dough can be formed into cookies or stored in the refrigerator for up to 4 days.

- Preheat oven to 350°F. Line 2 rimmed baking sheets with parchment paper.

- Scoop dough out of the bowl (I like to use a medium ice cream scoop) and roll the dough into 2-inch balls. Place 8 balls on each baking sheet, leaving 2 inches between each ball. Flatten the balls with the palm of your hand, making them all about ½ inch thick. Place 1 baking sheet of cookies in the refrigerator while baking the other sheet.

- Bake cookies, one sheet at a time, on center rack of oven for 15 to 18 minutes each. To help the cookies bake evenly, rotate the baking sheet every 4 minutes or so. The finished cookies will be golden brown around the edges and slightly soft in the center. Let cool on the baking sheet for 15 minutes. The cooled cookies can be stored in an airtight container for up to 3 days.

OLIVIA'S OLD-FASHIONED CHOCOLATE CHIP COOKIES

This recipe, Macrina's version of the traditional Toll House classic,
makes the best chocolate chip cookies I've ever tasted. The recipe is actually named after two
special Olivias: my daughter and the grandmother of our pastry chef, Karra Wise.

Makes 16 cookies

2¼ cups unbleached all-purpose flour
1 teaspoon baking soda
1 teaspoon salt
3 cups semi-sweet chocolate chips
8 tablespoons (1 stick) unsalted butter, at room temperature
½ cup vegetable shortening, at room temperature
¾ cup granulated sugar
¾ cup light brown sugar
2 eggs
1 teaspoon pure vanilla extract

- Combine flour, baking soda, and salt in a medium bowl. Add chocolate chips and mix well with a spoon. Set aside.

- Combine butter, shortening, granulated sugar, and brown sugar in the bowl of your stand mixer. Using the paddle attachment, mix on medium speed for about 5 minutes, until the mixture is smooth and pale in color. Add 1 egg and mix until incorporated. Scrape down the sides of the bowl, then add the remaining egg and vanilla extract. Continue mixing until incorporated, about 1 minute. Remove the bowl from the mixer and scrape down the sides of the bowl again.

- Using a rubber spatula, fold half of the dry ingredients into the dough. After the first batch is fully incorporated, fold in the rest of the dry ingredients and continue folding until all of the flour has been absorbed. Scrape down the sides of the bowl and cover it with plastic wrap. Chill in the refrigerator for at least 1 hour. At this point the dough can be formed into cookies or stored in the refrigerator for up to 4 days.

- Preheat oven to 350°F. Line 2 rimmed baking sheets with parchment paper.

- Scoop dough out of the bowl (I like to use a medium ice cream scoop) and roll the dough into 2-inch balls. Place 8 balls on each baking sheet, leaving 3 inches between each ball. Flatten the balls with the palm of your hand to about 1 inch thick. Place 1 sheet of cookies in the refrigerator while baking the other sheet.

- Bake cookies, 1 sheet at a time, on center rack of oven for 15 to 18 minutes each. To help the cookies bake evenly, rotate the baking sheet very 4 minutes or so. The finished cookies will be golden brown around the edges, and still light in the center. Let cool on the baking sheet for 15 minutes. The cooled cookies can be stored in an airtight container for up to 3 days.

SOUR CHERRY SHORTBREAD

These flavorful butter cookies are easy to make, and the dough can be cut into all kinds of festive shapes. They make great holiday gifts and will last in an airtight container for up to one month.

Makes 3 dozen cookies

1 cup light brown sugar
½ cup cornstarch
3½ cups unbleached all-purpose flour
1 teaspoon salt
16 ounces (4 sticks) unsalted butter, chilled and cut into ¼-inch pieces
¾ cup dried tart cherries, coarsely chopped
1 tablespoon pure vanilla extract
Powdered sugar

- Combine brown sugar and cornstarch in the bowl of your stand mixer. Using the paddle attachment, mix on low speed for about 30 seconds to break up any clumps.

Creating Olivia's Cookie

One of the best things about creating a new recipe is naming it. I generally like to keep the names simple and descriptive, but sometimes you just have to have fun with it. A good example is pastry chef Karra Wise's Chocolate Eros Cake, which we make every Valentine's Day. The name doesn't necessarily tell you what the cake tastes like, but it sure gets your attention. A personal favorite of mine is Olivia's Old-Fashioned Chocolate Chip Cookies, affectionately named after my daughter.

When my daughter was still in her stroller, we would often pass an afternoon by going on an adventure. We toured our neighborhood, looking at flowers, pointing out all the different colors we saw, and observing the other children. Halfway through our strolls we would stop for a juice and a cookie. We had some pretty good cookies together, but I had trouble finding just the right one. I wanted Olivia to know the kind of cookie my mom used to make, still warm, bursting with oozing chocolate chips.

The truth was that at the time we didn't even make a cookie like that at Macrina. We had plenty of great cookies, but not the simple classic I was craving. So Karra and I got together and using the basic Toll House recipe as our starting point, came up with a winner. The name selection was easy, and the cookie quickly became our biggest seller. As an added bonus, I now have the pleasure of hearing customers say, "I'll have an Olivia's."

Add flour and salt and mix for another 30 seconds. Drop in butter and continue mixing on low speed until the mixture is coarse and crumbly. Stop mixing as soon as the dough starts to come together. Add cherries and vanilla and mix just until the cherries are evenly distributed, 20 to 30 seconds.

- Pull dough from bowl onto a floured work surface and divide it into 2 equal pieces. Place 1 piece of dough on a sheet of parchment paper and roll the dough out ¼ inch thick. Lift parchment paper onto a rimmed baking sheet and cover with plastic wrap. Repeat with remaining piece of dough. Chill both baking sheets in the refrigerator for at least 1 hour.

- Preheat oven to 325°F.

- Remove baking sheets from the refrigerator. Using a sharp knife, cut the dough into 2-inch diamonds. Each sheet of dough should yield about 16 cookies. (You can also use your favorite cookie cutters to create a variety of shapes. Baking time will vary depending on the size of the cookies, so try to keep the sizes consistent.) Remove any excess dough and spread the cookies out on the parchment-lined baking sheets, leaving about 1 inch between the cookies. Place 1 sheet of cookies in the refrigerator while baking the other sheet

- Bake cookies, 1 sheet at a time, on center rack of oven for 20 to 25 minutes each. (Larger cookies will take longer.) To help the cookies bake evenly, rotate the baking sheet every 4 minutes or so. Keep a watchful eye on smaller cookies to make sure they don't burn. The finished cookies will be golden brown on all sides, including the bottoms. Let cool on the baking sheet for at least 20 minutes, then dust with powdered sugar.

ROASTED WALNUT & ANISE BISCOTTI

We've been using this recipe at the bakery since the day we opened. Unlike a lot of traditional, harder biscotti that need to be dunked, these are light and crisp.

Makes 24 cookies

1 cup walnut halves
½ teaspoon anise seeds
1½ cups unbleached all-purpose flour
½ teaspoon baking powder
¼ teaspoon salt
4 tablespoons unsalted butter, at room temperature
¼ cup canola oil
½ cup granulated sugar
2 eggs
1 teaspoon pure vanilla extract

- Preheat oven to 350°F.
- Spread walnuts on a rimmed baking sheet and toast on center rack of oven for 7 to 10 minutes, or until golden brown. Let cool, then chop walnuts into medium pieces. Set aside.
- Toast anise seeds in a small sauté pan over medium heat until seeds are light brown and fragrant. Pour seeds onto a cutting board, let cool, then coarsely chop. (You can also chop the seeds in a clean coffee grinder.)

- Combine chopped walnuts, anise seeds, flour, baking powder, and salt in a medium bowl. Mix with a whisk until evenly distributed. Set aside.

- Combine butter, oil, and sugar in the bowl of your stand mixer. Using the paddle attachment, mix on low speed for 1 minute until the ingredients begin to come together. Increase speed to medium and mix for about 5 minutes, or until the mixture is light in texture and pale in color. Add 1 egg and mix until incorporated. Scrape down the sides of the bowl, then add the remaining egg and vanilla extract. Continue mixing until incorporated, about 1 minute. Remove the bowl from the mixer and scrape down the sides of the bowl again.

- Line 2 baking sheets with parchment paper.

- Using a rubber spatula, fold half of the dry ingredients into the dough. After the first batch is fully incorporated, fold in the rest of the dry ingredients until all of the flour has been absorbed. Coat your hands with flour and pull dough from bowl onto a floured work surface. Pat the dough into a 3 x 12-inch rectangle, about 1 inch thick. Cut the rectangle in half crosswise and place the halves on the prepared baking sheets. Cover with plastic wrap and chill in the refrigerator for 30 minutes.

- Preheat oven to 350°F.

- Bake biscotti logs, 1 sheet at a time, on center rack of oven for 40 minutes each. To help the logs bake evenly, rotate the baking sheet every 10 minutes or so. The finished logs will be golden brown and slightly firm to the touch. Leave oven on.

- Cool logs at least 10 minutes, then transfer them to a cutting board. Using a sharp knife, cut each of the logs crosswise into ½-inch-thick biscotti. Lay biscotti, cut sides down, on the lined baking sheets, about 1½ inches apart. Bake biscotti, one sheet at a time, for 10 minutes, then turn each biscotti over and bake the other side for another 10 minutes. Biscotti should be a deep, golden brown and feel firm and dry. Let cool on the baking sheet for 20 minutes. These biscotti will keep for 1 to 2 weeks in an airtight container.

ALMOND & ORANGE BISCOTTI

These traditional Italian biscotti are nice and crisp,
perfect for dipping in coffee or your favorite tea.

Makes 16 cookies

1 cup whole almonds
1¾ cups unbleached all-purpose flour
½ cup semolina flour
1½ teaspoons baking powder
2 tablespoons freshly grated orange zest
8 tablespoons (1 stick) unsalted butter, at room temperature
1 cup granulated sugar
2 eggs

- Preheat oven to 350°F.

- Spread almonds on a rimmed baking sheet and toast on center rack of oven for 10 minutes. The almonds will become fragrant and will darken slightly. Let cool and chop coarsely.

- Combine chopped almonds, flours, baking powder, and orange zest in a medium bowl. Mix with a whisk until evenly distributed. Set aside.

- Combine butter and sugar in the bowl of your stand mixer. Using the paddle attachment, mix on medium speed for 2 to 3 minutes. Add 1 egg and mix until incorporated. Scrape down the sides of the bowl, then add the remaining egg. Continue mixing until incorporated, about 1 minute. Remove the bowl from the mixer and scrape down the sides of the bowl again.

- Line 2 rimmed baking sheets with parchment paper.

- Using a rubber spatula, fold half of the dry ingredients into the dough. After the first batch is fully incorporated, fold in the rest of the dry ingredients until all of the flour has been absorbed, 1 to 2 minutes. Coat your hands with flour and pull dough from bowl onto a floured work surface. Sprinkle a little flour over the dough, then pat it into a 3 x 14-inch rectangle, about 1 inch thick. Cut the rectangle in half crosswise and place the halves on the prepared baking sheets. If the rectangles lose their shape when lifted, lightly flour your hands and pat them back into shape. Cover with plastic wrap and chill in the refrigerator for 30 minutes.

- Preheat oven to 350°F.

- Bake biscotti logs, 1 sheet at a time, on center rack of oven for 35 to 40 minutes each. To help the logs bake evenly, rotate the baking sheet every 10 minutes or so. The finished logs will puff slightly and be golden brown and slightly firm to the touch. Leave oven on.

- Cool logs at least 10 minutes, then transfer them to a cutting board. Using a sharp knife, cut each log crosswise into ¾-inch-thick biscotti. Lay biscotti, cut sides down, on the lined baking sheets, about 1½ inches apart. Bake biscotti, 1 sheet at a time, for 10 minutes, then turn each biscotti over and bake the other side for another 10 minutes. Biscotti should be a deep, golden brown and feel firm and dry. Let cool on the baking sheet for 20 minutes. These biscotti will keep for 1 to 2 weeks in an airtight container.

FRUIT & OAT BARS

The secret to these popular bars is the high quality of the preserves. I recommend using freezer preserves, jams made from fruit that is picked at the height of its season and immediately frozen. These preserves manage to retain their bright, vivid color when cooked, making the oat bars even more enticing. If you can't find freezer preserves, use the highest quality jarred preserves available.

Makes 12 bars

1 recipe Sweet Almond Dough (*page 130*), at room temperature
2½ cups raspberry freezer preserves
12 tablespoons (1½ sticks) unsalted butter, chilled
1¼ cups light brown sugar
1¼ cups unbleached all-purpose flour
1¼ cups rolled oats

- Preheat oven to 325°F. Oil a 13 x 9 x 2¼-inch baking pan.

- Using your fingers, press the dough into the prepared pan, covering the bottom and ¾ inch of the sides with a ¼-inch layer of dough. Chill in the refrigerator for 30 minutes.

- Line the chilled crust with a piece of parchment paper and fill it with dried beans or baking weights (see photo, page 127). Bake crust on center rack of oven for 20 to 25 minutes, or until the edges are golden brown. Carefully remove the paper and beans and check to see if the bottom of the shell is dry. If it is still moist, place it back in the oven (without the baking weights) and bake for another 2 or 3 minutes. Let cool. Leave the oven on.

- Using a rubber spatula, cover the crust with raspberry preserves.

- Cut butter into ¼-inch pieces and place them in a medium bowl. Add sugar, flour, and oats. Using your fingers, mix the ingredients, working the butter into the flour until the ingredients are combined and the mixture is coarse and crumbly. Sprinkle the topping evenly over the preserves.

- Bake on center rack of oven for about 30 minutes, or until the topping is golden brown and the preserves are bubbling around the edges. Let cool at least 30 minutes, then cut into 3 x 4-inch bars.

CARAMEL PECAN BROWNIES

These moist brownies are as rich as can be. The dense chocolate-cake base is
packed with pecans, then smothered with decadent caramel sauce and chocolate chips.
If you have any leftovers (not likely!), they can be stored in the refrigerator for up to four days.
It's best to make the caramel sauce while the brownies are baking.

Makes 12 brownies

½ cup cocoa powder
1 cup unbleached all-purpose flour
2 cups granulated sugar
1 pound (4 sticks) unsalted butter, at room temperature
4 eggs
2 teaspoons pure vanilla extract
1¾ cups coarsely chopped pecans
1 recipe Caramel Sauce *(recipe follows)*
¼ cup white chocolate chips, coarsely chopped
¼ cup bittersweet chocolate chips, coarsely chopped

- Preheat oven to 325°F. Oil a 13 x 9 x 2¼-inch baking pan.

- Sift cocoa powder and flour into a medium bowl and mix with a whisk until combined. Set aside.

- Combine sugar and butter in the bowl of your stand mixer. Using the paddle attachment, mix on medium speed for about 5 minutes, until the mixture is smooth and pale in color. Add eggs 1 at a time, making sure each egg is fully incorporated before adding another. It's a good idea to scrape down the sides of the bowl after mixing in each egg. Add vanilla extract with the last egg and continue mixing until incorporated, about 1 minute. Remove the bowl from the mixer and scrape down the sides of the bowl again.

● Using a rubber spatula, fold half of the cocoa powder–flour mixture into the batter. After the first batch is fully incorporated, fold in the rest of the mixture and continue folding until all of the flour has been absorbed.

● Pour the batter into the prepared baking pan and spread it evenly with a rubber spatula. Scatter pecans over the top of the batter. Bake on center rack of oven for 30 to 35 minutes, or until center is just set. The center should still be slightly soft. Let cool 15 minutes. This is a good time to prepare the Caramel Sauce.

● Pour warm Caramel Sauce evenly over the pan of brownies. Sprinkle the chopped white and bittersweet chocolate chips over the top of the caramel. The chocolate will melt into the caramel. To finish the brownies, use a skewer to create a pretty line pattern in the caramel: Drag the skewer through the caramel, creating horizontal lines ½ inch apart. Rotate the pan halfway and use the skewer to create vertical lines at ½-inch intervals across the horizontal lines. Chill in the refrigerator for 2 hours to set the caramel, then cut into 12 bars.

CARAMEL SAUCE

Makes approximately 2 cups

2 cups granulated sugar
1 cup water
1 cup heavy cream
4 tablespoons unsalted butter

● Combine sugar and water in a medium heavy-bottomed saucepan. Mix with a whisk to dissolve the sugar, then bring to a simmer over medium heat. While the mixture is heating, brush the sides of the pan with a pastry brush to keep sugar crystals from forming. Repeat this process often, about every 3 minutes, while heating the sauce. After a few minutes the liquid will start turning light brown and then a deep amber color. If one side of the pan darkens quicker than the other, jiggle the pan to mix the liquid. Add cream, taking care to avoid the steam that will rise from the pan. Mix with a whisk until cream is incorporated and the sauce has thickened. Add butter and continue whisking until combined. Let cool slightly, but use while it is still warm.

BITTERSWEET CHOCOLATE BROWNIES

This is my favorite brownie recipe. Unlike the classic dense and chewy brownies that most of us grew up with, these have a light and airy texture. I've heard some customers describe them as chocolate cotton candy.

Makes 9 brownies

5 ounces unsweetened chocolate, coarsely chopped
12 tablespoons (1½ sticks) unsalted butter, at room temperature
1½ cups granulated sugar
2 tablespoons unbleached all-purpose flour
6 eggs
Powdered sugar

- Combine chocolate and butter in a medium stainless steel bowl. Place bowl on top of a saucepan filled with 2 inches of simmering water, making sure that the bottom of the bowl does not come in contact with the water. It's important that the water be just simmering; if it's too hot it will scorch the chocolate. Stir with a rubber spatula until chocolate and butter have melted and reached a smooth consistency. Remove the bowl from the heat and let cool to room temperature.

- Preheat oven to 325°F. Oil a 9-inch square baking pan.

- Place sugar and flour in the bowl of your stand mixer and mix with the paddle attachment for 30 seconds on low speed. Increase speed to medium and add eggs, one at a time, making sure each egg is fully incorporated before adding another. Scrape down the sides of the bowl frequently.

- With the mixer on low speed, drizzle in the cooled, melted chocolate. Scrape the bowl with a rubber spatula to make sure you get all of the chocolate. Increase speed to medium and mix for about 1 minute, or until the batter is mousse-like in texture.

- Pour the batter into the prepared baking pan and spread it evenly with a rubber spatula. Bake on center rack of oven for 30 to 35 minutes, or until the center is just set. Let cool on a wire rack.

- After the brownies have completely cooled, dust them with powdered sugar. Cut into 3 x 3-inch bars, cleaning the knife between cuts. It's best to enjoy these brownies the day they are baked, but they can be stored at room temperature for up to 1 day. The brownies will become very dense and fudge-like if kept in the refrigerator.

MACRINA CAFE FAVORITES

Macrina Cafe Favorites

Macrina Cafe is where all of my passions come together, from my love of baking and the fun I have serving customers to my desire to build a community gathering place. It's also the face of our business and the place where all of the staff's hard work has a chance to shine and be appreciated. I've always wanted to build a place where people feel at home, and the fact that customers come back day after day makes me feel that we're doing a pretty good job. Many of our regular customers have become friends, and quite a few first dates have taken place over a pastry and a cup of joe. We've even seen one or two marriage proposals.

The inspiration for Macrina Cafe came from a small bakery I visited in Prato, Italy. The place was called Barni, and it had a storefront filled with fresh-baked breads, cookies, and prepared foods. Up one step and through a doorway was the cafe, a busy little place filled with regulars enjoying their meals at jam-packed communal tables. One look inside and I couldn't wait to sit down with a plate of my own.

I made my selection from a chalkboard hanging over an open kitchen counter, and then had the pleasure of peering into the kitchen itself. Five or six women were hard at work cooking the food and plating up orders as they came in. Everything on the menu was either roasted or slow-simmered—I loved the sight and smells of all those bubbling pots. My order came up in a matter of minutes, and I made my way to one of the tables, feeling like a member (at least temporarily) of their community.

Macrina has been fortunate to attract many talented chefs over the years, men and women who have worked hard to make our cafe the success that it is. This section is filled with dishes from past and present chefs, as well as recipes I developed myself. You'll find recipes that showcase my philosophy about food: Prepare simple, satisfying dishes from fresh, local, organic, and seasonal ingredients. Make the Corn Chowder with fresh summer corn and pink potatoes. The secret to this recipe is boiling the cobs in the stock, releasing all of their natural sweetness. Or bake a comforting Butternut Squash & Apple Galette, spiced up with Gorgonzola cheese. For breakfast in bed, try Cinnamon French Toast, made from a homemade Classic Brioche Loaf and topped with warm cinnamon glaze. Or pair a slice of tasty Bacon, Leek & Gruyère Quiche with a strong cup of coffee.

Chapter 12

BRUNCH

Gingerbread Crêpes with Citron Ricotta, Cranberry Compote
& Vanilla Syrup

Macrina's Fried Egg Sandwich

Breakfast Strata with Grilled Portobello Mushrooms,
Fontina & Roasted Onions

Old-Fashioned Buttermilk Waffles with Fresh Berries & Cream

Cinnamon French Toast with Ricotta Filling

German Pancake with Apples, Rum & Brown Sugar

Egg Scramble with Delicata Squash, Spinach, Smoked Provolone
& Beurre Blanc Sauce

Bacon, Leek & Gruyère Quiche

Brunch was not part of the original plan for Macrina Cafe. We knew we would have our hands full preparing a daily variety of morning pastries and breads and couldn't imagine serving plated breakfasts. But it didn't take long for our plans to change. The cafe is located in the heart of a bustling residential neighborhood, and when it opened good breakfast spots were few and far between. Soon after we opened our doors, customers were quick to let us know what they wanted. They loved the breakfast pastries we offered, but what they were craving was a weekend brunch. A couple of months later we developed the basic brunch menu that is still with us today. The lines get long from time to time, but it's worth the wait.

Rustic breads and pastries are the backbone of our business, and working them into our brunch menu came naturally. French Toast? No problem, but would you like that made with Macrina Casera, Classic Brioche, Challah, Panettone, or Rustic Potato Loaf? A basket of pastries? Would you like Rocket Muffins, Cherry Almond Scones, Morning Rolls, Hazelnut Orange Pinwheels, or a variety of Buttermilk Biscuits? The options are endless when you have your own bakery. We try to use as many regional purveyors as possible for other items on our brunch menu, searching out local providers for fresh bacon, sausage, smoked salmon, and all of our produce.

This chapter features recipes for some of our most popular brunch dishes. We've included the wildly popular Fried Egg Sandwich as well as our Buttermilk Waffles and German Pancake. Some of the dishes require a little extra preparation, much of which can be done the night before. If you can't spend part of your weekend with us in Belltown, these recipes will help satisfy your cravings. Serve any one of them with a basket of fresh baked pastries, and you can't go wrong.

GINGERBREAD CRÊPES WITH CITRON RICOTTA, CRANBERRY COMPOTE & VANILLA SYRUP

Jeanine Riss, one of our former chefs, created these crêpes for a special Christmas Eve brunch at our cafe. They were a big hit, selling out earlier than expected. Jeanine found it best to prepare and fill the crêpes one day in advance. That way, all she had to do in the morning was prepare the compote and syrup and reheat the crêpes before serving.

Serves 4

FOR THE CRÊPES:
1 cup unbleached all-purpose flour
2 tablespoons granulated sugar
1 teaspoon ground ginger
1 teaspoon cinnamon
¼ teaspoon ground cloves
1 ⅓ cups whole milk
2 eggs
2 tablespoons molasses
3 tablespoons unsalted butter, melted
Canola oil

FOR THE CITRON RICOTTA FILLING:
2 cups ricotta cheese
½ cup granulated sugar
½ cup candied citron*
1 teaspoon freshly grated orange zest

FOR THE CRANBERRY COMPOTE:
2 cups fresh cranberries
½ cup water
¾ cup granulated sugar
1 tablespoon freshly grated orange zest
2 tablespoons unsalted butter

FOR THE VANILLA SYRUP:
1 cup pure maple syrup
1 vanilla bean

Powdered sugar
*available at specialty stores and some supermarkets

PREPARING THE CRÊPES:

- Combine flour, sugar, ginger, cinnamon, and cloves in a medium bowl. Toss together and set aside.

- In a separate medium bowl, combine milk, eggs, and molasses, and mix with a whisk. Slowly drizzle the milk mixture into the bowl of flour, whisking as you pour. When ingredients are fully combined, whisk in 1 tablespoon of the melted butter. Cover bowl with plastic wrap and place in the refrigerator for 2 hours.

- Heat a small (7-inch) nonstick sauté pan over medium heat and brush with a little canola oil. Ladle in just enough crêpe batter to evenly cover the bottom of the pan, about 2 tablespoons. Lift and tilt the pan to spread out the batter more quickly. Cook until edges start to turn brown, about 1 minute, then flip the crêpe over with a spatula and cook the other side. Transfer finished crêpe to a large plate and cover crêpe with a piece of parchment paper. Repeat with the rest of the batter, placing paper between each crêpe as you finish. You should have 8 crêpes.

PREPARING THE CITRON RICOTTA FILLING AND ASSEMBLING THE CRÊPES:

- Combine ricotta cheese, sugar, candied citron, and orange zest in a medium bowl and mix well with a wooden spoon.

- Line a rimmed baking sheet with parchment paper.

- Lay the crêpes out on a work surface and scoop equal portions of citron filling onto the center of each crêpe. Roll each of the crêpes into a log and place them, seam sides down, on the prepared baking sheet. Brush tops with the remaining melted butter. (It may be necessary to reheat the butter.)

- At this point the crêpes can be wrapped with plastic wrap and stored in the refrigerator overnight. If you are ready to eat, move on to the next step.

PREPARING THE CRANBERRY COMPOTE:

- Combine cranberries, water, sugar, and orange zest in a medium saucepan. Cook over medium heat until cranberries begin to burst, 5 to 7 minutes. Remove pan from heat and drop in butter, stirring until butter is melted and evenly distributed. Set aside.

PREPARING THE VANILLA SYRUP:

- Pour maple syrup into a medium saucepan. Cut vanilla bean in half lengthwise and, using the tip of a sharp knife, scrape seeds out of each half and add them to the pan.

- Drop opened bean pods into the syrup for extra flavor and simmer over low heat for 10 to 15 minutes. Remove bean pods and set aside.

FINISHING THE CRÊPES:

- Preheat oven to 350°F.
- Place baking sheet of crêpes on center rack of oven and bake for 10 minutes. Crêpes will be heated through and golden brown on the edges.
- While crêpes are baking, reheat the cranberry compote and the vanilla syrup.
- Place 2 crêpes in the center of each plate and top with a generous scoop of compote. Drizzle warm syrup around the edges of the crêpes, then garnish the plate with a little powdered sugar. Serve while still warm.

MACRINA'S FRIED EGG SANDWICH

Many of our regular customers would be in an uproar if we replaced this mainstay of our weekly brunch menu. The combination of grilled potato bread, melted Muenster cheese, and spicy tomato sauce makes this dish habit forming!

Serves 4

1 medium red onion
2 tablespoons olive oil
Kosher salt
Freshly ground black pepper
2 tablespoons balsamic vinegar
1 loaf Rustic Potato Loaf *(page 33)*
6 tablespoons unsalted butter, at room temperature
¼ cup Dijon mustard
4 slices Muenster cheese
8 eggs
1 cup Spicy Tomato Sauce *(recipe follows)*

- Preheat oven to 350°F.

- Peel onion and cut lengthwise into 8 wedges. Place wedges on a rimmed baking sheet, drizzle olive oil over the wedges, and season with a little salt and pepper. Roast on center rack of oven for 20 to 25 minutes, or until edges are golden brown. Remove from oven and spoon balsamic vinegar over hot onions. Set aside to cool.

- Cut 8 generous (½-inch-thick) slices of Rustic Potato Loaf and lightly butter 1 side of each slice. (Use 4 tablespoons of the butter for 8 slices of bread.)

- Heat a cast-iron skillet or nonstick frying pan to medium heat. Place 2 slices of bread, buttered sides down, on the heated surface. Spread a little Dijon mustard on top of 1 piece and place a slice of Muenster cheese on the other piece. (Make sure the slice of cheese doesn't hang over the sides of the bread.)

- While bread is grilling, place ½ tablespoon of the remaining butter in another nonstick frying pan and place over medium heat. Fry 2 eggs in the butter. (I recommend serving them over-medium.) Season eggs with a little salt and freshly ground black pepper. Slide the cooked eggs on top of the mustard-coated slice of potato bread, then lift both slices of bread onto a dinner plate. Top the eggs with one quarter of the roasted onions and a generous portion (about ¼ cup) of warm Spicy Tomato Sauce. Finish the sandwich by flipping the cheese-topped slice of bread over onto the egg-and-tomato-sauce-topped slice. Cut the sandwich in half diagonally. Repeat with remaining bread and eggs.

Spicy Tomato Sauce

You can also use this sauce to jazz up scrambled eggs or toss it with your favorite pasta.

Makes about 1 cup

1 dried pasilla pepper*
2 tablespoons olive oil
½ medium yellow onion, diced
2 garlic cloves, thinly sliced
1 tablespoon ground cumin
1 tablespoon ground coriander
6 Roma tomatoes, chopped
¼ cup chopped fresh cilantro leaves
Kosher salt
Freshly ground black pepper

available in specialty shops and some supermarkets

- Place dried pepper in a small bowl, cover with boiling water, and soak for 10 to 15 minutes. Let cool, drain well, then remove the core and seeds from the pepper. Coarsely chop and set aside.

- Place olive oil in a medium saucepan and heat to medium-low. Add the onion and cook, covered, for about 5 minutes, or until translucent. Stir in the garlic, cumin, and coriander, and cook for another 1 to 2 minutes. Add tomatoes and chopped pasilla to the pan and increase heat to medium. Simmer for 10 to 15 minutes.

- Remove from heat and add cilantro. Season to taste with salt and freshly ground black pepper. This sauce is best served warm. After the sauce has completely cooled, it can be stored in an airtight container for up to 4 days in the refrigerator.

BREAKFAST STRATA WITH
GRILLED PORTOBELLO MUSHROOMS,
FONTINA & ROASTED ONIONS

We make a version of this strata every weekend at our cafe. It's also a popular carryout item for customers on their way out of town. One couple told me they like to take some with them when they go hiking in the nearby Cascade Mountains. It's a good idea to assemble this strata the evening before you want to serve it, then all you'll have to do in the morning is bake it.

Serves 4 to 6

3 cups half-and-half

7 eggs

Kosher salt

1½ teaspoons white pepper

3 medium portobello mushroom caps, cleaned

½ cup olive oil

2 garlic cloves, finely chopped

1 tablespoon chopped fresh rosemary

Freshly ground black pepper

1 medium yellow onion, diced

8 cups oven-dried white bread cubes (about 1½ loaves cut into 1-inch cubes)

2½ cups grated fontina cheese

¼ cup chopped fresh Italian parsley

- Combine half-and-half, eggs, 1½ teaspoons of the kosher salt, and white pepper in a medium bowl. Mix with a whisk until fully blended. Cover bowl and place in the refrigerator.

- Preheat oven to 325°F. Line a rimmed baking sheet with parchment paper.

- Heat a cast-iron skillet to medium-high. When the skillet starts to smoke, brush mushrooms with a little of the olive oil and lay them, top sides down, on the skillet. Cook mushrooms just until lightly brown, then turn them over and brown the other sides.

- Transfer mushrooms to the prepared baking sheet and sprinkle garlic and ½ tablespoon of the rosemary over the tops. Season with a little kosher salt, freshly ground black pepper, and a drizzle of the remaining olive oil. Roast mushrooms on center rack of oven for about 10 minutes, or until they are tender to the touch. Let cool for 10 minutes, then cut into ½-inch-square pieces. Set aside.

- Pour remaining olive oil into a large sauté pan and bring to medium heat. Add onion and the remaining ½ tablespoon of rosemary and season with salt and freshly ground black pepper. Cook for 8 to 10 minutes, or until onions are golden brown and caramelized. Set aside.

- Brush a 9-inch square baking dish with olive oil. Place half of the bread cubes in the bottom of the dish, then layer half of the mushrooms, onions, fontina cheese, and parsley on top. Add the remaining bread cubes and top with the rest of the mushrooms, onions, cheese, and parsley.

- Remove custard from the refrigerator and pour over the bread cubes, filling the dish to just below the top. Place a dinner plate on top of the bread cubes to weigh them down and help them absorb all of the moisture. Set aside for 20 minutes or store in the refrigerator overnight.

- Preheat oven to 325°F.

- Remove the plate from the strata and cover the baking dish with aluminum foil. Poke 2 small vent holes in opposite corners of the foil. Bake strata on center rack of oven for 1 hour, then carefully remove the foil and continue baking for another 15 minutes. Finished strata will be golden brown and the custard will be set in the center. Let cool slightly and serve warm.

OLD-FASHIONED BUTTERMILK
WAFFLES WITH
FRESH BERRIES & CREAM

One of the best waffles I ever had was at San Francisco's Sears Fine Food on Union Square. What I loved most about it was that it stayed crisp long after it had cooled, and even after I smothered it with butter and maple syrup. In that tradition, our brunch chef, Amy Pinkis, created this waffle recipe for us.

Serves 4

1 cup semolina flour

⅓ cup whole-wheat flour

3 tablespoons fine cornmeal

2 teaspoons baking soda

1 tablespoon light brown sugar

5 tablespoons granulated sugar

½ teaspoon kosher salt

2 eggs

1 ⅓ cups buttermilk

4 tablespoons unsalted butter, melted and slightly cooled

2 cups (1 pint) fresh raspberries

2 cups (1 pint) fresh blackberries

2 teaspoons freshly grated lemon zest

1 cup heavy cream
1 tablespoon pure vanilla extract
½ cup pure maple syrup
Canola oil for brushing waffle iron

- Combine semolina flour, whole-wheat flour, cornmeal, baking soda, brown sugar, 1 tablespoon of the granulated sugar, and salt in a medium bowl. Mix with a whisk and set aside.

- Separate the eggs, placing the yolks in one bowl and the whites in another. Add buttermilk and melted butter to the bowl of egg yolks. Mix with a whisk. In a slow stream, add the buttermilk mixture to the bowl of dry ingredients, mixing with a whisk to dissolve all lumps.

- Using a whisk or hand-held mixer, whip the egg whites until medium-firm peaks form. Gently fold the whipped egg whites into the bowl of batter with a rubber spatula and continue folding until there are no visible streaks of white.

- Combine raspberries, blackberries, lemon zest, and 3 tablespoons of the remaining granulated sugar in a medium bowl. Toss well and set aside.

- In another medium bowl, combine heavy cream, vanilla extract, and remaining tablespoon of granulated sugar. Mix with a whisk for 4 or 5 minutes, just until cream is softly whipped, then place in the refrigerator until ready to serve.

- Preheat your waffle iron.

- Pour maple syrup into a small saucepan and warm over low heat. Keep warm until ready to serve.

- Oil the preheated waffle iron. Ladle waffle batter onto iron and cook until golden and crispy. The amount of batter and cooking time will depend on your individual waffle iron, but you should have enough batter for at least 4 waffles. Transfer finished waffle to a heated plate and repeat with remaining waffle batter. Pile berries in the center of each waffle and top with a generous spoonful of whipped cream. Drizzle warm maple syrup around edges of the waffle and serve.

Cinnamon French Toast
with Ricotta Filling

French toast is one of the best uses of leftover breads that I can think of, and at the bakery we're lucky to have a wide range of options to choose from. This recipe calls for Classic Brioche Loaf, but feel free to experiment with your favorite loaves.

Serves 4

FOR THE RICOTTA FILLING:
1 cup ricotta cheese
2 tablespoons granulated sugar
1 tablespoon freshly grated lemon zest

My Favorite Breakfast

Everyone has his or her favorite breakfast restaurant. Mine is located in my hometown of Portland, Oregon, a town famous for many things. Personally I think it should be famous for being the birthplace of the original "Original Pancake House." This white house, with its green striped awnings, sits just off one of Portland's freeway exits, where it calls to me each time I pass through the city. Inside, the familiar faces of the never-changing wait staff greet customers with smiles and strong coffee. This is breakfast at its best.

The childhood meals I had at the Original Pancake House defined breakfast for me, and influence me to this day. I can remember eating a bowl of sweet Oregon strawberries, served with a pitcher of real cream and a bowl of powdered sugar. Other favorites included the famous Apple Cinnamon Pancake, which required a thirty-minute wait and a hearty appetite. No problem. The pancake was five inches high and smothered with cinnamon glazed apples, which drew the attention of everyone in the restaurant as it arrived. I've been searching for a similar recipe for years, a version of which can be found in this chapter (see page 188) and on our cafe's brunch menu.

I still love going out to breakfast, though I don't get to visit the Original Pancake House as often as I would like. But the next time you're in Portland, I recommend stopping by.

FOR THE CINNAMON TOPPING:

½ cup light brown sugar
½ cup granulated sugar
2 tablespoons cinnamon
½ teaspoon ground nutmeg
8 tablespoons (1 stick) unsalted butter, at room temperature
¼ cup pure maple syrup

FOR THE FRENCH TOAST:

3 eggs
1 teaspoon pure vanilla extract
1 tablespoon light brown sugar
2½ cups whole milk
1 Classic Brioche Loaf (*page 43*)
¼ cup canola oil
2 nectarines, pitted and cut into ¼-inch slices
4 sprigs fresh mint
Powdered sugar

PREPARING THE RICOTTA FILLING:

- Combine ricotta, sugar, and lemon zest in a medium bowl. Mix well and set aside. This filling can be made in advance and stored, covered, in the refrigerator for up to 2 days.

PREPARING THE CINNAMON TOPPING:

- Combine all of the ingredients in a small saucepan and place over medium heat. Stir frequently until butter is melted and all of the ingredients are combined, about 2 minutes. Set aside.

PREPARING THE FRENCH TOAST:

- Combine eggs, vanilla extract, brown sugar, and milk in a medium bowl. Mix with a whisk, then pour into a shallow baking pan.

- Cut 4 generous (about 1½ inches thick) slices from the Classic Brioche Loaf. Using a sharp paring knife, cut a pocket into the side of each slice. Try not to cut all the way through the slices. Fill each pocket with one quarter of the ricotta filling, taking care not to tear through the bread.

- Preheat oven to 400°F. Line a rimmed baking sheet with parchment paper.

- Preheat a large sauté pan over medium heat and add half of the canola oil. Gently dredge 2 slices of stuffed brioche in the pan of batter, making sure all sides are evenly coated. Lay slices in the preheated pan and cook until both sides are golden brown, then transfer them to the prepared baking sheet. Add remaining canola oil to the sauté pan and repeat process with remaining slices.

- Spoon the warm cinnamon topping onto the browned slices of French toast and bake on center rack of oven for about 5 minutes, until the topping starts to bubble at the edges and a thin crust has formed on top of the bread.

- Place French toast on 4 plates and top with nectarine slices and fresh mint. Using a spoon, scoop any remaining cinnamon glaze off the baking sheet and drizzle it over the French toast. Dust plates with a little powdered sugar and serve.

GERMAN PANCAKE WITH APPLES, RUM & BROWN SUGAR

Our version of a German pancake is started on your stove top, then finished in the oven. This recipe calls for apples, but you could substitute peaches, plums, or bananas.

Serves 2

3 eggs
¾ cup whole milk
1 tablespoon pure vanilla extract
¾ cup unbleached all-purpose flour
2 tablespoons granulated sugar
¼ teaspoon kosher salt
4 tablespoons unsalted butter
2 Granny Smith apples, peeled and cored
½ cup light brown sugar
2 teaspoons cinnamon
¼ cup dark rum
Powdered sugar

- Preheat oven to 400°F.

- Combine eggs, milk, and vanilla extract in a medium bowl. Mix with a whisk and set aside.

- In another medium bowl, combine flour, granulated sugar, and salt and mix with a wooden spoon. Set aside.

- Melt 2 tablespoons of the butter in an oven safe 9-inch sauté pan. Remove from heat and let cool for 3 minutes. Add bowl of wet ingredients to bowl of dry ingredients and mix well with a whisk, making sure to dissolve all lumps. Pour most of the melted butter into bowl of batter, leaving just enough butter in the pan to coat the bottom. Mix butter into the batter with a whisk.

- Place the butter-coated sauté pan over medium heat. When butter starts to sizzle (but not turn brown), pour in the pancake batter. Cook for 2 to 3 minutes, just until the edges of the pancake start to turn brown. Place pan on center rack of oven and bake for about 20 minutes. The finished pancake will be fluffy and golden brown.

- While pancake is baking, slice each of the apples into 12 pieces. Place remaining 2 tablespoons of butter, brown sugar, and cinnamon in a medium saucepan and cook over low heat until the mixture starts to bubble. Add rum and mix well. Drop in the apples and mix with a spoon to coat all of the slices. Cook for about 15 minutes, until slices are fork-tender, then cover and remove from heat.

- Remove the pancake from the oven and loosen the edges with a spatula. Remove pancake from pan and place in center of a large serving platter. Pour cooked apples onto center of pancake and dust the edges with powdered sugar. Serve hot.

James Beard Brunch

In April of 1999 I had the honor of cooking at the James Beard House in New York City. James Beard, the legendary food writer, had long been a hero of mine and I had read all of his books, so when I was invited to prepare a "Baker's Brunch" (menu follows on page 193) at his esteemed home I didn't hesitate for a second. I gathered together my pastry chef at the time, Katie Fuller, and my café chef, Jeanine Riss, and we sat down to plan our menu. Before long we were packing boxes of Northwest goodies and were on our way.

Cooking at the James Beard House has one famous challenge—lack of space. Guest chefs need to arrive with most of their preparations done in advance. Luckily my good friend Amy Scherber, owner of Amy's Breads (and author of a fantastic cookbook of her own), offered us some kitchen space at her Chelsea Market bakery. Not only was the bakery close to the Beard House, but we were also able to buy all of our last-minute supplies right there in the Market.

We started working the day before the big event, pre-baking tart shells and crêpes, rolling out croissant dough, and preparing mixes for biscuits and coffee cakes. Then came the morning of the brunch, and we had to figure out how to get all that food over to the Beard House. It would have taken three cab rides, but once again Amy helped out, offering the use of one of her delivery vans. We were able to transport everything in a matter of minutes. Then it was time to get back to work.

We didn't waste any time after we arrived in the kitchen. Katie got busy baking Raspberry & Brown Sugar Coffee Cakes, Apple Frangipane Braids, and Buttermilk Biscuits. Jeanine went straight to the grill, searing her handmade sausages and marking slices of brioche. I was hard at work on the hors d'oeuvres, miniature Pressed Ham Sandwiches and Crab Canapés, to name just two. We worked at a crazy pace, but finished in time to test the sparkling wine that we were serving at the brunch. It was a perfect match, and a perfect pick-me-up.

Guests enter the James Beard House through the kitchen. This would be a little unsettling in a busy restaurant, but on that day it was a treat. We were able to meet our guests as they arrived and offer them a sampling of what to expect. The brunch lasted three hours, starting with the savory hors d'oeuvres and ending with Strawberry Rhubarb Tartlets. It was a lot of fun and a great success, the only complaint being that people couldn't stop eating.

Egg Scramble with Delicata Squash, Spinach, Smoked Provolone & Beurre Blanc Sauce

We like to change our brunch "scramble" every weekend so that we can highlight the finest local produce available at the time. This combination, topped with rich Beurre Blanc Sauce, is one of my favorites.

Serves 2

4 eggs
1 small (about 8 ounces) Delicata squash
1 teaspoon chopped fresh thyme
3 tablespoons olive oil
Kosher salt
Freshly ground black pepper
4 slices Rustic Baguette *(page 13)*
2 tablespoons unsalted butter, at room temperature
2 cups chopped fresh spinach
2 garlic cloves, finely chopped
2 slices smoked provolone cheese
Beurre Blanc Sauce *(recipe follows)*
2 tablespoons chopped fresh Italian parsley

- Crack eggs into a medium bowl and mix with a whisk. Place in the refrigerator until needed.

- Preheat oven to 375°F. Line a rimmed baking sheet with parchment paper.

- Remove stem from squash and cut it in half lengthwise. Scoop out any seeds with a spoon, then cut each half into ¼-inch slices, leaving the skin on. In a medium bowl, combine squash slices, thyme, and 2 tablespoons of the olive oil. Toss until slices are evenly coated, then spread slices evenly on the prepared baking sheet. Season with a little salt and pepper. Bake on center rack of oven until slices are tender, about 15 minutes. Set aside to cool.

- Heat a 9-inch sauté pan over medium heat. Butter both sides of the baguette slices and cook, turning once, until both sides are golden brown. Place 2 slices each onto 2 plates and set aside.

- Make Beurre Blanc Sauce just before starting the next step.

- Remove bowl of eggs from the refrigerator. Add remaining 1 tablespoon of olive oil to the sauté pan and heat to medium-high. Place spinach in the pan and cook for about 30 seconds. Add the garlic and toss together. When garlic starts to smell sweet (after 1 to 2 minutes), add the eggs and stir with a wooden spoon until cooked, 2 to 3 minutes (depending on how firm you like the eggs). Season to taste with salt and freshly ground black pepper.

- Divide scrambled eggs between the 2 plates, covering the toasted bread. Top eggs with a slice of provolone. Lay pieces of roasted squash on top of the cheese, then ladle hot Beurre Blanc Sauce over all. Garnish with chopped Italian parsley.

BEURRE BLANC SAUCE

Makes approximately ¾ cup

1 tablespoon canola oil
2 tablespoons finely diced shallots
1 cup dry white wine
½ teaspoon chopped fresh thyme
8 ounces (2 sticks) unsalted butter, at room temperature
Kosher salt
Freshly ground black pepper

- Pour canola oil into a medium saucepan and bring to medium-low heat. Add shallots and cook for 1 to 2 minutes, until shallots are translucent. Add wine and thyme and bring to a simmer. Let cook until wine has reduced to about ¼ cup, approximately 15 minutes.

- Reduce heat to low and add a small amount of butter, about 1 tablespoon. Stir with a whisk until butter melts and is blended into the sauce. Whisking continuously, continue adding pieces of butter until all of the butter has been incorporated and the sauce has thickened. Make sure the sauce doesn't get too hot; if it boils, the sauce will separate and you'll have to start all over. Season to taste with salt and freshly ground black pepper. *Note: It's best to serve this sauce immediately. Remove the pan from the heat, leaving it on the stovetop to stay warm, and prepare the eggs. Stir sauce with a whisk one more time before serving.*

The Baker's Brunch
at James Beard House

April 11, 1999

Pressed Ham Sandwiches

Organic Oregon Cheddar & Crab Canapés

Walnut Crostini with Tuscan White Bean Purée, Arugula, and Agrumato Oil

Pacific Echo Brut

Gratin of Seasonal Fruits and Citrus Sabayon

Basket of Macrina's Breakfast Pastries
(Raisin Brioche, Apple Frangipane Braid, Raspberry & Brown Sugar Coffee Cake, Mini Buttermilk Biscuit)

Smoked Copper River Salmon & Grilled Asparagus on Buttered Brioche

Chestnut Crêpes with Fresh Ricotta, Tart Cherries, and Muscadet Grapes Served with House Sausage

Pacific Echo Crémant

Sliver of Fudge Pie with Soft Vanilla Ice Cream

Petite Strawberry Rhubarb Tartlet

BACON, LEEK & GRUYÈRE QUICHE

Quiche is making a comeback! Serve alongside fresh fruit or a simple green salad.

Makes 1 (9-inch) quiche

5 slices bacon
3 medium leeks
3 tablespoons olive oil
Kosher salt
Freshly ground black pepper
2 eggs
2 egg yolks
1 cup heavy cream
1 cup whole milk
½ teaspoon ground white pepper
1 teaspoon chopped fresh thyme
1 teaspoon chopped fresh Italian parsley
2 ounces (about 4 slices) Gruyère cheese, chopped or grated
1 pre-baked (9-inch) Flaky Pie Dough tart shell *(page 129)*

- Cut bacon into ¼-inch pieces and place in a medium sauté pan. Cook over medium heat until fat is rendered and bacon is golden brown. Remove bacon with a slotted spoon and drain on paper towels.

- Remove most of the green portion of the leeks and discard. Cut remaining white portions in half lengthwise. Rinse leeks well under running water, then cut into ¼-inch slices. (You should have about 3 cups of sliced leeks.)

- Heat olive oil in a medium sauté pan over medium heat. Add the sliced leeks and season with salt and black pepper. Cook until leeks are tender, 3 to 5 minutes. Remove from heat.

- Preheat oven to 325°F.

- Combine eggs, egg yolks, heavy cream, milk, ½ teaspoon kosher salt, white pepper, thyme, and parsley in a medium bowl. Mix well with a whisk.

- Evenly spread bacon, leeks, and Gruyère cheese over the bottom of the pre-baked tart shell. Place shell on a rimmed baking sheet, then fill the shell with the custard mixture. Carefully transfer the baking sheet to the center rack of the oven and bake until custard is set and lightly browned on top, about 45 minutes. Remove from oven and let cool on a wire rack for 15 minutes before serving.

Chapter 13

LUNCH

Macrina's Organic Greens Salad with Balsamic Vinaigrette

French Lentil Soup with Roasted Tomatoes & Peppers

Corn Chowder with Pink Potatoes & Cream

Tuscan Tomato & Fennel Soup with White Beans

Butternut Squash & Apple Galette

Roasted Tomato & Olive Galette with Fontina

Salmon Paillard on Mixed Greens with Mustard Vinaigrette

Roasted Goat Cheese Salad with Vintner's Vinaigrette

Orecchiette Salad with Roasted Beets, Fennel & Toasted Almonds

Orzo Salad with Cucumber, Bell Peppers, Basil & Feta

Chicken Tagine with Lemon & Olives

Sweet Potato Gnocchi with Sage Cream & Romano Cheese

Egg Salad Sandwich on Greek Olive Bread with
Roasted Tomatoes & Anchovies

Every morning Macrina opens its doors to a flood of people anticipating their morning coffee, fresh pastries, and fruit salads. It's a busy, casual scene. But by eleven o'clock the room is transformed. The tables are set with linen napkins and freshly printed copies of our daily menu. Dessert specials are described on the chalkboard, loaves of fresh bread are chosen for service, and waiters ask our chef about the daily specials. The "please wait to be seated" sign goes up, and it's time for lunch.

The format of our lunch menu never changes, but the daily selection is rarely duplicated. Offerings depend on what's fresh and available from our suppliers, changing dramatically with each season. For example, some days we rearrange the entire menu because our friend Merv Dykstra has dropped off cases of fresh produce from farms in eastern Washington. A simple salad or dessert can be suddenly transformed by the arrival of Merv's nectarines. Lunch fare at Macrina isn't fancy, but I like to think it's soul satisfying. We make use of simple preparations, accentuating the natural flavors of each ingredient. This chapter includes a wide range of recipes from our café, from hearty soups and simple salads to comfort food and picnic favorites. There's a dish for every season. Enjoy!

Macrina's Organic Greens Salad with Balsamic Vinaigrette

Filled with a variety of flavors, this simple salad of local organic greens accompanies every entrée served at our café.

Serves 4

1 medium red onion
¼ cup olive oil
Kosher salt
Freshly ground black pepper
2 tablespoons balsamic vinegar
½ cup whole almonds
1 tablespoon freshly grated lemon zest
10 ounces organic salad greens, washed and dried
½ cup Balsamic Vinaigrette *(recipe follows)*
12 olives (your favorite assortment)

- Preheat oven to 350°F.

- Peel onion and cut lengthwise into 8 wedges. Place wedges on a rimmed baking sheet, drizzle 2 tablespoons of the olive oil over the wedges, and season with a little salt and pepper. Roast on center rack of oven for 20 to 25 minutes, or until edges are golden brown. Remove from oven and spoon balsamic vinegar over hot onions. Set aside to cool. Leave oven on.

- Spread almonds on a rimmed baking sheet and toast for about 15 minutes, or until golden brown. Let cool for 20 minutes. Place toasted almonds in a small bowl with the remaining 2 tablespoons of olive oil and lemon zest. Toss ingredients together to coat almonds, then season with salt and pepper to taste.

- Combine salad greens and Balsamic Vinaigrette in a large bowl and toss until greens are coated. Divide greens among 4 salad plates and garnish each salad with a wedge of roasted onion, toasted almonds, and olives.

BALSAMIC VINAIGRETTE

We've been using this vinaigrette recipe since tossing the first salad at our café.

Makes approximately 1¼ cups

2 tablespoons chopped fresh Italian parsley
1 tablespoon Dijon mustard
1½ teaspoons chopped garlic
¼ cup balsamic vinegar
1 teaspoon freshly grated lemon zest
½ cup canola oil
¼ cup extra virgin olive oil
Kosher salt
Freshly ground black pepper

• Combine parsley, mustard, garlic, vinegar, and lemon zest in a medium bowl. Mix with a whisk to combine. Add canola oil in a slow stream, whisking as you pour in the oil. Add olive oil in the same manner. Season to taste with salt and pepper, then store, covered, in the refrigerator for up to 5 days.

FRENCH LENTIL SOUP WITH ROASTED TOMATOES & PEPPERS

This soup recipe is one of many brought to Macrina by the talented Chef Kim Abrams-Marshall. Enjoyed in our cozy café, it's a perfect comfort food on a drizzly Seattle day. We like to serve the soup with a few slices of crostini topped with goat cheese and a drizzle of good olive oil. If you can't find French green lentils at your supermarket you can substitute regular lentils.

Serves 4 to 6

4 Roma tomatoes
¾ cup olive oil
Kosher salt
Freshly ground black pepper
10 garlic cloves, peeled
1 medium yellow onion, diced
2 red bell peppers, diced
1 celery rib, diced
1½ tablespoons ground cumin

1½ tablespoons ground coriander seed
1½ cups French green lentils*
8 to 10 cups vegetable stock
1 tablespoon chopped fresh Italian parsley
1 teaspoon chopped fresh thyme
*available in specialty shops and some supermarkets

- Preheat oven to 400°F. Line a rimmed baking sheet with parchment paper.

- Wash and core the tomatoes, then cut them into 12 pieces each. Combine chopped tomatoes and ¼ cup of the olive oil in a bowl and toss together. Pour tomatoes onto the prepared baking sheet and spread into an even layer. Season with salt and pepper and roast on center rack of oven for about 15 minutes. Set aside.

- Place 7 of the garlic cloves and another ¼ cup of the olive oil in a small saucepan. Bring to a simmer over low heat and cook until cloves are tender, approximately 15 minutes. Swirl the pan occasionally to keep the cloves from sticking to the pan. Transfer cooked garlic cloves to a small bowl and mash into a paste. Set aside.

- Pour the remaining ¼ cup of olive oil into a large, heavy-bottomed soup pot. Add diced onion, bell peppers, and celery. Cover pot and cook for 15 minutes over medium-low heat to sweat the vegetables, stirring occasionally. The onions will become translucent. Finely dice the 3 remaining garlic cloves and add to the soup pot along with the cumin and coriander. Continue cooking over medium-low heat for 1 minute, or until garlic smells sweet but is not brown.

- Add roasted tomatoes, mashed garlic, lentils, and 8 cups of the vegetable stock, and bring to a simmer. Cook soup for 45 to 50 minutes, or until lentils are tender, adding more stock as needed. If foam gathers on the surface of the soup, remove it with a spoon. Before serving, add parsley and thyme and season to taste with salt and pepper.

CORN CHOWDER WITH
PINK POTATOES & CREAM

This soup is a perfect way to celebrate the sweetness of ripe corn.
It can be made quickly and is light enough to enjoy on a warm summer evening.

Serves 4 to 6

2 tablespoons olive oil
1 medium yellow onion, diced
2 garlic cloves, finely diced
8 to 10 cups water
Kosher salt
4 ears fresh corn, shucked and cut in half crosswise
¼ cup heavy cream
4 medium red new potatoes, washed and chopped into ¼-inch pieces
1 tablespoon chopped fresh thyme
Freshly ground black pepper
½ cup sour cream
2 tablespoons freshly squeezed lime juice

- Pour the olive oil into a large, heavy-bottomed soup pot and add onion. Cover pot and cook for 15 minutes over medium-low heat to sweat the onion, stirring occasionally. The onions will become translucent. Add garlic and continue cooking over medium-low heat for 1 minute, or until garlic smells sweet but is not brown.

- Add 8 cups of the water and ½ teaspoon salt and bring to a boil. Carefully drop in the ears of corn and cook until kernels are tender, 4 to 6 minutes. Remove corn and set aside to cool for 5 minutes.

- Remove kernels from the cobs with a knife, then place the cobs and half of the kernels back in the soup pot. Cook over medium heat for 30 minutes, then remove the cobs and discard. Add the heavy cream, potatoes, and thyme, and simmer over medium heat until potatoes are tender, adding more water as needed, about 15 minutes. Season to taste with salt and pepper. Add the remaining kernels of corn just before serving.

- In a small bowl, combine ½ teaspoon salt, sour cream, and lime juice. Mix well and drizzle over steaming bowls of soup.

Tuscan Tomato & Fennel Soup with White Beans

This is a frequently requested recipe from the collection of our chef, Kim Abrams-Marshall. She likes to pair the rich tomato soup with a gooey grilled cheese sandwich made with smoky bacon and roasted tomatoes.

Serves 4 to 6

1 cup dried white beans
2 bay leaves
¼ cup olive oil
1 medium yellow onion, diced
2 medium fennel bulbs, diced
4 garlic cloves, finely diced
1 tablespoon ground fennel seed
2 tablespoons chopped fresh thyme
10 Roma tomatoes
6 to 8 cups vegetable stock
½ cup chopped fennel fronds
Kosher salt
Freshly ground black pepper
¼ cup Aioli *(recipe follows)*

- Soak beans in water overnight.

- Drain beans and place in a medium saucepan. Cover with water and add bay leaves. Simmer over medium heat for about 20 minutes, or until beans are slightly tender. Reserve 1 cup of the cooking liquid, drain beans, and set aside.

- Combine olive oil, onion, and fennel in a large, heavy-bottomed soup pot. Cover pot and cook for 15 minutes over medium-low heat to sweat the vegetables, stirring occasionally. The onions will become translucent. Add garlic, fennel seed, and thyme. Cover pot and continue cooking over medium-low heat for 1 minute, or until garlic smells sweet but is not brown.

- Wash and core the tomatoes, then cut them into 12 pieces each and add them to the soup. Increase heat to medium and cook for 20 to 30 minutes, or until tomatoes are fully cooked and falling apart. Add 6 cups of the vegetable stock and the reserved bean-cooking liquid. Bring to a boil, then simmer over medium heat, uncovered, for 20 minutes to concentrate the flavors. Add more stock as needed.
- Add the cooked white beans and chopped fennel fronds, and season to taste with salt and pepper. Ladle soup into bowls and garnish with a little Aioli.

AIOLI

Makes approximately 1 cup

2 garlic cloves, diced
2 egg yolks
1 teaspoon Dijon mustard
2 teaspoons freshly squeezed lemon juice
1 cup canola oil
Kosher salt
Cayenne pepper

- In a medium bowl, combine garlic, egg yolks, mustard, and lemon juice. Mix well with a whisk. Add canola oil in a slow stream, whisking as you pour in the oil. Continue whisking until the sauce has emulsified and thickened slightly. Season to taste with salt and cayenne pepper. Store in airtight container for up to 3 days in the refrigerator.

Butternut Squash & Apple
Galette

*During the bakery's first months of operation I had the pleasure of
meeting dozens of wonderful customers. One woman, visiting from New York,
came twice a day for what she called her "necessities." We became friends, and a few months
later she mailed me an article showcasing savory galettes, or free-form folded tarts. "These
would be perfect in your café," she wrote across the bottom. We started experimenting with
the recipes—and have been serving our versions ever since. At Macrina, our galettes have
a crust of Flaky Pie Dough, encasing a sweet or savory filling. Try a small slice as
part of an appetizer plate or enjoy a large piece with a dinner salad.*

Serves 8 to 10

2 Granny Smith apples
½ teaspoon ground allspice
1 teaspoon cinnamon
¼ teaspoon ground cloves
2 tablespoons unsalted butter
3 cups Roasted Butternut Squash *(page 85)* or canned pumpkin
2 tablespoons light brown sugar
3 eggs
½ teaspoon kosher salt
1 tablespoon finely chopped fresh sage
½ recipe Flaky Pie Dough *(page 127)*, chilled
Egg wash made with 1 egg and 1 teaspoon water
2 ounces Gorgonzola cheese
1 tablespoon coarsely chopped fresh Italian parsley

- Line a rimmed baking sheet with parchment paper.

- Core and peel the apples and cut into ½-inch wedges. Place wedges in a medium
  bowl and toss with half of the allspice, half of the cinnamon, and half of the ground
  cloves.

- Melt butter in a medium saucepan over medium-low heat, then add the spiced
  apples and continue cooking for another 5 minutes, or until apples are tender. Set
  aside to cool.

- Combine butternut squash purée with the remaining allspice, cinnamon, and cloves in a large bowl. Add brown sugar, eggs, salt, and sage, and mix with a whisk to fully blend the ingredients.

- Form chilled pie dough into a ball and place it on a lightly floured work surface. Flatten ball slightly, then roll it into a 14-inch circle, about ⅛ inch thick. Carefully lift it onto the prepared baking sheet. Spoon squash mixture onto center of circle and spread to cover about 8 inches, leaving a 3-inch border. Place a single layer of apples in concentric circles on top of the squash filling. Lift border over top of the filling, tucking and folding the dough to create a gathered, or pleated, finish (see photos, below). Lift each of the folds up and brush underneath with egg wash to seal the crust. Brush all exposed dough with egg wash, then sprinkle Gorgonzola cheese and parsley on top. Place the baking sheet in the refrigerator and chill for 30 minutes.

- Preheat oven to 375°F.

- Remove tart from refrigerator and bake on center rack of oven for 55 to 60 minutes, or until crust is golden brown. Let cool on baking sheet for 20 minutes.

ROASTED TOMATO & OLIVE GALETTE WITH FONTINA

The filling in this galette recipe is a perfect showcase for all kinds of summer vegetables. Sweet, ripe tomatoes are roasted separately and added to the top of the tart just before serving. Roasting the tomatoes intensifies their flavor and keeps the filling from getting too wet.

Serves 8 to 10

2 cups grated fontina cheese
2 cups ricotta cheese
3 eggs
Kosher salt
1 teaspoon chopped fresh oregano

1 teaspoon chopped fresh thyme
Freshly ground black pepper
½ recipe Flaky Pie Dough *(page 127)*, chilled
Egg wash made with 1 egg and 1 teaspoon water
5 Roma tomatoes
⅓ cup extra virgin olive oil
8 leaves fresh arugula
1 cup kalamata olives, pitted and halved
1 teaspoon freshly grated lemon zest

- Line 2 rimmed baking sheets with parchment paper.

- Combine fontina cheese, ricotta, eggs, 1 teaspoon kosher salt, oregano, thyme, and a little freshly ground black pepper in a large bowl. Mix with a whisk to fully blend ingredients. Set aside.

- Form chilled pie dough into a ball and place it on a lightly floured work surface. Flatten ball slightly, then roll it into a 14-inch circle, about ⅛ inch thick. Carefully lift it onto a prepared baking sheet. Spoon ricotta mixture onto center of circle and flatten to cover 10 inches, leaving a 2-inch border. Lift border over top of the filling, tucking and folding the dough to create a gathered, or pleated, finish (see photos, left). Lift each of the folds up and brush underneath with egg wash to seal the crust. Brush all exposed dough with egg wash, then place the galette in the refrigerator and chill for at least 30 minutes.

- Preheat oven to 375°F.

- Wash and core the tomatoes, then cut them into 12 pieces each. Combine chopped tomatoes and ¼ cup of the olive oil in a bowl and toss together. Pour tomatoes onto a prepared baking sheet and spread into a single layer. Season with salt and pepper. Roast on center rack of oven for 35 to 40 minutes, or until edges are deep brown. Set aside to cool. Leave oven on.

- Remove tart from refrigerator and bake on center rack of oven for 55 to 60 minutes, or until crust is golden brown. Let cool on the baking sheet for 20 minutes.

- Cut or tear arugula leaves into 1-inch pieces and place in a bowl with olives, fresh lemon zest, and the remaining olive oil. Add a little salt and pepper, and toss together. Arrange arugula mixture on center of galette and scatter roasted tomatoes over the top. Serve at room temperature.

SALMON PAILLARD ON MIXED GREENS
WITH MUSTARD VINAIGRETTE

Macrina's first café chef, Ed Sata, understood the essence of what we were striving for, and his dishes defined our style. This recipe was one of his most popular and showcases some of the Northwest's local products. The roasted red peppers are readily available in cans and jars and in the deli section of many supermarkets.

Serves 4

8 ounces organic salad greens, washed and dried

12 leaves fresh basil, torn into small pieces

½ cup fresh cilantro leaves

4 (4-ounce) salmon fillets, with skin and bones removed

½ cup unbleached all-purpose flour

Kosher salt

Freshly ground black pepper

2 tablespoons canola oil

2 tablespoons unsalted butter

About 3 tablespoons Mustard Vinaigrette *(recipe follows)*

2 roasted red bell peppers, peeled, seeded, and cut into ½-inch-wide strips

¼ cup pine nuts, toasted

12 olives (your favorite assortment)

- Combine salad greens, half of the basil, and half of the cilantro in a large bowl. Toss together and set aside. Combine the remaining basil and cilantro in a small bowl.

- Place one of the salmon fillets in the center of a 10 x 10-inch piece of plastic wrap and fold one side of the plastic wrap over the salmon to cover it. Tap the salmon with a mallet or heavy frying pan to flatten it until it is ¼ to ½ inch thick. Flatten the remaining pieces.

- Pour flour into a pie pan. Carefully unwrap each piece of salmon and season 1 side of each fillet with salt and freshly ground black pepper. Gently press one quarter of the basil-cilantro mixture onto the seasoned side of each fillet. Dredge both sides of the fillets in flour and brush off any excess with your fingers. Set aside.

- Heat 1 tablespoon of the canola oil and 1 tablespoon of the butter in a large sauté pan over medium heat. Add 2 pieces of salmon and cook until golden brown, about 2 minutes, then gently turn them and cook for an additional 2 minutes. Set cooked salmon aside. Add the remaining canola oil and butter to the pan and cook the remaining 2 pieces of salmon.

• Toss the bowl of salad greens with just enough Mustard Vinaigrette to coat all of the leaves. Divide the salad among 4 plates and set the salmon fillets off-center on the greens. Garnish each plate with roasted red peppers, pine nuts, and olives. Drizzle a little more vinaigrette over the salmon and serve.

MUSTARD VINAIGRETTE

Makes 1 cup

1 tablespoon Dijon mustard
1 tablespoon sherry vinegar
1 tablespoon finely chopped shallots
1 teaspoon honey
1 teaspoon chopped fresh thyme
¾ cup extra virgin olive oil
Kosher salt
Freshly ground black pepper

• In a medium bowl, combine mustard, vinegar, shallots, honey, and thyme, and mix well with a whisk. Continue whisking and add the olive oil in a slow stream. Whisk until the dressing has emulsified, then season to taste with salt and freshly ground black pepper. Store in an airtight container for up to 5 days in the refrigerator.

ROASTED GOAT CHEESE SALAD WITH VINTNER'S VINAIGRETTE

One summer, while working at a restaurant on Nantucket Island, I read every James Beard book that I could get hold of. The Vintner's Vinaigrette for this salad was inspired by a recipe in Beard's Delights & Prejudices, *written in the 1960s.*

Serves 4

2 tablespoons chopped fresh oregano
2 tablespoons chopped fresh Italian parsley
1 teaspoon chopped fresh rosemary
8 ounces goat cheese, chilled
¼ cup unbleached all-purpose flour
1 egg
½ cup bread crumbs
4 tablespoons unsalted butter
8 ounces organic salad greens, washed and dried
About 4 to 5 tablespoons Vintner's Vinaigrette *(recipe follows)*
20 slices crostini *(page 26)*

- Combine oregano, parsley, and rosemary in a small bowl. Cut goat cheese into 4 equal pieces, then coat each piece with the mixed herbs. Pour flour into a small bowl. Dredge the pieces of herb-coated cheese in flour and brush off any excess with your fingers.

- Crack egg into a small bowl and beat with a fork. Pour bread crumbs into a small bowl. Using a pastry brush, gently coat each piece of cheese with egg, then cover with bread crumbs, making sure each piece is completely coated with crumbs. Place coated pieces of cheese on a plate and chill in the refrigerator until you are ready to assemble the salad.

- Preheat oven to 350°F.

- Melt butter in a medium saucepan over medium-low heat. (Make sure you are using a saucepan with an oven-safe handle.) Remove cheese from the refrigerator and place all 4 pieces in the bubbling butter. Cook until lightly brown on both sides, then place the pan in the oven and cook for 3 to 5 minutes more.

- While the cheese is in the oven, place salad greens in a large bowl and toss with Vintner's Vinaigrette. Divide greens among 4 dinner plates, then place a piece of hot cheese in the center of each plate. Drizzle a little more vinaigrette over the goat cheese and garnish each plate with homemade crostini. Serve while cheese is still warm.

Vintner's Vinaigrette

Makes approximately 1¼ cups

2 cups red wine
1 bay leaf
1 garlic clove, peeled
½ teaspoon Dijon mustard
½ teaspoon chopped garlic
¼ cup red wine vinegar
1 teaspoon chopped fresh lemon zest
¼ cup fresh Italian parsley
¼ cup extra virgin olive oil
¼ cup canola oil
Kosher salt
Freshly ground black pepper

- Combine red wine, bay leaf, and garlic clove in a medium saucepan (make sure that you are not using an aluminum pan). Cook over low heat until the wine has reduced to one fourth of its original volume. Remove bay leaf and garlic, then pour wine reduction into a small bowl and set aside to cool.

- Combine mustard, chopped garlic, vinegar, lemon zest, parsley, and the cooled wine reduction in the bowl of your food processor. Blend for about 2 minutes, making sure that all of the ingredients are finely chopped. With the blades turning, slowly drizzle in olive oil and canola oil. Blend until the dressing is emulsified. Season to taste with salt and pepper. Store in an airtight container for up to 5 days in the refrigerator.

ORECCHIETTE SALAD WITH ROASTED BEETS, FENNEL & TOASTED ALMONDS

We prepare a wide range of take-out foods at our retail cafés, including sage-roasted chickens, quiche and galettes, green salads, and focaccia. One of my favorites is this Orrechiette Salad from Chef Kim Abrams-Marshall. This particular recipe calls for roasted beets and fennel, but try using your favorite fresh vegetables year round.

Serves 4 to 6

2 medium golden beets, washed
4 tablespoons extra virgin olive oil
Kosher salt
Freshly ground black pepper
¾ cup whole almonds
2 cups dry orecchiette pasta
1 cup thinly sliced radicchio
½ cup thinly sliced fennel bulb
¼ cup chopped fennel fronds
½ cup diced scallions
¼ cup chopped fresh Italian parsley
⅓ cup Lemon Vinaigrette *(recipe follows)*

- Preheat oven to 350°F.

- Place washed beets in the center of a large piece of aluminum foil. Drizzle with 2 tablespoons of the olive oil and season with a little salt and pepper. Gather up the edges of the foil and seal the beets inside a pouch. Bake on center rack of oven for about 1 hour, or until beets are tender when poked with a fork. Let cool, then peel the beets and chop to a medium dice. Set aside. Leave oven on.

- Spread almonds on a rimmed baking sheet and toast for 15 minutes, or until golden brown. (This can be done while the beets are roasting.) Let almonds cool, then coarsely chop and set aside.

- Fill a large saucepan two-thirds full of water. Add a pinch of kosher salt and bring to a boil. Drop in pasta and simmer for 10 to 12 minutes, or until tender. Remove the pan from the heat and drain the pasta in a colander, then run cold water over the pasta for a few minutes until cooled. Shake the colander to remove excess water and transfer cooled pasta to a medium bowl. Toss in the remaining 2 tablespoons of olive oil to keep the pasta from sticking together.

- Add the diced beets, toasted almonds, radicchio, fennel bulb and fronds, scallions, and parsley. Drizzle in Lemon Vinaigrette and toss all ingredients together. Season to taste with kosher salt and freshly ground black pepper. Cover and store in the refrigerator for up to 2 days.

LEMON VINAIGRETTE

Makes approximately 1¼ cups

1 tablespoon Dijon mustard
2 teaspoons red wine vinegar
⅓ cup freshly squeezed lemon juice
1 teaspoon honey
1 tablespoon freshly grated lemon zest
1 garlic clove, finely chopped
1 teaspoon kosher salt
¼ teaspoon white pepper
¾ cup extra virgin olive oil

- Combine mustard, vinegar, lemon juice, honey, lemon zest, garlic, salt, and pepper in a medium bowl. Mix well with a whisk. Add olive oil in a slow stream, whisking as you pour in the oil. Continue whisking until the dressing has emulsified, then cover and store in the refrigerator for up to 4 days.

✓Orzo Salad with ~~Cucumber,~~ Bell Peppers, Basil & Feta

This is the most popular of all our take-out salads. Pack this up with a loaf of rustic bread and a wedge of your favorite cheese, and you have a perfect picnic.

Serves 4 to 6

1 cup walnut halves
~~1 cucumber~~
1 red bell pepper
1 yellow bell pepper
Kosher salt
1½ cups dry orzo pasta
2 tablespoons extra virgin olive oil
~~½ cup kalamata olives, pitted and halved~~
½ cup diced scallions
¼ cup chopped fresh basil
¼ cup chopped fresh Italian parsley
1¼ cups crumbled feta cheese
⅓ cup Lemon Vinaigrette *(page 211)*
Freshly ground black pepper

- Preheat oven to 350°F.

- Spread walnuts on a rimmed baking sheet and toast on center rack of oven for about 10 minutes, or until golden brown. Let cool, then coarsely chop and set aside.

- Peel and core cucumber and cut it into ½-inch cubes. Core the red and yellow peppers and cut them into ½-inch-square pieces. Set aside.

- Fill a large saucepan two-thirds full of water. Add a pinch of salt and bring to a boil. Drop in pasta and simmer for 3 to 5 minutes, or until tender. Remove the pan from the heat and drain the pasta in a colander, then cool the pasta by running cold tap water over the colander for a few minutes. Shake the colander to remove excess water and transfer the cooled pasta to a medium bowl. Toss with olive oil to keep the pasta from sticking together.

- Add the toasted walnuts, cucumber, peppers, olives, scallions, basil, parsley, and feta. Drizzle in Lemon Vinaigrette and toss well. Season to taste with salt and pepper. Cover and store in the refrigerator for up to 2 days.

CHICKEN TAGINE WITH LEMON & OLIVES

The word tagine *refers to a shallow Moroccan clay cooking pot used for making stews. It's a wonderful way of cooking if you happen to have one of the pots, but for this recipe I like to use a shallow cast-iron skillet. Slow cooking, as well as a combination of aromatic herbs and spices, makes this recipe irresistible. Serve with extra slices of your favorite bread for catching every last drop. To achieve the most robust flavors possible, be sure to marinate the chicken for two hours before cooking.*

Serves 4

½ cup freshly squeezed lemon juice

2 tablespoons ground cumin

2 tablespoons ground coriander

2 tablespoons ground turmeric

¼ teaspoon cayenne pepper

4 (6-ounce) boneless chicken breasts, cut into 1-inch-square pieces

2 medium yellow onions

¾ cup unbleached all-purpose flour

Kosher salt

Freshly ground black pepper

6 tablespoons olive oil

4 garlic cloves, chopped

1 teaspoon peeled and grated ginger

1 cup dry white wine

3 tablespoons freshly grated lemon zest

2 cups chicken stock

4 medium new potatoes, washed and quartered

1 cup kalamata olives, pitted and halved

1 loaf rustic bread

Extra virgin olive oil for brushing bread

¼ cup chopped fresh Italian parsley

¼ cup chopped fresh cilantro leaves

½ cup chopped scallions

- Combine lemon juice, 1 tablespoon of the cumin, 1 tablespoon of the coriander, 1 tablespoon of the turmeric, and ⅛ teaspoon of the cayenne pepper in a medium bowl. Mix with a whisk, then add the chicken and toss well. Cover bowl with plastic wrap and marinate chicken in the refrigerator for about 2 hours.

- Peel onions, cut in half lengthwise, and cut into ¼-inch-thick slices. Set aside.
- Place flour in a shallow pan and season with a little salt and pepper. Dredge each of the chicken pieces in flour and brush off any excess with your fingers.
- Pour olive oil into a large cast-iron skillet and place over medium-high heat. When oil is hot, sauté the floured chicken until golden on all sides. Remove chicken and set aside. Reduce heat to medium and add the sliced onions. Cook for 2 to 5 minutes, then add garlic, remaining cumin, coriander, turmeric, and cayenne and all of the ginger. Sauté for another 2 minutes to release all the flavors.
- Add the white wine and deglaze the pan by using a wooden spoon to scrape up any dark or browned bits from the bottom of the pan. Continue simmering until wine has reduced by half its volume. Add lemon zest and chicken stock and simmer for another 20 minutes.
- To the skillet, add the sautéed chicken, potatoes, and olives. Simmer until potatoes are tender, about 20 minutes.
- While the tagine is simmering, cut bread into 1-inch slices and brush each side with a little olive oil. In a separate pan, sauté the slices over medium heat until golden brown on both sides. Place 2 slices of bread in center of each plate.
- Just before serving the tagine, add parsley, cilantro, and scallions and season to taste with salt and pepper. Spoon generous servings over the slices of toasted bread.

SWEET POTATO GNOCCHI WITH SAGE CREAM & ROMANO CHEESE

Our first chef, Ed Sata, moved here from sunny Los Angeles during a particularly dreary Seattle winter and was immediately excited by the challenge of creating warm comfort food for our shivering lunch clientele. One of Ed's first attempts, gnocchi, was such a big hit that it became a weekly special, with customers lining up every Thursday to see what kind he had prepared for them. This recipe was inspired by Ed's work. Try it as a shared appetizer or add a simple salad for an entrée.

Serves 4

½ cup walnut halves
1½ pounds Red Garnet sweet potatoes, washed
Kosher salt
Freshly ground black pepper
½ teaspoon granulated sugar
2 eggs
1¼ cups unbleached all-purpose flour
2 tablespoons unsalted butter
3 tablespoons finely diced shallots
1 cup dry white wine
18 fresh sage leaves
3 cups heavy cream
1 cup grated Romano cheese
8 Fried Sage Leaves (*recipe follows*)

- Preheat oven to 350°F.

- Scatter walnuts on a rimmed baking sheet and toast for about 10 minutes, or until golden brown. Let cool, then coarsely chop and set aside for garnish. Increase oven temperature to 375°F.

- Cut sweet potatoes in half lengthwise and place them, cut sides up, on a rimmed baking sheet. Bake for about 1 hour, or until fork tender. Cut potatoes in half again lengthwise and return to oven for another 30 minutes. (They need to be good and dry.) Remove from oven and let cool for about 20 minutes. Peel away the skins and pass the warm flesh through a ricer or food mill into a medium bowl.

- To the bowl of sweet potato add ½ teaspoon kosher salt, ¼ teaspoon pepper, and sugar and mix well with a wooden spoon. Make a well in the center of the sweet potatoes and crack eggs into the well. Beat eggs together with a fork, then start folding them into the mixture by pulling small amounts of sweet potatoes into the center. Continue until eggs are fully incorporated into the sweet potatoes.

- Add flour to the bowl and fold together with a fork. Knead slightly with your hands, then pull dough onto a floured work surface and form into a 2-inch-thick log. You may need to add a little flour if dough is extra sticky. Divide the log into 4 equal pieces, then roll each piece into a 1-inch-thick log. Using a sharp knife, cut each log into 1-inch pieces.

- Have ready a large bowl of ice water. Bring a large saucepan of water to a full boil and add a pinch of salt. Drop in one quarter of the pieces and simmer for about 4 minutes, or until the gnocchi float to the surface. Transfer cooked gnocchi to bowl of ice water to stop the cooking process. After gnocchi have cooled, remove them from the water with a slotted spoon and spread them evenly on a rimmed baking sheet. Repeat with remaining gnocchi. Set cooled gnocchi aside.

- Place butter in a large saucepan and melt over medium heat. Add shallots and cook for 1 to 2 minutes, until translucent. Add white wine and simmer until liquid has reduced to about ¼ cup. Add sage leaves and cream and simmer over low heat for about 30 minutes, or until volume has reduced to approximately 2 cups. Season to taste with salt and pepper. Drop in the gnochhi and toss gently. Cook for another 2 to 3 minutes over low heat, taking care not to over-cook the gnocchi. Divide among 4 plates and top with toasted walnuts, grated Romano cheese, and Fried Sage Leaves. Serve immediately.

FRIED SAGE LEAVES

*Try adding Fried Sage Leaves to a variety of pasta dishes and soups,
or just enjoy them as a snack.*

Olive oil
Fresh sage leaves, washed and stemmed
Kosher salt

- Fill a small sauté pan with ½ inch of olive oil and heat to medium-high. Gently drop sage leaves into the oil and fry until dark green. The leaves will sizzle but shouldn't turn brown. Remove fried leaves with a slotted spoon and transfer to paper towels to drain and cool. Sprinkle with a little kosher salt.

Egg Salad Sandwich on Greek Olive Bread with Roasted Tomatoes & Anchovies

My inspiration for this sandwich came from a visit to Alice Waters'
Café Fanny, located next door to Acme Bread's retail bakery in Berkeley, California.
Café Fanny serves remarkably satisfying, simple dishes, made from the finest local
ingredients. The sandwich I had for lunch was made with Acme's delicious
Levain bread, but I think a good rival is our Greek Olive Loaf.

Makes 2 (open-faced) sandwiches

2 Roma tomatoes
Kosher salt
4 eggs
1½ tablespoons Dijon mustard
3 tablespoons Homemade Mayonnaise *(recipe follows)*
1 tablespoon finely chopped shallots
1 teaspoon chopped fresh oregano
1 tablespoon chopped fresh Italian parsley
Freshly ground black pepper
4 slices Greek Olive Loaf *(page 17)*
2 tablespoons unsalted butter, at room temperature
8 leaves arugula
4 anchovy fillets, sliced in half lengthwise
4 kalamata olives, pitted and coarsely chopped

- Preheat oven to 400°F. Line a rimmed baking sheet with parchment paper.

- Quarter tomatoes lengthwise and lay slices on the prepared baking sheet. Sprinkle
  a little salt over the tomatoes and bake on center rack of oven for 25 to 30 minutes,
  or until edges are deep brown. Remove from oven and set aside to cool.

- Place eggs and a pinch of salt in a medium saucepan and cover with water. Bring water to a boil over medium heat. Once the water has boiled, cover the pan and remove it from the heat. Let pan stand for 11 minutes, then drain eggs and run cold water into the pan until eggs are cooled.

- Chop hard-boiled eggs to a medium dice and place in a medium bowl. Add mustard, mayonnaise, shallots, oregano, and parsley, and mix well. Season to taste with a little salt and freshly ground black pepper. Place in the refrigerator to chill.

- Toast or broil 4 large slices of Greek Olive Loaf until light brown, then butter one side of each slice. Arrange 2 leaves of arugula on the buttered side of each piece of toast, then top each slice with one quarter of the egg salad. Garnish each slice with equal portions of roasted tomatoes, anchovies, and olives. Place 2 slices each onto 2 plates.

HOMEMADE MAYONNAISE

A sandwich simply isn't complete without fresh mayonnaise.

Makes approximately 1 cup

2 egg yolks
1 teaspoon Dijon mustard
2 teaspoons freshly squeezed lemon juice
1 cup canola oil
Kosher salt
White pepper

● Combine egg yolks, mustard, and lemon juice in a medium bowl. Mix well with a whisk. Add canola oil in a slow stream, whisking as you pour in the oil. Continue whisking until the oil is fully incorporated and thickened. Season to taste with salt and white pepper. Store in an airtight container for up to 3 days in the refrigerator.

THE HOLIDAY TABLE

THE HOLIDAY TABLE

Holiday baking has always been a tradition in my family. As soon as the leftover Thanksgiving turkey had been eaten and there was enough room in the refrigerator, my mother would start preparing and storing her Christmas cookie doughs. This was quite an ordeal, as our family usually made three or four different kinds of cookies, as well as lefsa, krumkaka, stollen, and rosettes, all from recipes my mother had learned from my grandmother. Relatives and friends could look forward to receiving a basket of our holiday goodies every year.

The year Macrina opened, I asked my mom to come in and teach the pastry crew exactly how to make her cookies. It had been ten years since I had been home to bake with her, and I couldn't remember a lot of her special touches. She drove up from Portland, Oregon, with her special Christmas apron, and went to work with the staff. Our equipment was a little different from what she had at home. I remember that she kept saying, "Well, these cookies aren't perfect or fancy or anything." But I thought they looked "perfectly" homemade and delicious, which is what we were striving for at the bakery. Years later, my mother is teaching her four granddaughters how to make the same cookies, and they can still be found in our pastry case every Christmas.

The Thanksgiving and Christmas holidays are the busiest time of year for us at Macrina. Preparations start as early as September, with our first "holiday meeting." The lead bakers and retail managers sit down with me to talk about past holidays, reminiscing about favorite items such as the Winter Pear Crowne and the Harvest Pie. We also toss around all kinds of new ideas, and after a lot of discussion and recipe testing, we come up with the season's list of offerings.

This chapter includes the most popular of these holiday recipes. At Macrina they are most commonly prepared for Thanksgiving and Christmas, but there's no reason they can't be enjoyed all year long. The Chocolate Cherry Heart Bread, for example, is a perfect Valentine's Day gift and makes decadent French toast. Try the Sweet & Spicy Nuts or the Baked Brie en Croûte at your next party, or slice up a Roasted Pear Galette for a unique appetizer. When the holiday season arrives, serve a fresh Maple Pecan Pumpkin Pie or—my personal favorite—the easy-to-prepare Holiday Tart.

One of the biggest joys of operating our neighborhood bakery is the knowledge that our products are part of so many personal celebrations. I love seeing our pink boxes, packed with cookies, tarts, and more, being carried home for the holidays. By offering these recipes, we are taking this concept one step further.

Chapter 14

SAVORY BITES

Porcini Harvest Loaf

Holiday Fougasse

Winter Pear Crowne

Fig & Cranberry Chutney

Baked Brie en Croûte

Roasted Pear Galette with Chèvre & Pomegranates

Sweet & Spicy Nuts

PORCINI HARVEST LOAF

*This savory bread is a variation of our popular Rustic Potato Loaf (page 33).
For this recipe we've added a little whole-wheat flour, fresh herbs, and flavorful porcini
mushrooms. It's perfect alongside roast turkey or prime rib. Try making leftovers into
croutons for topping winter soups, or slice the loaf for a great grilled cheese sandwich.*

Makes 1 large loaf

1¼ pounds russet potatoes
1 tablespoon kosher salt
¼ cup dried porcini mushrooms
2 teaspoons dried yeast
2 tablespoons extra virgin olive oil
1 teaspoon chopped fresh oregano
1 teaspoon chopped fresh rosemary
1 teaspoon chopped fresh Italian parsley
½ cup whole-wheat flour
2¾ cups unbleached all-purpose flour
Spray bottle of water

- Scrub potatoes thoroughly and cut into 1-inch chunks. Place potatoes and 1 tea-spoon of the kosher salt in a medium saucepan and cover with water. Bring water to a boil, reduce heat, and simmer potatoes for 15 to 20 minutes, or until they are tender when poked with a knife. Measure out ¾ cup of potato water and set aside. Drain potatoes in a colander and leave them to cool and dry for 20 minutes.

- Place dried mushrooms in a small bowl and cover with the warm potato water. Let soak for 10 minutes, then drain, reserving the soaking liquid. Squeeze excess liquid from the mushrooms, chop them coarsely, and set aside.

- Pour the soaking liquid into a small saucepan and warm slightly over low heat. Pour the just-warm liquid into a small bowl and sprinkle yeast over the top. Mix with a whisk until yeast is dissolved and let stand for 5 minutes while yeast blooms.

- Place drained and cooled potatoes in the bowl of your stand mixer. Using the pad-dle attachment, mix on low speed for 1 minute to mash the potatoes. Add olive oil and mix for about 30 seconds. Pour in the yeast mixture and mix until fully com-bined, 1 to 2 minutes. Switch to the hook attachment and add chopped mushrooms, oregano, rosemary, parsley, whole-wheat flour, all-purpose flour, and remaining 2 teaspoons of salt. Mix on low speed for 1 minute, then increase speed to medium and mix for another 10 to 11 minutes. Dough will appear firm at first but will become wetter as mixing continues. Check for elasticity by flouring your fingers and stretching some of the dough. The dough should stretch about 2 inches without breaking.

- Pull dough from bowl onto a floured work surface and form it into a ball. Place ball in an oiled medium bowl and cover with plastic wrap. Let dough sit in a warm room, about 70°F, for about 1¼ hours. Dough will almost double in size.

- Pull dough from bowl onto a floured surface and flatten it with your hands. Form dough into a ball by repeatedly pulling the edges upwards onto the center of the mass. Let the loaf rest on the counter, seam side down, for 2 minutes. Line a medium bowl with a lightly floured dishtowel and place loaf, seam side up, in the center. Fold ends of towel over top of loaf to prevent a skin from forming on the surface. Let proof at room temperature for 40 to 45 minutes. Loaf will increase about 50 percent in size and feel spongy to the touch.

- Place a baking stone on center rack of oven and preheat to 400°F. While oven is preheating, cut a small (about 4-inch-tall) mushroom-shaped stencil out of a piece of paper.

- Carefully unwrap the loaf and place it, seam side down, on a lightly floured counter or baker's peel. Gently brush excess flour off the loaf with your fingers. Place mushroom stencil on the center of the loaf and dust the top of the loaf with a little all-purpose flour. Remove the stencil, leaving a mushroom shape on the surface of the loaf. Using a sharp knife, score 4 shallow lines around the mushroom shape, framing it. Moving quickly, place loaf in center of baking stone and heavily mist inside of oven with spray bottle of water. Bake loaf for about 45 minutes, misting the oven once more after the first 5 minutes. The finished loaf will be golden brown and sound hollow when tapped on the bottom. Let cool on a wire rack for at least 30 minutes.

HOLIDAY FOUGASSE

Stuffed with Gorgonzola cheese and walnuts, this loaf makes a unique appetizer for holiday gatherings. Its festive leaf shape always grabs attention.

Makes 1 loaf

1 recipe Classic Italian Loaf dough *(page 22)*
⅓ cup walnut halves
¾ cup crumbled Gorgonzola cheese
1 tablespoon chopped fresh thyme
Semolina flour or cornmeal
Egg wash made with 1 egg and 1 teaspoon water
Extra virgin olive oil
Coarse sea salt
Spray bottle filled with water

- Prepare Classic Italian Loaf dough through the mixing process and let proof as instructed for 2 hours. Dough will almost double in size.

- Preheat oven to 350°F.

- While dough is proofing, scatter walnuts on a rimmed baking sheet and toast on center rack of oven for about 10 minutes, or until golden brown. Let cool and chop coarsely.

- In small bowl, combine walnuts, Gorgonzola, and half of the thyme. Mix with a spoon and set aside.

- Prepare a rimmed baking sheet by lightly dusting it with semolina flour or cornmeal.

- Pull dough from bowl onto a floured surface and flatten with your hands. Pat dough into a rectangle measuring about 8 x 20 inches and position it so that a long side is facing you. Sprinkle the cheese and nut mixture over the left half of the dough, leaving a 1-inch border around the mixture (photo 1). Brush a little egg wash around the filling. Fold the other half of the dough over the filling and pinch the edges of the dough together to seal the filling inside (photo 2). Place the loaf on the prepared baking sheet and cover with plastic wrap. Let proof in a warm room, 70 to 75°F, for 1 hour. The loaf will increase 50 percent in size.

- Place a baking stone on center rack of oven and preheat to 400°F.

- Remove plastic from loaf and position the baking sheet so that a short side of the loaf is facing you. Now it's time to give the Fougasse its signature shape. The goal

1

2

3

4

5

6

7

here is to create a pattern loosely resembling the veins in a leaf. Using a sharp knife, cut 3 angled 2½-inch slashes into the left half of the rectangle, spacing the slashes about 4 inches apart and 1 inch from the edge of the dough (photo 3). Be sure to cut all the way through the dough. Repeat this procedure on the right half of the rectangle (photos 4 & 5). Make sure that your cuts do not run into each other or the loaf will fall apart.

- Gently lift the loaf onto a baker's peel or flat cookie sheet. Stretch the left and right sides of the loaf outwards slightly to open up the slashes. (Each slash should open about 1 inch; photo 6.) If nuts or cheese start to fall out of the openings in the dough, insert your fingers into the slashes and pinch the dough together to seal the ingredients back inside. Grab the center of the far edge and stretch it a couple of inches away from you to help create the leaf shape (photo 7).

- Brush the top of the loaf with extra virgin olive oil and sprinkle with remaining thyme and a little coarse sea salt. Moving quickly, slide the loaf onto center of baking stone and mist inside of oven with a spray bottle of water. Bake for 30 to 40 minutes, misting the oven twice more during the first 15 minutes. The finished loaf will be golden brown and sound hollow when tapped on the bottom. Cool on a wire rack for 30 minutes.

WINTER PEAR CROWNE

*The recipe for this classic French loaf was brought to the bakery by Evan Andres,
one of Macrina's former lead bakers. The addition of sweet pears, one of the Northwest's
signature fruits, has made it a must-have for many of Seattle's holiday tables.
I recommend using ripe Bartlett pears.*

Makes 2 crown-shaped loaves

2 ripe Bartlett pears
⅓ cup warm filtered water
2 teaspoons dried yeast
1 tablespoon plus 1 teaspoon honey
2 eggs
4½ cups unbleached all-purpose flour
2 teaspoons kosher salt
½ teaspoon freshly ground black pepper
Spray bottle of water

- Peel and core pears, then coarsely chop them. Place one third of the pears in a small bowl and set aside. Place the remaining pears in a food processor and purée until smooth. Set aside.

- Combine water, yeast, and honey in the bowl of your stand mixer. Mix with a whisk until yeast has fully dissolved, then let sit for 5 minutes while yeast blooms.

- Add eggs and puréed pears to the bowl and using the paddle attachment, mix on low speed until ingredients are combined, about 1 minute. Add flour, salt, and pepper, and mix on low speed for 1 minute to start bringing the dough together. Switch to the hook attachment and mix on medium speed for 10 to 12 minutes. Dough will form a loose ball around the base of the hook and will stretch easily.

- Pull dough from bowl onto a floured work surface and flatten it with your hands. Form dough into a rectangle, approximately ½ inch thick, and position it so that a long side is facing you. Scatter the chopped pears over the surface of the dough. Starting with the closest long end, roll dough away from you into a log. Make sure the log is resting on its seam, then fold the ends underneath, meeting in the center to form a loosely shaped ball. Place the ball, seam side down, in an oiled medium bowl. Cover with plastic wrap and let proof in a warm room, 70 to 75°F, for 2 hours. Dough will almost double in size.

- Uncover bowl and dimple the surface of the dough with your fingers to release excess air bubbles. Next, give dough what bakers call a turn: Stretch each of the dough's four edges outward and then back onto the center (see photos, page 14). Turn the left and right sides first, followed by the top and bottom. Flip the entire ball over, placing it seam side down in the bowl, and cover again with plastic wrap. Let proof in a warm room for another 2 hours. Dough will double in size.

- Pull dough from bowl onto a floured work surface and flatten it with your hands. Divide dough in half and form each piece into a ball by repeatedly pulling the edges upwards and onto the center of the mass. Let the loaves rest on the counter, seam sides down, for about 2 minutes. Place the loaves, seam sides up, on a heavily floured rimmed baking sheet. Cover with plastic wrap and let proof at room temperature for about 1 hour, until loaves rise 50 percent.

- Place baking stone on center rack of oven and preheat to 385°F.

- To create the crown shape, place 2 fingers in the center of a loaf and press down until you have broken through to the baking sheet. Rotate loaf around your fingers until you have created a 3-inch hole in the center of the loaf. Invert loaf onto a lightly floured counter or baker's peel and repeat with remaining loaf. (If your baking stone will hold only one loaf, leave the remaining loaf on the baking sheet and cover it with plastic wrap. Do not form it into a crown until it can be baked. Store it in the refrigerator while the other loaf bakes and remove it 10 minutes before baking to warm it up a little.)

- Using a sharp knife, score a shallow line (about ¼ inch deep) around the tops of the loaves. Moving quickly, place the loaves on the baking stone and mist inside of oven with water. Bake for 40 to 45 minutes, misting the oven twice more during the first 15 minutes. The finished loaves will be a deep, golden brown and sound hollow when tapped on the bottom. Let loaf cool on a wire rack for 30 minutes.

FIG & CRANBERRY CHUTNEY

This Macrina staff favorite is a good accompaniment to roast turkey or ham.
It's also a nice way to brighten up your favorite sandwiches.

Makes 2½ cups

½ cup dried figs
½ cup white wine vinegar
¼ cup dark rum
¾ cup light brown sugar
2 tablespoons peeled and grated ginger
1½ teaspoons whole mustard seeds
¼ teaspoon ground cloves
¼ teaspoon chile flakes, ground
½ teaspoon kosher salt
½ cup seedless raisins
½ teaspoon finely chopped garlic
1 cup diced yellow onion
½ cup freshly squeezed orange juice
2 teaspoons freshly grated orange zest
2 cups fresh cranberries

- Cut figs into quarters and place them in a small bowl. Cover with hot water and let soak for 15 minutes. Drain and set aside.

- In a medium saucepan (not aluminum), combine vinegar, rum, brown sugar, ginger, mustard seeds, cloves, chile flakes, and salt and mix well with a whisk. Add raisins, garlic, onion, orange juice, and orange zest and bring to a simmer over medium heat. Simmer for 20 to 25 minutes, until the liquid has reduced by one third, stirring with a spoon frequently to keep the bottom from burning.

- Add the cranberries and soaked figs and continue cooking over medium heat for 10 to 15 minutes, or until cranberries just start to burst. Remove from heat and let cool slightly. If you are going to serve the chutney as a side dish, I recommend serving it slightly warm or at room temperature. Once completely cooled, the chutney can be covered and stored in the refrigerator for up to 6 days.

Baked Brie en Croûte

If you're looking for a unique cheese appetizer for your holiday party, this recipe is the one for you. Your guests will devour the ripe Brie, layered with roasted grapes and walnuts and encased in Flaky Pie Dough. I recommend baking two and keeping a spare in the freezer.

Makes an appetizer for 5 to 6 people

2 tablespoons coarsely chopped walnuts
¾ cup seedless red grapes, stemmed and washed
1 tablespoon extra virgin olive oil
1 tablespoon light brown sugar
2 teaspoons chopped fresh thyme
Kosher salt
Freshly ground black pepper
½ recipe Flaky Pie Dough *(page 127)*, chilled
1 (4-ounce) Brie wheel
Egg wash made with 1 egg and 1 teaspoon water

● Preheat oven to 375°F. Line 2 rimmed baking sheets with parchment paper.

● Place walnuts in a small sauté pan and toast over medium heat for 2 to 3 minutes, or until golden brown. Set aside to cool.

● Combine grapes and olive oil in a medium bowl and toss until grapes are coated. Place grapes on one of the prepared baking sheets and roast on center rack of oven for 10 to 15 minutes. This roasting intensifies and sweetens the flavor of the grapes. Remove from oven as soon as the grapes start to burst.

● Using a rubber spatula, scrape the warm grapes into a medium bowl. Add walnuts, brown sugar, and 1½ teaspoons of the thyme. Toss ingredients together, then season to taste with salt and pepper. Set bowl aside and let cool to room temperature.

● Cut off one quarter of the chilled pie dough and form it into a ball. Place the ball on a floured work surface and roll it out ⅛ inch thick. Trim the dough into a 4-inch circle and set it aside on a piece of parchment paper. Form the remaining dough into a ball and roll it out ⅛ inch thick. Trim the dough into a 10-inch circle, then lift it onto the remaining prepared sheet pan. Using a sharp knife or a cookie cutter, cut 3 small leaf shapes from the remaining scraps of dough and set them aside with the 4-inch circle of dough.

● Place Brie in the center of the 10-inch circle of dough, leaving a 3-inch border (The Brie wheel should be no more than 4 inches wide.) Using your hands, tightly pack the grape mixture on top of the Brie. Lift the border of dough on top of the filling, pleating the dough as you go, and brush a little egg wash under each of the pleats to seal them. There will be a small opening on top of the wrapped Brie, exposing some of the filling. Brush the top of the pastry dough with egg wash and center the 4-inch circle of dough over the opening. Gently press the 2 crusts together to create a tight seal, then turn the whole thing over, placing it seam side down on the baking sheet. Brush the sides and top of the Brie with egg wash and arrange the 3 leaves on top. Finally, brush the leaves with a little more egg wash and sprinkle them with the remaining thyme. Chill in the refrigerator for 30 minutes.

- Bake on center rack of oven for 20 to 25 minutes, or until crust is golden brown. If Brie starts oozing out through the crust, it has been baking too long or was not well sealed. Let cool briefly and serve warm.

- After baking, the Brie en Croûte can be stored in the freezer for up to 2 weeks. Make sure it is fully cooled, then double wrap it with plastic wrap before freezing. To re-heat Brie en Croûte, first defrost it in the refrigerator for 1 day, then place in a preheated 375°F oven for about 15 minutes.

Roasted Pear Galette
with Chèvre & Pomegranates

This rustic tart makes a great escape from the frequently heavy dishes of the holiday season. Serve it alongside a cup of your favorite soup and Macrina's Organic Greens Salad for a simple, satisfying meal. It also works well as a party appetizer.

Serves 8 to 10

2 ripe Bartlett pears, cored and halved
Canola oil
2 cups ricotta cheese
2 cups goat cheese
3 eggs
1 teaspoon kosher salt
1 teaspoon chopped fresh thyme
½ teaspoon chopped fresh rosemary
Freshly ground black pepper
½ recipe Flaky Pie Dough *(page 127)*, chilled
¼ cup fresh pomegranate seeds
1 tablespoon chopped fresh Italian parsley
Egg wash made with 1 egg and 1 teaspoon water

- Preheat oven to 375°F. Line a rimmed baking sheet with parchment paper.

- Preheat a cast-iron grill to medium-high. (If you don't have a grill, a large frying pan will be fine.) Cut pear halves into ½-inch-thick slices. Brush both sides of the slices with canola oil and lay them on the hot grill. Turn the slices over as soon as grill marks appear on the fruit. It's important that the fruit not get cooked all the way through. (If using a frying pan, cook the slices just until both sides are slightly browned.) Lay the grilled slices on a sheet of parchment paper and set aside to cool.

- Combine ricotta, goat cheese, eggs, salt, thyme, and rosemary in a large bowl. Season with a little pepper and mix well with a whisk. Set aside.

- Form chilled pie dough into a ball and place it on a floured work surface. Flatten the ball slightly and roll it into a 14-inch circle, about ⅛ inch thick. Carefully lift rolled dough onto the prepared baking sheet. Spoon ricotta mixture onto center of circle and flatten to cover 10 inches, leaving a 2-inch border. Lift border on top of the filling, tucking and folding the dough to create a gathered, or pleated, finish (see photos, page 204). Lift each of the folds up and brush underneath with egg wash to seal the crust. Brush all exposed dough with egg wash, then place the galette in the freezer to chill for 30 minutes.

- Remove tart from freezer and bake on center rack of oven for 30 minutes. Remove tart from oven and lay the cooled pear slices on top of the tart. I like to spread them out in a flower-like pattern, with the tips of the slices meeting in the center of the tart. Return the tart to the oven and bake for another 10 to 15 minutes, or until crust is golden brown. Let cool on the baking sheet for 20 minutes. Garnish the tart with pomegranate seeds and chopped parsley. The galette is best served slightly warm. Wrap any leftovers with plastic wrap and store in the refrigerator for up to 2 days.

Sweet & Spicy Nuts

Jeanine Riss, one of our past chefs, brought this holiday recipe to Macrina. We start getting requests for the nuts in early November and don't stop making them until after the New Year is rung in. They're great for parties, and can be stored in an airtight container for up to two weeks. But fat chance you'll have any leftovers!

Makes 4 cups of nuts

1 cup whole almonds
1 cup whole peanuts
1 cup whole pecans
1 cup walnut halves
1 teaspoon cinnamon
½ teaspoon ground allspice
¼ teaspoon ground cardamom
½ teaspoon ground ginger
¼ teaspoon freshly ground black pepper
½ teaspoon cayenne pepper
½ teaspoon kosher salt
½ cup honey
½ cup light corn syrup

- Preheat oven to 350°F. Line a rimmed baking sheet with parchment paper, then brush the top of the parchment paper with canola oil.

- Combine almonds, peanuts, pecans, and walnuts in a medium bowl.

- Combine cinnamon, allspice, cardamom, ginger, black pepper, cayenne pepper, and salt in a small bowl. Mix well with a spoon, then pour the spice mixture over the nuts and toss together thoroughly.

- Combine honey and corn syrup in a medium saucepan and place over low heat. Stirring frequently, heat just until mixture is warm. Pour the warm mixture over the nuts and toss together (it's best to use your hands) until nuts are evenly coated.

- Pour the nuts onto the prepared baking sheet and spread them into single layer. Bake on center rack of oven for 15 to 20 minutes, or until nuts take on a rich mahogany color. Let nuts cool completely. At this point they will have formed a single, crispy layer in the baking sheet. Break the nuts apart with your hands and store in an airtight container. Store in a cool place, as heat will melt the syrup on the nuts and make them sticky.

Chapter 15

SWEET TREATS

Chocolate Cherry Heart Bread
Panettone
Steamed Chocolate Pudding Cake
Holiday Tart
Maple Pecan Pumpkin Pie
Harvest Pie
Festive Gingerbread People
The Christmas Cookie Box

CHOCOLATE CHERRY HEART BREAD

This heart-shaped loaf was inspired by a Greek Christmas bread, but we actually sell more loaves on Valentine's Day and Mother's Day than we do at Christmas. Customers have been asking for this recipe for years, and I offer it now with one warning: The smell of this bread baking will draw a large crowd, so be prepared to share.

Makes 1 loaf

⅓ cup dried tart cherries
1 cup hot water
1 tablespoon brandy
1 tablespoon pure vanilla extract
½ teaspoon pure almond extract
¼ cup whole almonds
1¼ teaspoons anise seeds
1½ teaspoons dried yeast
⅓ cup granulated sugar
¼ cup Natural Sour Starter *(page 7)*, at room temperature
1 egg
2¾ cups unbleached all-purpose flour
½ teaspoon kosher salt
3 tablespoons unsalted butter, at room temperature
2 ounces bittersweet chocolate, coarsely chopped
Egg wash made with 1 egg and 1 teaspoon water
Powdered sugar

- Combine cherries, water, brandy, vanilla extract, and almond extract in a small bowl. Mix with a spoon and set aside to steep for 20 minutes.

- Preheat oven to 350°F.

- Scatter almonds on a rimmed baking sheet and toast on center rack of oven for 10 to 12 minutes, or until golden brown. Let cool, then coarsely chop and set aside.

- Place anise seeds in a small sauté pan and toast over medium heat for 1 to 2 minutes, or until slightly darkened and fragrant. Transfer to a cutting board and let cool, then coarsely chop and add to the chopped almonds. (You can also chop the seeds in a coffee or spice grinder.)

- Drain the marinated cherries, reserving the liquid, and set cherries aside. Pour the marinating liquid into a medium saucepan and warm slightly over low heat. Pour the just-warm liquid into the bowl of your stand mixer and sprinkle yeast over the top. Mix with a whisk to dissolve yeast. Let bowl sit for 5 minutes while yeast blooms.

- Add sugar, Natural Sour Starter, and egg and using the paddle attachment, mix on low speed until ingredients are combined, about 1 minute. Add flour and salt and continue mixing on low for 1 to 2 minutes. Switch to the hook attachment. Increase speed to medium and start adding small pieces of the butter. Continue mixing for a total of 5 to 7 minutes. At this point the dough will have a satiny finish and should stretch easily. Let dough rest in the bowl for 5 minutes to relax the gluten.

- To the bowl of dough, add the anise seeds, almonds, marinated cherries, and chopped chocolate. Mix on low speed just long enough to distribute the new ingredients, 2 to 3 minutes. If the cherries are particularly wet, you may need to add a couple more tablespoons of flour.

- Pull dough from bowl onto a floured work surface and form it into a ball. Place ball in an oiled medium bowl and cover with plastic wrap. Let sit in a warm room, 70 to 75°F, for 2 hours. Dough will almost double in size.

- Line a rimmed baking sheet with parchment paper.

- Remove dough from bowl and place on a floured work surface. Flatten dough with your hands to release excess air bubbles. Form the dough into a 10 x 6-inch rectangle and position it so that a long side is facing you. Now it's time to form the dough into a heart (see photos, below). Using a sharp paring knife, cut a small slit (about 1½ inches) down the center of the far side of the dough, cutting all the way through the dough. This will make it easier to form the heart shape. Slide your hands underneath the bottom corners of the rectangle and fold them up to meet in the center of the dough, creating the lower point of the heart. Gently stretch the upper corners outward and pat them into shape, finishing off the heart. Pinch together any seams

in the dough. Invert the heart onto the prepared baking sheet and cover with plastic wrap. Let proof in a warm room for about 1 hour.

- While loaf is proofing, preheat oven to 350°F.

- The loaf is ready to bake when it has increased 50 percent in size and is pillow-like to touch. Brush the top of the loaf with egg wash and bake on center rack of oven for 25 to 30 minutes. The top of the loaf will have a mahogany color and the base will be deep brown. Let cool for at least 30 minutes on a wire rack, then dust the loaf with powdered sugar. Any leftovers can be wrapped in plastic wrap and stored at room temperature for 2 to 3 days.

PANETTONE

Macrina's version of this Italian Christmas bread was inspired by a recipe in Carol Field's wonderful book The Italian Baker. *The loaf is studded with candied citrus and dried fruits and enriched with eggs and butter. It's irresistible. Nowadays it's easy to find decorative paper baking molds, but I prefer to bake these loaves in clay flowerpots, which look beautiful and make great holiday gifts. Making this dough is a two-step process that can't be rushed, but the finished loaves are more than worth the wait. You will need four three-inch clay flowerpots for this recipe.*

Makes 4 loaves

FOR THE STARTER DOUGH:
12 tablespoons (1½ sticks) unsalted butter, at room temperature
¾ cup warm filtered water
2 tablespoons dried yeast
⅓ cup granulated sugar
3 eggs
2 tablespoons freshly grated orange zest

1½ tablespoons freshly grated lemon zest
3 tablespoons honey
1 tablespoon pure vanilla extract
2½ cups unbleached all-purpose flour

FOR THE FINAL DOUGH:
1½ cups golden raisins
12 ounces (3 sticks) unsalted butter, at room temperature
3 eggs
4 egg yolks
1¼ cups granulated sugar
2 teaspoons kosher salt
4½ cups unbleached all-purpose flour
¾ cup candied citron, cut into ¼-inch pieces
¾ cup candied orange peel*
Egg wash made with 1 egg and 1 teaspoon water

available at specialty stores and some supermarkets

PREPARING THE STARTER DOUGH:

- Cut butter into small pieces and set aside.

- Combine warm water, yeast, and sugar in the bowl of your stand mixer. Mix with a whisk to dissolve yeast. Let sit for 5 minutes while yeast blooms.

- Add butter, eggs, orange zest, lemon zest, honey, vanilla extract, and flour. Using the hook attachment, mix on low speed to start bringing the ingredients together. After about 1 minute, increase speed to medium and mix for 5 to 7 minutes. Transfer dough to an oiled medium bowl and cover with plastic wrap. Let sit in a warm room, 70 to 75°F, for 2 hours. The dough will almost double in size.

PREPARING THE FINAL DOUGH:

- While the starter dough is proofing, place raisins in a small bowl and cover with hot water. Let soak for 20 minutes to plump the raisins, then drain the raisins and wrap them in a dishtowel to absorb any excess water. Set aside.

- Cut butter into small pieces and set aside.

- When the starter dough has finished proofing, remove the plastic and punch down the dough with lightly floured hands.

- Combine eggs, yolks, and sugar in the bowl of your stand mixer and mix well with a whisk. Add the starter dough, salt, and flour. Using the hook attachment, mix on low speed until all of the ingredients are combined, 2 to 3 minutes. Scrape down the sides of the bowl with a rubber spatula. Increase speed to medium and start adding small pieces of butter. This will take 3 to 4 minutes. Mix on medium speed for another 10 to 12 minutes. The dough will have a satiny finish and should stretch easily. Let dough rest in the bowl for 5 minutes to relax the gluten.

- Add the soaked raisins, citron, and candied orange peel to the bowl. Mix on low speed until the new ingredients are evenly distributed, scraping down the sides of the bowl frequently with a rubber spatula. If necessary, add 1 or 2 tablespoons of flour to help bring the dough together.

- Transfer the finished dough to an oiled medium bowl and cover with plastic wrap. Let sit in a warm room for 3 to 4 hours. Dough will almost double in size.

- While dough is proofing, prepare 4 (3-inch) clay flowerpots: Thoroughly wash the pots and dry them in a preheated (335°F) oven for 5 minutes. Let the pots cool to room temperature, then brush the insides with canola oil and line the bottom and sides with pieces of parchment paper. The parchment paper should extend 1½ inches above the rims of the pots.

- Line a rimmed baking sheet with parchment paper.

- Pull dough from bowl onto a floured work surface and divide it into 4 equal pieces. Form each piece of dough into a ball by repeatedly pulling the edges of the dough upwards onto the top of the mass. Fit the balls of dough, seam sides down, into the prepared clay pots. Gently press the dough to make sure the bottoms of the pots are filled with dough and that there are no air pockets. Place pots on the prepared baking sheet and cover with plastic wrap. Let proof for 45 minutes to 1 hour. Dough will rise to the top of the parchment papers.

- Position oven rack so that it is second from the bottom rung. Preheat oven to 335°F.

- Using a razor blade or sharp knife, score a shallow cross over the top of each loaf. Brush the loaves with egg wash, then place the baking sheet in the oven. Bake for about 1½ hours, or until loaves are deep golden brown on top. Remove one of the loaves from the oven and gently lift the loaf out of the clay pot to see if the sides are golden brown. If not, return the loaf to the pot and continue baking for a few more minutes. Let finished loaves cool in the pots for at least 45 minutes before serving. Wrapped in plastic, these moist loaves will last for several days at room temperature.

STEAMED CHOCOLATE PUDDING CAKE

This is probably the most delicious cake I have ever tasted. It's rich with chocolate and butter
but is not overly sweet. If you don't already have one, you'll need to purchase an eight-cup
steamed-pudding mold for this recipe. Make sure you find one with a snug-fitting lid.
I recommend serving this cake slightly warm, with generous spoonfuls of whipped cream.

Makes 1 (8-cup) pudding cake

1 pound (4 sticks) unsalted butter
10 ounces unsweetened chocolate, coarsely chopped
1½ cups granulated sugar
¾ cup hot freshly brewed espresso or strong coffee
5 eggs
1½ teaspoons unbleached all-purpose flour

- Prepare an 8-cup steamed-pudding mold by thoroughly brushing the insides with melted butter.

- Place 1 pound of butter in a medium saucepan and start melting it over medium-low heat. Clarify the butter by continuously skimming off all of the white particles that form on the surface. Take care not to over-heat the butter or it will turn brown. When the butter is golden and clear, after about 45 minutes, it is ready to be used. When finished, you should have 1½ cups of clarified butter.

- Combine clarified butter and chocolate in a medium bowl. Place bowl on top of a saucepan filled with 2 inches of simmering water, making sure that the bottom of the bowl does not come into contact with the water. It's important that the water be just simmering, as the ingredients will scorch if the water is too hot. Stir ingredients with a rubber spatula until all of the chocolate has melted and reached a smooth consistency. Remove bowl from heat and let cool until chocolate is slightly warm.

- Place sugar and hot coffee in a medium bowl and stir with a whisk until sugar is dissolved. Let cool to room temperature.

- Separate eggs, placing whites in a medium bowl. Add yolks to the coffee mixture and mix well with a whisk. Pour coffee mixture into the bowl of melted chocolate and fold the ingredients together with a rubber spatula.

- Using a whisk or hand-held mixer, whip egg whites until medium-stiff peaks form. Add flour in the final minutes of whipping, incorporating it evenly into the whites. Gently fold the egg whites, one third at a time, into the chocolate mixture. Continue folding the batter until there are no visible white streaks. Pour batter into the prepared pudding mold and cover securely with the mold's lid.

- Place a 1-inch-high trivet or rack in a roasting pan, and pour hot water into the pan until the water is level with the top of the trivet. (An alternative to the trivet would be to mold a 1 x 3-inch disk out of aluminum foil.) Set the pudding mold on top of the trivet, then cover the top of the roasting pan with foil, making sure the edges of the pan are tightly sealed. Poke two small holes in opposite corners of the foil to vent the steam.

- Place roasting pan on top of a burner and turn heat to medium-low. Gently simmer the pudding on the stovetop for 45 minutes. After the first 20 minutes, carefully peel back a corner of the foil to make sure there is still water in the pan. (Be careful not to burn yourself with the steam.)

- Preheat oven to 325°F.

- Add more water to the roasting pan if needed and continue steaming. After a total of 45 minutes, remove the foil from the pan and open the pudding mold. The pudding should be set (not jiggly) on the top and the edges.

- Place pudding, uncovered, on center rack of oven and bake for 10 to 15 minutes. The cake will puff up during the final minutes of baking. Gently remove from the oven and let cool for 45 minutes. The cake will collapse a little, but hopefully it won't crack. Place a serving plate on top of the pudding mold and carefully invert them both, releasing the pudding cake onto the plate.

HOLIDAY TART

This pecan-filled Christmas tart is a particular favorite of mine.
The fresh orange zest and tangy cranberries are perfectly balanced by the sweet custard filling.
It's easy to prepare and guaranteed to be a hit at any holiday party.

Makes 1 (10-inch) tart

1 cup chopped pecans
3 eggs
⅔ cup light brown sugar
⅔ cup light corn syrup
4 tablespoons unsalted butter, melted and cooled to room temperature
½ teaspoon salt
1 tablespoon brandy
2 teaspoons freshly grated orange zest
1 pre-baked (10-inch) Flaky Pie Dough tart shell (*page 129*)
1¼ cups fresh cranberries
Powdered sugar

- Preheat oven to 350°F.

- Spread pecans on a rimmed baking sheet and toast in the oven for 5 to 10 minutes, or until golden brown. Let cool and set aside. Reduce oven temperature to 325°F.

- Combine eggs, brown sugar, corn syrup, melted butter, salt, brandy, and orange zest in a medium bowl. Mix with a whisk until ingredients are combined. Set aside.

- Place pre-baked tart shell on a rimmed baking sheet. Scatter toasted pecans and cranberries in the tart shell, then pour in the custard mixture. Place baking sheet on center rack of oven and bake the tart for 35 to 40 minutes. The custard will be set in the center and slightly brown on top. Let cool on a wire rack for 30 minutes, then remove the sides of the pan. I like to dust powdered sugar around the outer edge of the tart before serving.

MAPLE PECAN PUMPKIN PIE

*Everyone has his or her favorite Thanksgiving pie, from pumpkin to pecan to
all-American apple. For this recipe, I combine puréed pumpkin with butternut squash and
finish it off with sweet Maple Pecan Topping. The addition of butternut squash adds
a natural sweetness to the pie and gives it a dark, richer color.*

Makes 1 (9-inch) pie

½ recipe Flaky Pie Dough *(page 127)*
1 cup canned pumpkin puree
1 cup Roasted Butternut Squash *(page 85)*
¼ cup light brown sugar
2 tablespoons honey
2 tablespoons pure maple syrup
1 teaspoon cinnamon
½ teaspoon salt
½ teaspoon ground nutmeg
1 tablespoon peeled and grated ginger
¼ teaspoon ground cloves
¼ cup semolina flour
3 eggs
1 cup buttermilk
1 tablespoon brandy
1 recipe Maple Pecan Topping *(recipe follows)*
Powdered sugar

- Coat your hands with flour and shape the pie dough into a ball. Working on a floured surface, flatten the ball slightly, then roll out the dough ⅛ inch thick. Fit the rolled dough into a 9-inch pie pan, then trim the edges of the dough to leave a 1-inch over-hang around the pan. Fold the overhanging dough under itself, creating a double-thick crust around the edge of the pie shell. Crimp with your fingers (see photos, page 136), then chill in the refrigerator or freezer for at least 30 minutes.

- Preheat oven to 375°F.

- Line the chilled pie shell with an oversized piece of parchment paper and fill it with dried beans or baking weights *(page 127)*. Bake on center rack of oven for 25 to 30 minutes, or until edges are golden brown. Remove the shell from the oven and let it sit for 15 to 20 minutes before removing the paper and beans. Check to see if the bottom of the shell is done. If the bottom still looks wet, return it to the oven for 2 to 3 minutes. If bubbles appear on the bottom of the crust, carefully depress them with a dishtowel, taking care to avoid the escaping steam. The entire pie shell should have a light, golden brown color. Let cool completely before filling.

- Reduce oven temperature to 325°F. Line a rimmed baking sheet with parchment paper.

- Combine pumpkin, squash, brown sugar, honey, maple syrup, cinnamon, salt, nutmeg, ginger, cloves, and semolina flour in a medium bowl. Mix with a whisk or hand-held mixer until ingredients are thoroughly combined, about 1 minute. Add eggs, buttermilk, and brandy and continue mixing until incorporated.

- Place pre-baked pie shell on the prepared baking sheet and pour the filling into the shell. Bake pie on center rack of oven for 55 to 60 minutes, or until the center is just set.

- Remove pie from the oven and spoon Maple Pecan Topping on top. Gently spread topping evenly over the pie, taking care not to push the topping down into the fragile pie filling. Return the pie to the oven and bake for another 20 to 25 minutes. The topping will be set and golden brown. Let pie cool to room temperature, then dust the edges with a little powdered sugar.

MAPLE PECAN TOPPING

This simple topping can be put together at the last minute or it can be made
a day in advance and stored, covered, in the refrigerator. Adding this topping transforms
a traditional pumpkin pie into something extra special.

Makes enough topping for 1 (9-inch) pie

1 egg
2 tablespoons honey
2 tablespoons light brown sugar
1 tablespoon unsalted butter, melted
3 tablespoons pure maple syrup
1 cup coarsely chopped pecans
1 tablespoon brandy

- Combine all ingredients in a small bowl and mix with a spoon until thoroughly blended.

A Thanksgiving to Remember

Andrew Cleary, the bakery's General Manager and my assistant on this book, remembers one Thanksgiving that didn't go the way he had planned.

"Perhaps my fondest Macrina memory is one most people would want to forget. It was Thanksgiving eve 1999, and we had just pulled the last of our pumpkin pies from the ovens. Our entire pastry team had worked overtime to produce a record number of pies, and all that was left was to wait for them to cool and then box them up.

"I volunteered to transport the pies from our kitchen to our retail location next door. After loading eighty steaming desserts onto a baker's rack, I said my goodbyes and rolled the pies out the door. Everything went well for the first quarter block, then disaster struck. One of the wheels fell into a tiny hole in the concrete, and I watched in horror as the rack tipped over (in slow motion, I swear), spilling Thanksgiving onto the sidewalk. I couldn't move. This isn't happening! After thirty seconds I ran into the bakery, yelling for help at the top of my lungs.

"Leslie was the first out the door, followed closely by Karra and Heather, two of the pastry cooks who'd already worked overtime to make the pies. One by one they looked at the pile of pies, then at me, and back again at the wreckage. After a respectful moment of silence we scooped up the mess, wiped our eyes, and got to work. Pie dough was mixed, squash was roasted, more shells were rolled. I stood in the corner grating fresh ginger—my punishment.

"One by one the bakers went home, and Leslie and I were left to finish the job. We baked through the night, accompanied by our favorite CDs and endless cups of coffee. We were actually enjoying ourselves. At 4 a.m., just as the daily papers were being delivered and our morning crew was arriving for work, we once again pulled the last of our pies from the ovens. A few hours later they were carried to homes and tables across the city. We had done it. We had survived."

Harvest Pie

We've made many versions of this winter pie over the years, but this recipe has become the most popular of the bunch. I like serving it alongside pumpkin pie at Thanksgiving and at family dinners all through the autumn and winter months.

Makes 1 (9-inch) pie

½ recipe Sesame Almond Dough *(page 132)*, chilled
½ cup whole almonds
2 Granny Smith apples
2 ripe Bartlett pears
1 cup fresh cranberries
2 cups granulated sugar
1 tablespoon peeled and grated ginger
1 teaspoon cinnamon
½ teaspoon ground nutmeg
¼ teaspoon ground cloves
1 tablespoon freshly squeezed lemon juice
⅓ cup cornstarch
1 recipe Sesame Almond Streusel Topping *(recipe follows)*

- Form the chilled dough into a ball and place it on a floured work surface. Roll the dough out to a 13- to 14-inch circle, about ⅛ inch thick. Using a long knife or offset spatula, gently release the rolled dough from the work surface. Fold the dough in half to make it easier to lift and fit it into a 9-inch pie pan, trimming away all but 1 inch of overhanging dough. (This dough is fragile but resilient. If it cracks, simply pinch and press the dough together with your fingers.) Fold the overhanging dough under itself, creating a double-thick crust around the rim of the pan. Next, crimp the dough every inch or so with your fingers, creating a decorative pattern around the edge. Chill in the freezer for ½ hour.

- Preheat oven to 350°F.

- Line the chilled pie shell with a piece of parchment paper and fill it with dried beans or baking weights (see photo, page 127). Bake on center rack of oven for 25 to 30 minutes, or until crust is golden brown. Carefully remove the paper and beans and set pie shell aside to cool. Leave the oven on.

- Scatter almonds on a rimmed baking sheet and toast on center rack of oven for 10 to 12 minutes, or until golden brown. Let cool, then chop coarsely and set aside.

- Peel and core apples and pears and cut them into 1-inch chunks. In a large bowl, combine apples, pears, almonds, cranberries, sugar, ginger, cinnamon, nutmeg, cloves, and lemon juice. Toss well with your hands, then pour the filling into a large colander. Set the colander inside the mixing bowl and let the filling sit at room temperature for 1 hour to drain excess liquid from the fruit.

- Remove the colander from the bowl and pour the drained pie filling back into another large bowl. Pour the collected fruit juices into a small saucepan and cook over medium-low heat until thick and syrupy, 15 to 20 minutes. Transfer to a small bowl and let cool slightly.

- Preheat oven to 350°F.

- Add the cooled, thickened fruit juices and the cornstarch to the bowl of pie filling. Mix well with a spoon, then scoop the filling into the pre baked pie shell. Mound the filling with your hands, making sure there are no air pockets. Top with an even layer of Sesame Almond Streusel Topping and place pie on a rimmed baking sheet.

- Place baking sheet on center rack of oven and bake for approximately 1½ hours. The topping will be golden brown and the filling will be bubbling around the edges. Let cool on a wire rack for at least 1 hour before serving.

Sesame Almond Streusel Topping

Makes enough topping for 1 (9-inch) pie

¼ cup whole almonds

¼ cup sesame seeds

8 tablespoons (1 stick) unsalted butter, chilled and cut into ½-inch pieces

1 cup unbleached all-purpose flour

½ cup rolled oats

¾ cup granulated sugar

¼ teaspoon pure almond extract

- Preheat oven to 350°F.

- Spread almonds and sesame seeds on separate rimmed baking sheets and toast on center rack of oven until golden brown, about 10 minutes (almonds may take a few minutes more than sesame seeds). Let cool, then chop almonds to medium-fine.

- Combine almonds, sesame seeds, butter, flour, oats, sugar, and almond extract in the bowl of your stand mixer. Using the paddle attachment, mix on low for 2 to 3 minutes, until mixture is coarse and crumbly.

• At this point the topping is ready to use. If you are making the topping in advance and want to store it, place the topping in an airtight container and keep it in the refrigerator for up to 2 days. The topping will form a block when chilled, so I recommend grating it over the pie with a cheese grater when you're ready to use it.

FESTIVE GINGERBREAD PEOPLE

Cookie decorating is one of the best ways I know to get into the holiday spirit, and even though we end up making hundreds of these gingerbread people at the bakery every Christmas, our pastry bakers never seem to run out of new decorating ideas. The first cookies of the season usually start out with simple frosting outlines and dots for facial features, but after a few dozen cookies have been finished, we start seeing sassy shirts with matching skirts, swim suits, or surfer shorts with tank tops. Anything goes when you're decorating these cookies, which is what makes them so much fun. Invite your friends over, kids and grownups alike, and jump-start the season with a cookie decorating party of your own.

Makes 6 to 8 (6-inch) cookies

FOR THE COOKIES:
3⅓ cups unbleached all-purpose flour
2 teaspoons baking soda
2 teaspoons cinnamon
2 teaspoons ground allspice
¼ teaspoon cayenne pepper
1¾ cups light brown sugar
¾ cup solid vegetable shortening, at room temperature
2 eggs
¼ cup honey
⅓ cup molasses
2 tablespoons peeled and grated ginger

FOR THE FROSTING:
1 cup powdered sugar
1 tablespoon filtered water
Food coloring

PREPARING THE COOKIES:

- Sift flour, baking soda, cinnamon, allspice, and cayenne pepper into a medium bowl. Mix with a spoon until ingredients are evenly distributed.

- Place sugar and shortening in the bowl of your stand mixer. Using the paddle attachment, mix on low for about 30 seconds to start bringing the ingredients together. Increase speed to medium and continue mixing for 5 to 8 minutes, or until the mixture is smooth and pale in color. Add eggs, one at a time, making sure the first egg is fully incorporated before adding the second. Add honey, molasses, and ginger and mix on medium for about 30 seconds. Scrape down the sides of the bowl with a rubber spatula and mix for another 30 seconds to make sure the ingredients are evenly distributed. Remove the bowl from the mixer and scrape down the sides one more time.

- Fold half of the dry ingredients into the batter with a rubber spatula. After the first batch is incorporated, fold in the rest of the dry ingredients and continue folding just until all of the flour has been absorbed.

- Using a rubber spatula, scrape dough from bowl onto a large piece of plastic wrap. Dust your hands with a little flour and pat the dough into a block, then wrap it tightly in the plastic wrap and chill in the refrigerator for 1 to 2 hours.

- Preheat oven to 325°F. Line 2 rimmed baking sheets with parchment paper.

- Place chilled dough on a floured work surface and roll it out ½ inch thick. Using a 6-inch cookie cutter, make as many gingerbread people as you can and place them on the prepared baking sheets. These cookies will spread out a little bit during baking, so leave a 2-inch space between each cookie. Roll the scraps of dough into a ball and roll it out again. You should be able to cut a few more cookies from the dough.

- Bake cookies, 1 sheet at a time, on center rack of oven for 20 to 25 minutes. To help the cookies bake more evenly, rotate the baking sheet every 5 minutes or so. Let cool completely before decorating. These cookies can be made 2 or 3 days before a decorating party and stored in an airtight container.

PREPARING THE FROSTING:

- Place powdered sugar in a medium bowl and add water. Mix with a spoon until the mixture is smooth and all the sugar is dissolved. Add just a little bit of food coloring and mix well. You can always add more coloring if you need it. Cover the bowl with plastic wrap and store at room temperature for up to 1 day.

- Repeat the steps to create more colors. For white frosting, omit the food coloring.

- Fit pastry bags with fine tips. Using a rubber spatula, fill the bags with the frostings.

- After all of the cookies have been decorated, let them sit for 2 hours at room temperature so the frosting can set. These cookies will last for up to 2 weeks in an airtight container, but it's important that they be stored in a single layer. If stacked, the frosting will soften and stick to the next cookie. I like to place individual cookies in cellophane bags and tie them with ribbons for festive holiday gifts.

THE CHRISTMAS COOKIE BOX

Every year the pastry cooks at Macrina put together a Christmas Cookie Box containing four types of holiday cookies. One of the cookie varieties changes annually, but the following three are always included. These recipes have been handed down to me through my mother's family, and I wouldn't dream of changing them.

SWEDISH OVERNIGHTS
Prepare this dough 1 day before baking.

Makes 3 dozen cookies

8 ounces (2 sticks) unsalted butter, at room temperature
1 cup powdered sugar, sifted
1 egg, separated
1 teaspoon pure vanilla extract
2¼ cups unbleached all-purpose flour
1 cup finely chopped walnuts
Sugar crystals in your favorite colors

- Combine butter and sugar in the bowl of your stand mixer. Using the paddle attachment, mix on low speed for about 30 seconds. Increase speed to medium and mix for another 5 to 7 minutes, or until the mixture is smooth and pale in color. Add the egg yolk and vanilla extract and mix for about 30 seconds. Scrape down the sides of the bowl with a rubber spatula and mix for another 30 seconds, making sure egg and vanilla are thoroughly incorporated. Remove bowl from mixer and scrape down the sides of the bowl again.

- Using a rubber spatula, fold half of the flour into the dough. After the first batch is fully incorporated, fold in the other half and continue folding until all of the flour has been absorbed, 1 to 2 minutes.

- Pull dough from bowl onto a floured surface and divide it in half. Roll each half into a log about 1½ inches thick, and place the logs on separate pieces of parchment paper. (The parchment paper needs to be at least 4 inches longer than the logs.) Brush the logs with the egg white, then scatter half of the walnuts over each log. Roll the logs back and forth until they are completely coated in nuts. Roll each log up within its parchment paper. Finish by twisting the ends of the paper to create a seal. Chill logs in the refrigerator overnight.

- Preheat oven to 325°F. Line 2 rimmed baking sheets with parchment paper.

- Unwrap the logs and using a sharp knife, cut them into ½-inch-thick coins. Place the cookies on the prepared baking sheets, leaving 1 inch between each cookie. Brush the top of each cookie with a tiny bit of water and sprinkle festive sugar crystals on top.

- Bake on center rack of oven, 1 sheet at a time, for 20 to 25 minutes. To help the cookies bake evenly, rotate the baking sheet every 4 minutes or so. The finished cookies will be golden brown on the edges and pale in the center. Let cookies cool completely on the baking sheet. They can be stored in an airtight container for up to 1 month at room temperature.

MEXICAN WEDDING BALLS

Makes 3 dozen cookies

1½ cups whole almonds
12 ounces (3 sticks) unsalted butter, at room temperature
⅓ cup granulated sugar
1 tablespoon pure vanilla extract
3¼ cups unbleached all-purpose flour
2 cups powdered sugar, sifted

- Preheat oven to 350°F.

- Scatter almonds on a rimmed baking sheet and toast on center rack of oven for approximately 10 minutes, or until golden brown. Let cool, then finely chop and set aside.

- Combine butter and sugar in the bowl of your stand mixer and using the paddle attachment, mix on low speed for about 30 seconds. Increase speed to medium and mix for another 5 to 7 minutes, or until the mixture is smooth and pale in color. Add vanilla extract and mix for about 30 seconds, making sure vanilla is fully incorporated. Remove the bowl from the mixer and scrape down the sides of the bowl.

- Place almonds and flour in a medium bowl and toss together. Using a rubber spatula, fold half of the dry ingredients into the bowl of batter. After the first batch is fully incorporated, fold in the other half and continue folding until all of the dry ingredients have been absorbed, 1 to 2 minutes. Cover bowl with plastic wrap and chill in the refrigerator for 1 hour.

- Preheat oven to 325°F. Line 2 rimmed baking sheets with parchment paper.

- Scoop small amounts of dough out of the bowl (I like to use a small ice cream scoop), and roll the dough into 1½-inch balls. Place the balls on the prepared baking sheets, about 1 inch apart, pressing them down lightly to create a flat bottom on each cookie.

- Bake on center rack of oven, 1 sheet at a time, for 15 to 20 minutes, or until the cookies just start to color. To help the cookies bake evenly, rotate the baking sheet every 4 minutes or so. Let the cookies cool slightly on the baking sheet, then toss them in powdered sugar. Lay the sugar-coated cookies on a clean baking sheet to finish cooling. Finally, after the cookies are fully cooled, toss them in powdered sugar once again. They can be stored in an airtight container for up to 1 month at room temperature.

ANGEL THUMBPRINTS

Makes 4 dozen cookies

12 tablespoons (1½ sticks) unsalted butter, at room temperature
¾ cup solid vegetable shortening, at room temperature
1 cup granulated sugar
1 cup light brown sugar
3 eggs
1½ teaspoons pure vanilla extract
1½ teaspoons pure almond extract
3¼ cups unbleached all-purpose flour
¼ teaspoon salt
2 cups finely chopped pecans
¾ cup raspberry preserves

- Line 2 baking sheets with parchment paper.

- Combine butter, shortening, granulated sugar, and brown sugar in the bowl of your stand mixer. Using the paddle attachment, mix on low speed for about 30 seconds. Increase speed to medium and mix for another 5 to 7 minutes, or until the mixture is smooth and pale in color. Add the eggs, 1 at a time, making sure each egg is fully incorporated before adding another. After the last egg is added, scrape down the sides of the bowl with a rubber spatula. Add the vanilla extract and almond extract, and mix for about 30 seconds, making sure egg and extracts are thoroughly incorporated. Remove bowl from mixer and scrape down the sides of the bowl again.

- Using a rubber spatula, fold half of the flour and the salt into the dough. After the first batch is fully incorporated, fold in the other half and continue folding until all of the flour has been absorbed, 1 to 2 minutes.

- Pour pecans onto a plate or pie pan. Scoop small amounts of dough out of the bowl (I like to use a small ice cream scoop) and roll the dough into quarter-sized balls. (If the dough is too sticky to handle, cover the bowl with plastic wrap and chill the dough in the refrigerator for 15 minutes.) Roll each of the balls in the chopped pecans and place them on the prepared baking sheets, leaving about 1 inch between each cookie. Use your thumb to press down on the center of each cookie, flattening them about halfway. Place baking sheets in the refrigerator and chill for 30 minutes.

- Preheat oven to 325°F.

- Bake on center rack of oven, 1 sheet at a time, for 15 minutes. To help the cookies bake evenly, rotate the baking sheet every 4 minutes or so. Remove the cookies from the oven and using a small spoon, slightly dimple the center of each cookie to make sure the "thumbprints" are big enough to hold the preserves. Top each cookie with ½ teaspoon of raspberry preserves, then return the cookies to the oven. Bake for another 5 to 7 minutes, or until the cookies are golden brown and the jam has just set. Do not let the jam start to bubble. Let cool completely. The best way to store these cookies is to lay them flat in a single layer. If you want to stack them in a tin or cookie jar, place a small piece of parchment paper between each layer to keep the jam from sticking. The cookies can be stored in an airtight container for up to 1 month at room temperature.

Most-Requested Recipes

Morning Glory Muffins
Fresh Fruit Coffee Cake
New Flaky Pie Dough
Macrina's Tuxedo Cake
Chocolate Walnut Tart
Ribollita with Seasoned Croutons
Sesame Millet Bread
Blackburn Wheat Bread

Since the first edition of this book was released in 2003, I've kept a list of the requests we've received for new recipes. And now, with this new chapter, I have been given an opportunity to fulfill a few of those requests. To begin with, I offer you Morning Glory Muffins. This muffin, bursting with fresh apples, carrots, and pineapple, has become our most popular. We also serve a different variety of Fresh Fruit Coffee Cake every day, showcasing seasonal fresh fruit. The recipe presented here is easy to prepare and is perfect for weekend brunch.

Everyone I know loves chocolate cake, and we are always creating new varieties for the menu at Macrina. One of the first cakes we ever offered, our Tuxedo Cake, has become our most popular and has earned a place of honor on the cover of this book. We create different versions of this cake throughout the year and the recipe here, lightened by whipped cream and ripe raspberries, is one of my personal favorites.

Every year, in preparation for the holiday season, our pastry cooks create special new desserts to feature in our list of offerings. Some are made only once, and others become annual crowd pleasers. The Chocolate Walnut Tart falls into this second category. This rich and decadent dessert can be made in less than an hour and is guaranteed to satisfy your sweet tooth.

My baking philosophy has always been to stay true to a recipe's origins, and I stand firmly behind that goal. But, obviously, it is also important to consider food allergies and nutritional value when deciding what food to put on our tables. With that in mind, I accepted the challenge of developing more recipes that took into account gluten intolerance, the dangers of trans fats, and the popularity of a vegan diet. In this new chapter you will find recipes for our new gluten free Sesame Millet Bread and the vegan Blackburn Wheat Bread. Both are recent additions to our retail shelves. I have also updated our popular Flaky Pie Dough recipe, replacing old-fashioned vegetable shortening with a newly available variety of palm fruit shortening, which contains no trans fats and yields wonderful results.

MORNING GLORY MUFFINS

This is by far our most popular muffin, and customers have been requesting the recipe for years.
I prefer fresh pineapple when possible, but the unsweetened, canned variety works just fine.

Makes 12 muffins

½ cup seedless raisins
⅓ cup walnut halves
2 cups unbleached all-purpose flour
½ cup granulated sugar
2¼ teaspoons cinnamon
1½ teaspoons baking soda
¼ teaspoon salt
1 medium carrot, grated
1 Granny Smith apple, peeled and grated
¾ cup chopped pineapple
3 eggs
¼ cup canola oil
6 tablespoons unsalted butter, melted
1 tablespoon freshly squeezed lemon juice
1 teaspoon pure vanilla extract
½ cup shredded, unsweetened coconut
⅓ cup coarse raw sugar

- Preheat oven to 350°F. Brush the insides of a muffin tin with canola oil.

- Place raisins in a small bowl and cover with hot tap water. Let sit for 10 minutes while raisins plump, then drain and squeeze out excess liquid with your hands. Set aside. Place walnuts on a rimmed baking sheet and toast until golden brown, about 15 minutes. Let cool, then chop coarsely and set aside.

- Sift flour, granulated sugar, cinnamon, baking soda, and salt into a medium bowl. Mix gently with a wooden spoon and set aside. In a separate medium bowl, combine raisins, walnuts, carrot, apple, pineapple, eggs, canola oil, melted butter, lemon juice, vanilla extract, and coconut, and mix with a wooden spoon until combined. Add dry ingredients and continue stirring just until all the dry ingredients are moistened. It's important not to overmix.

- Scoop batter into oiled muffin tin, filling the cups to the top. Sprinkle coarse raw sugar on tops of muffins and bake on the center rack of the oven for 40 to 45 minutes. The finished muffins will be deep brown. Let cool for 20 minutes, then slide a fork down the side of each muffin and gently lift it from the pan.

FRESH FRUIT COFFEE CAKE

This is what weekend mornings are made for. Shuffle into the kitchen in your pajamas and mix up this recipe while the coffee brews. Pop the pan in the oven, pour a cup of java, grab the paper from the front porch, and crawl back into bed until the aroma of fresh coffee cake draws you back into the kitchen. Need I say more? To make the best possible cake, use fresh fruit picked at the height of its growing season.

Makes 1 bundt cake

3 cups unbleached all-purpose flour
1½ teaspoons baking soda
¾ teaspoon salt
2 cups ripe fruit (whole berries or fruit cut into ½-inch pieces)
12 tablespoons (1½ sticks) unsalted butter, at room temperature
1 cup granulated sugar
½ cup light brown sugar
2 eggs
1½ teaspoons pure vanilla extract
1½ cups buttermilk
Edible flowers and powdered sugar, for garnish (optional)

- Preheat oven to 350°F. Oil a 12-cup bundt pan.

- Sift flour, baking soda, and salt into a large bowl and toss with your hands to combine. Remove ¼ cup of the flour mixture and set bowl aside.

- In a separate medium bowl, combine fruit and the reserved ¼ cup of flour mixture. Toss until fruit is evenly coated, and set aside. Tossing the fruit in flour helps keep it from sinking to the bottom of the coffee cake—a true disaster!

- Combine butter, granulated sugar, and brown sugar in the bowl of your stand mixer. Mix with the paddle attachment for 5 to 8 minutes on medium speed. The mixture will become smooth and pale in color. Add eggs, one at a time, making sure the first egg is fully mixed into the batter before adding the other. After the second egg is incorporated, add vanilla extract and mix for 1 minute. Scrape down the sides of the bowl with a rubber spatula and mix for another 30 seconds to make sure all of the ingredients are fully incorporated. Remove the bowl from the mixer.

- Alternately add small amounts of flour mixture and buttermilk to the batter, mixing with a wooden spoon just until all dry ingredients are incorporated. Gently fold in the flour-coated fruit, making sure the fruit is evenly distributed through the batter. Spoon batter into the prepared bundt pan, filling two-thirds of the pan.

- Bake on the center rack of the oven for 1 hour and 30 minutes, or until top is golden brown. Check the center of the coffee cake with a skewer. It will come out clean when the cake is done. Let cool in pan for 45 minutes.

- Loosen the sides of the cake with a sharp knife. Place a serving plate, upside down, on top of the cooled bundt pan and invert the pan to remove the cake.

- This delicious coffee cake is perfect just the way it is, but I like to jazz up the presentation with a few fresh, edible flowers and a dusting of powdered sugar.

NEW FLAKY PIE DOUGH

Nonhydrogenated shortenings, like the one used in this recipe, tend to soften quicker than traditional vegetable shortenings do when they reach room temperature. Therefore, it is important to always work with this pie dough while it is cold. If the dough reaches room temperature, it will become difficult to handle and will fall apart. Unlike our original Flaky Pie Dough recipe (page 127), this dough is best prepared in a stand mixer. If mixing by hand, it will take considerably longer to cut all of the butter into the flour.

Makes enough dough for 2 double-crusted (9-inch) pies,
or 2 (10-inch) rustic galettes or tarts

5¼ cups unbleached all-purpose flour
1 tablespoon kosher salt
14 ounces (3½ sticks) unsalted butter, chilled and cut into ¼-inch pieces
¾ cup palm fruit shortening, chilled*
1 cup ice water
**available in specialty shops and some supermarkets*

- Combine flour and salt in the bowl of your stand mixer. Add half of the butter and, using the paddle attachment, pulse a few times by quickly turning the mixer on and off. (This is a way of gradually cutting the butter into the flour without sending the flour skyward.) Add remaining butter and continue pulsing until the mixture is coarse and crumbly, 2 to 3 minutes.

- Break up shortening and add it in small pieces. Pulse until dough is crumbly again. Add ice water all at once and mix on low speed for about 30 seconds, just until water is incorporated.

- Dust your hands with flour and pull dough from the bowl onto a lightly floured work surface (chilled marble is ideal). Divide dough into 2 pieces and pat into blocks. Wrap them tightly in plastic wrap and chill in the refrigerator for at least 1 hour. Since this recipe makes enough dough for 2 pies, I like to double-wrap one and freeze it for future baking.

- For further handling and baking instructions, please see the original Flaky Pie Dough recipe.

Creating Our New Flaky Pie Dough

I have been a member of the Seattle chapter of Les Dames d'Escoffier (an international organization of women working in the food industry) for many years, and have found it to be a wonderful source of mentorship, camaraderie, and resource sharing. Recently I attended a Les Dames–sponsored program featuring authors Kim Severson and Cindy Burke, who wrote *The Trans Fats Solution*. Like all of us, I had been hearing a lot about the dangers of trans fats in the news. But it wasn't until I attended this lecture that I truly understood the need for alternatives to hydrogenated shortening and fats.

Macrina's original recipe for Flaky Pie Dough (see page 127) uses a combination of butter and vegetable shortening, which I believe creates the best texture and flavor. I was hoping to eliminate the vegetable shortening without compromising the quality. First, I went to our supplier, Seattle's Glory Bee Foods, in search of an alternative to vegetable shortening. Glory Bee offers a wide variety of organic flours, nuts, and other baking ingredients, and as it turned out, they had a new product called organic palm fruit shortening. They suggested I give it a try.

Palm fruit shortening is processed using only steam, high temperatures, and a mechanical press. No chemicals are used in the process. It is naturally solid at room temperature and needs no refrigeration. It is lower in saturated fat than butter and is free of cholesterol and trans fatty acids. Palm fruit shortening should not be confused with palm kernel oil, which is high in saturated fats and should be avoided. I was thrilled to find this healthy alternative.

Our bakers and I experimented and found that the palm fruit shortening worked well in our cookies and biscotti. But the big test was incorporating it into our pie dough. We discovered that palm fruit shortening does bake differently than the hydrogenated shortening I was accustomed to, in that it holds more moisture while baking. To compensate, we ended up reducing the amount of shortening used in the recipe and increasing the amount of butter. This healthier version of our original recipe yields nice results. Just as chefs have a responsibility to support sustainable resources such as agriculture, bakers need to incorporate advances in nutritional awareness whenever possible.

Macrina's Tuxedo Cake

From birthdays to wedding celebrations, this elegant cake is one of our most popular special-occasion cakes. The combination of fresh raspberries and Lightly Sweetened Whipped Cream offers a perfect balance to the rich Chocolate Ganache. When fresh raspberries are out of season, try substituting a layer of quality raspberry preserves.

Makes 1 (9-inch) layer cake

1 cup dark cocoa powder

2 cups boiling water

2½ cups cake flour

1½ teaspoons baking soda

½ teaspoon baking powder

½ teaspoon salt

8 ounces (2 sticks) unsalted butter, at room temperature

2 cups granulated sugar

3 eggs

1 tablespoon pure vanilla extract

Vanilla Syrup *(page 112)*

Chocolate Ganache, at room temperature *(recipe follows)*

Lightly Sweetened Whipped Cream *(page 106)*

2 cups (1 pint) fresh raspberries

White Chocolate Frosting, at room temperature *(page 117)*

Edible flowers and granulated sugar, for garnish (optional)

- Preheat oven to 325°F. Prepare 2 (9 x 3-inch) cake pans by brushing the insides with oil and lining the bottoms with 10-inch circles of parchment paper. Set aside.

- Sift cocoa powder into a medium bowl. Carefully pour in boiling water and mix with a whisk until cocoa is dissolved. Set aside to cool.

- Into a separate medium bowl, sift flour, baking soda, baking powder, and salt. Toss with your hands to combine, and set aside.

- Combine butter and sugar in the bowl of your stand mixer. Using the paddle attachment, mix on low speed for 1 to 2 minutes. Increase speed to medium and mix for about 5 minutes to cream the butter. The mixture will become smooth and pale in color. Start adding eggs, one at a time, taking care to mix in each addition fully before adding the next. After the last egg is incorporated, add vanilla extract and mix for another 30 seconds. Scrape down the sides of the bowl with a rubber spatula and mix for another 30 seconds to make sure all ingredients are fully incorporated.

- Add about one-sixth of the wet cocoa mixture and one-sixth of the dry ingredients to the bowl, and pulse a few times by quickly turning the mixer on and off just until combined. Repeat 5 times, until all ingredients are incorporated, scraping down the sides with a rubber spatula between additions.

- Divide batter equally between the prepared pans and place them on the center rack of the oven. Bake for 35 to 40 minutes, or until deep brown. Test center with a skewer to make sure it's done. It will come out clean when the cake is finished. Remove from the oven and let cool in the pans on a wire rack for at least 1 hour.

- Invert the cooled cakes to remove them from the pans. If they stick, run a sharp knife around the sides of the cakes to release them from the pans. Peel the parchment paper off the bottoms of the cakes. To ensure an elegant, level cake, use a sharp bread knife to carefully cut the domed tops off of the cakes. (Discard pieces or save for snacking.) Next, gently cut each cake horizontally into 2 equal layers, creating a total of 4 layers from the 2 cakes. Place one layer on a serving plate or cardboard cake circle and brush it with a little Vanilla Syrup. Spread half of the Chocolate Ganache evenly over the layer, about ¼-inch thick. Top with another cake layer and brush with Vanilla Syrup. Spread Lightly Sweetened Whipped Cream evenly over the layer and sprinkle raspberries on top, reserving a few for garnish. Top with another cake layer, brush again with Vanilla Syrup, and spread on the remaining ganache. Add the final cake layer. Place a dollop of White Chocolate Frosting on top of the cake and spread it ⅛-inch thick, spreading any excess frosting down the sides. Spread a little more frosting on the sides until the entire cake has what bakers call a crumb coat—a thin underlayer of frosting that keeps crumbs out of the final layer of frosting. Chill cake in refrigerator for 20 to 30 minutes. The remaining frosting can stay at room temperature while the cake chills.

- Remove the cake from the refrigerator and, using an offset spatula, add a final, smooth layer of frosting. I like to finish this cake with sugar-dusted berries and flowers, which are easy to prepare. (Simply brush the berries or fresh flowers with a little beaten egg white and dust with granulated sugar. Then let them dry on a wire rack.) Store the finished cake in your refrigerator for up to 2 days. The cake is best enjoyed at room temperature, so remove it from the refrigerator 1 to 2 hours before serving.

CHOCOLATE GANACHE

Makes enough to fill 1 (9-inch) layer cake

2 cups heavy cream
8 ounces semi-sweet chocolate, coarsely chopped (or chips)
8 ounces bittersweet chocolate, coarsely chopped (or chips)

- Pour cream into a medium saucepan and place over medium heat. As soon as it begins to boil, turn off the heat and add chocolate. Mix constantly with a whisk until chocolate is melted. Using a rubber spatula, transfer ganache into a small bowl and set aside to cool. This ganache can be made in advance and stored for up to 1 week in your refrigerator, but it will need to reach room temperature to be spreadable.

CHOCOLATE WALNUT TART

I've been fine-tuning this recipe over the years, making little changes here and there, and have finally arrived at what I feel is a superb version. It's delicious and easy to prepare at the last minute, especially if you have an unbaked tart shell ready to go in the freezer.

Makes 1 (10-inch) tart

1 cup walnut halves
¼ cup granulated sugar
¼ cup light brown sugar
½ cup light corn syrup
2 egg yolks
1 egg
¼ teaspoon salt
1 tablespoon pure vanilla extract
8 tablespoons (1 stick) unsalted butter, melted
1 pre-baked (10-inch) tart shell, made with Flaky Pie Dough *(page 127)* or New Flaky Pie Dough *(page 262)*
⅓ cup semi-sweet chocolate chips
Lightly Sweetened Whipped Cream *(page 106)*

- Preheat oven to 350°F.

- Place walnuts on a rimmed baking sheet and toast until golden brown, about 15 minutes. Let cool and set aside.

- Combine granulated sugar, brown sugar, corn syrup, egg yolks, egg, salt, vanilla extract, and melted butter in a medium bowl. Mix with a whisk until ingredients are combined, and set aside.

- Place cooled, pre-baked tart shell on a rimmed baking sheet. Scatter walnuts and chocolate chips evenly in tart shell, then pour in sugar mixture. Use a rubber spatula to scrape remaining batter from the bowl, and gently spread mixture evenly over walnuts and chocolate. The tart shell should be filled to just below the top. Place the baking sheet on the center rack of the oven and bake for 25 to 30 minutes. The top of the tart will be golden brown. Let cool on a wire rack for 10 to 20 minutes, then remove the sides of the pan. Serve each warm slice with a spoonful of Lightly Sweetened Whipped Cream.

RIBOLLITA WITH SEASONED CROUTONS

This marriage of vegetable soup and yesterday's bread is a classic Tuscan combination. One of our chefs, Brandon Wicks, makes the dish into a meal by adding savory sausage and chicken.

Makes 4 servings

½ cup dried cannelloni beans
3 tablespoons extra virgin olive oil
1 pound Italian sausage links (chicken or pork)
4 thin slices pancetta (about 3 ounces), diced
1 medium yellow onion, diced
2 medium carrots, peeled and diced
1 medium fennel bulb, cut into large dice
3 celery ribs, diced
1 medium parsnip, peeled and diced
2 garlic cloves, finely diced
4 Roma tomatoes, cored and diced
½ small head green cabbage, coarsely chopped
2 tablespoons chopped fresh rosemary
1 tablespoon chopped fresh thyme
8 cups chicken or vegetable stock
1 (6-ounce) boneless, skinless chicken breast
¾ cup red wine
2 tablespoons sherry vinegar
Kosher salt
Freshly ground black pepper
3 cups Seasoned Croutons *(recipe follows)*
Extra virgin olive oil, for drizzling
2 tablespoons chopped fresh Italian parsley

- Soak beans in water overnight.

- Drain beans and set aside.

- Heat 1 tablespoon of olive oil in a medium sauté pan over medium-high heat. Add sausage links and cook until all sides are browned, about 10 minutes. Let cool, then cut links into 1-inch pieces and set aside.

- Combine remaining 2 tablespoons olive oil and pancetta in a large, heavy-bottomed soup pot. Cook over medium heat until fat is rendered and pancetta is golden brown.

Do not pour off the rendered fat. Add onion, carrot, fennel, celery, and parsnip. Cover the pot and sweat the vegetables over medium heat, stirring occasionally, for about 15 minutes or until vegetables are soft. Add garlic, tomatoes, cabbage, rosemary, and thyme, and cook, uncovered, for another 10 minutes.

- Add soaked beans, sausage, stock, chicken breast, red wine, and sherry vinegar, and bring to a boil. Simmer for 1 to 1½ hours, until beans are fully cooked, adding more stock or water as needed. If foam gathers on the surface of the soup, remove it with a spoon. Remove chicken breast from soup and set aside until it is cool enough to touch. Shred cooled chicken with your hands and return pieces to soup. Season to taste with salt and pepper.

- Divide croutons among 4 soup bowls, reserving about ½ cup. Ladle soup over croutons and garnish each serving with a drizzle of good olive oil, some Italian parsley, and the reserved croutons.

SEASONED CROUTONS

We use a lot of these savory croutons at our cafes. They're perfect for topping soups and salads, and can be stored in an airtight container for up to a week.

Makes 3 cups

2 tablespoons unsalted butter
3 tablespoons extra virgin olive oil
1 garlic clove, finely diced
3 cups white bread cubes (about ½ loaf), cut into ½-inch cubes
Kosher salt
Freshly ground black pepper

- Preheat oven to 350°F. Line a rimmed baking sheet with parchment paper.

- Melt butter in a small saucepan over medium-low heat. Add olive oil and garlic and continue cooking just until garlic is heated through, about 30 seconds. Remove from heat.

- Place bread cubes in a medium bowl. Pour in butter mixture and toss until bread cubes are evenly coated. Transfer cubes to rimmed baking sheet and spread evenly. Using a rubber spatula, scrape any remaining butter from the bowl and scatter over the bread cubes. Season to taste with a little salt and pepper.

- Bake on the center rack of the oven for 10 to 15 minutes, until croutons are golden brown. Let cool and enjoy.

Gluten-Free Baking

Customers started requesting a gluten-free loaf shortly after we opened our doors, and I am pleased to say we are finally offering one. We created our new Sesame Millet Bread (page 271) in response to the increasing awareness of gluten intolerance. Many people, as a result of allergies or chronic exposure, can no longer digest products that contain gluten. Very few commercially produced alternative products are available, so most individuals resort to baking at home.

My first task was researching and finding sources for alternative ingredients to the flours usually used at the bakery. I consulted with other bakers and read as much literature as I could find on the topic. It turns out there are more and more options for gluten-free baking, and many of the necessary ingredients are readily available at health food stores or the bulk section of your local supermarket.

One ingredient in our wheat-free loaf is millet, which is actually the seed of a tall grass. Ground into fine flour, it has great nutritional value and a sweet, nutty taste that doesn't overwhelm the flavor of the loaf. Millet flour goes bitter with time, so it's best to use the freshest available. Other ingredients to have on hand include tapioca flour, corn flour (not to be confused with semolina flour, which actually contains gluten), and garbanzo bean flour (also known as chick pea flour).

The challenge with this sort of baking is that the lack of gluten can result in very dense breads that don't rise well. You know the loaves I'm talking about—dense as bricks and just about as much fun to eat. One way to improve the texture of these loaves is to include an ingredient called xanthan gum. It is produced in a lab and effectively replaces the gluten in a recipe, allowing your loaves to rise. Xanthan gum is expensive, but a little goes a long way—so one package will last through many days of baking.

Here in Seattle, I was able to get almost everything I needed at my local Whole Foods store. Another great resource is bobsredmill.com, where customers can mail-order a wide range of baking supplies. Sources like these have helped gluten-free baking come a long way, and I hope to offer more new items in the future.

SESAME MILLET BREAD

This dense loaf is similar in appearance to quick breads, but it carries the same texture as classic, hearty, rustic loaves. I chose millet for its nutritional value and its likeness to sweet wheat flour. This bread is great for sandwiches. See Gluten-Free Baking (page 270) for more information on gluten-free alternatives.

Makes 1 (9 x 5-inch) loaf

¼ cup sesame seeds
¼ cup millet
2 cups warm filtered water
2½ teaspoons dried yeast
⅓ cup canola oil
1¼ cups millet flour
1 cup corn flour
1 cup garbanzo bean flour
1¼ cups tapioca flour
2 teaspoons xanthan gum
2 teaspoons kosher salt
Spray bottle of water

- Preheat oven to 350°F. Brush the inside of a 9 x 5 x 4-inch loaf pan with canola oil.

- Combine ½ teaspoon of sesame seeds and ½ teaspoon of millet in a small bowl and set aside. Spread remaining sesame seeds and millet on a rimmed baking sheet and place on center rack of oven. Toast until golden brown, about 10 minutes. Remove from oven and set aside to cool.

- Place warm water in the bowl of your stand mixer and sprinkle yeast on top. Mix with a whisk to dissolve the yeast. (If mixing by hand, combine warm water and yeast in a medium bowl and mix with a whisk.) Let rest for 5 minutes. The yeast will bloom and the mixture will look foamy. Add canola oil. Using the hook attachment, mix on low speed for 30 seconds. (If mixing by hand, add oil and mix with a whisk to combine.) Add the toasted sesame seeds and millet, millet flour, corn flour, garbanzo bean flour, tapioca flour, xanthan gum, and salt. Mix on low speed for 1 minute to combine ingredients. Increase speed to medium and mix for another 3 minutes. (If mixing by hand, add seeds, millet, flours, xanthan gum, and salt and mix with a wooden spoon until all ingredients are combined, several minutes). At this point the mixture will be quite moist and will look more like batter than traditional bread dough.

- Scoop the batter into the loaf pan with a rubber spatula. Using the rubber spatula, press down on the batter to make sure it extends to all corners of the pan, then smooth out the surface. Cover with plastic wrap and let proof in a warm room, 70 to 75°F, for 1 hour. Dough will rise to slightly above the top of the pan.

- While loaf is proofing, preheat oven to 375°F.

- Remove plastic and lightly mist top of loaf with a spray bottle of water. Sprinkle remaining sesame seeds and millet evenly on top. Place pan on the center rack of the oven and bake for approximately 1 hour. The top and sides of the finished loaf will be golden brown. Let cool in the pan on a wire rack for 10 minutes, then run a sharp knife around the sides of the loaf to release it from the pan. Invert the pan to remove the loaf, then continue cooling on a wire rack.

Blackburn Wheat Bread

This slightly sweet whole-grain loaf was inspired by Macrina staff member Chris Blackburn,
who eats an exclusively vegan diet. He suggested sweetening the bread with agave syrup,
instead of the more commonly used honey, to make it acceptable for vegans. See Gluten-Free
Baking (page 270) for more information on gluten-free and vegan alternatives.

Makes 1 (9 x 5-inch) braided loaf

⅓ cup flax seed
⅓ cup millet
2 cups warm filtered water
2½ teaspoons dried yeast
½ cup agave syrup sweetener*
⅓ cup canola oil
3¼ cups coarse whole-wheat flour
½ cup millet flour
½ cup barley flour
1 cup tapioca flour
2½ teaspoons kosher salt
Spray bottle of water
available in specialty shops and some supermarkets

- Preheat oven to 350°F. Measure out 1 teaspoon of flax seed and set aside for sprinkling on top of the loaf.

- Spread millet on a rimmed baking sheet and place on center rack of oven. Toast until golden brown, about 10 minutes. Remove from oven and transfer millet into a small bowl. Cover with ½ cup of warm water and let sit, uncovered, for 15 minutes. Set aside. Do not pour off water.

- Place remaining 1½ cups warm water in the bowl of your stand mixer and sprinkle the yeast on top. Mix with a whisk to dissolve the yeast. (If mixing by hand, combine warm water and yeast in a medium bowl and mix with a whisk.) Let rest for 5 minutes. The yeast will bloom and the mixture will look foamy. Add the rest of the flax seed, soaked millet (with water), agave syrup sweetener, canola oil, whole-wheat flour, millet flour, barley flour, tapioca flour, and kosher salt. Using the hook attachment, mix on low speed for 1 to 2 minutes to combine ingredients. Increase speed to medium and mix for about 10 minutes. (If mixing by hand, add flax seed, soaked millet, agave syrup sweetener, canola oil, flours, and kosher salt and mix with a wooden spoon until ingredients are combined. Knead with your hands for

10 to 12 minutes.) Dough will be wet at first but will eventually form a ball, pulling away from the base of the bowl. Finished dough will have a satiny finish and bounce back quickly when poked with a finger.

- Transfer dough to an oiled, medium bowl and cover with plastic wrap. Set bowl in a warm room, 70 to 75°F, and let rise for 1 hour. Dough will almost double in size.

- Brush the inside of a 9 x 5 x 4-inch loaf pan with canola oil.

- Pull dough from the bowl onto a floured surface and pat it into a rectangle with your hands. Divide dough into 3 equal pieces and roll each piece into a rope approximately 10 inches long. Line the strands up side by side and, starting at one end, braid the pieces (see photos in Raisin Brioche Twist recipe, page 44). Pinch the ends together to form a seal and fold the ends underneath.

- Lift the braid into the loaf pan and gently press down on the dough to make sure it extends to all corners of the pan. Cover with plastic wrap and let proof in a warm room for 45 minutes to 1 hour. Dough will rise to just above the top of the pan.

- While loaf is proofing, preheat oven to 350°F.

- Remove plastic and lightly mist top of loaf with a spray bottle of water. Sprinkle remaining teaspoon of flax seed evenly over the top. Place the pan on the center rack of the oven and bake for approximately 1 hour. The top and sides of the finished loaf will be deep golden brown. Let cool in the pan on a wire rack for 30 minutes, then run a sharp knife around the sides of the loaf to release it from the pan. Invert the pan to remove the loaf, then continue cooling on a wire rack.

INDEX

A – B

Aioli, 202

almonds
- Almond Cake with Mascarpone Cream & Fresh Blackberries, 122–24
- Almond & Orange Biscotti, 166–67
- almond syrup, 122, 124
- Apricot Frangipane Tart, 145–46
- Brown Sugar & Almond Coffee Cake, 81–82
- Cherry Almond Scones, 61–62
- Macringle, 75–76
- Mexican Wedding Balls, 254–55
- Orecchiette Salad with Roasted Beets, Fennel & Toasted Almonds, 210–11
- Plum & Almond Crumb Tart, 149–51
- Sesame Almond Dough, 132–33
- Sesame Almond Streusel Topping, 250–51
- Sweet Almond Dough, 130
- Sweet & Spicy Nuts, 236

anchovies
- Egg Salad Sandwich on Greek Olive Bread with Roasted Tomatoes & Anchovies, 217–18

Angel Thumbprints, 255–56

anise
- Currant Anise Scones, 62–63
- Roasted Walnut & Anise Biscotti, 164–65

appetizers
- Baked Brie en Croûte, 232–33
- Roasted Pear Galette with Chèvre & Pomegranates, 234–35
- Sweet & Spicy Nuts, 236

apple
- Apple Anadama Coffee Cake, 82–83
- Apple & Bing Cherry Galette, 141–42
- apple butter, 46–47
- Apple Cinnamon Monkey Bread, 46–47
- Butternut Squash & Apple Galette, 203–4
- German Pancake with Apples, Rum & Brown Sugar, 188–89
- Harvest Pie, 249–50

apple cider
- Cracked Wheat Walnut Cider Loaf, 35–36

apricot
- Apricot Frangipane Tart, 145–46
- Apricot Pecan Loaf, 15–16
- Chocolate & Apricot Cookies, 160–61
- Ricotta Biscuits with Dried Cherries, Apricots & Raspberries, 65–66

Bacon, Leek & Gruyère Quiche, 194

Baked Brie en Croûte, 232–33

baker's peel, *xviii*

baking
- with children, 34
- direct method, 31
- gluten-free, 270

baking sheets, rimmed, *xvii*

baking soda, 54

baking stone, *xv*

Balsamic Vinaigrette, 198

banana
- in Rocket Muffins, 57–58

basil
- Orzo Salad with Cucumber, Tomato, Basil & Feta, 212

beans
- Tuscan Tomato & Fennel Soup with White Beans, 201–2

Beard, James, Baker's Brunch, 190, 193

beets
- Orecchiette Salad with Roasted Beets, Fennel & Toasted Almonds, 210–11

bench scrapers, *xviii*

berries. *See individual entries*

Beurre Blanc Sauce, 192

biga, 19–20
- breads started with, 19–30
- Seed Dough, 21–22
- Traditional Biga Starter, 21

biscotti
- Almond & Orange Biscotti, 166–67
- Roasted Walnut & Anise Biscotti, 164–65

biscuits, 63–66

Cream Biscuits with Black Forest Ham and Romano Cheese, 64–65

Old-Fashioned Buttermilk Biscuits with Fresh Preserves, 63–64

Ricotta Biscuits with Dried Cherries, Apricots & Raspberries, 65–66

Bittersweet Chocolate Brownies, 170–71

Bittersweet Chocolate Gâteau, 105–6

blackberries
- Almond Cake with Mascarpone Cream & Fresh Blackberries, 122–24
- Old-Fashioned Buttermilk Waffles with Fresh Berries & Cream, 184–85

Blackburn Wheat Bread, 273–74

blowtorch, *xviii*

blueberries
- Blueberry Compote, 94
- Classic Blueberry Pie, 135–36
- Fresh Fruit Crostata, 136–38

bottle, spray, *xvii*

Brandied Cherries, 143

bread, 1–49, 271–74
- American standards, 31–40
- Apple Cinnamon Monkey Bread, 46–47
- Apricot Pecan Loaf, 15–16
- Blackburn Wheat Bread, 273–74
- Challah, 37–38
- Chocolate Cherry Heart Bread, 238–40
- Ciabatta Loaf, 27–28
- Classic Brioche Loaf, 43–44
- Classic Italian Loaf, 22–23
- Cracked Wheat Walnut Cider Loaf, 35–36
- Greek Olive Loaf, 17–18
- Guatemalan Hot Chocolate Bread, 48–49
- Holiday Fougasse, 226–28
- Macrina Casera Loaf, 11–12
- Macrina Pizzetta, 25–26
- Macrina's Fancy Focaccia, 24
- made in Italy, 2–3
- made with sour starter, 5–18
- Oatmeal Buttermilk Bread, 39–40
- Olivetta Loaf, 29–30